FORTY YEARS
AMONG THE STARS

by

COMMODORE
GEORGE W. ELDER

SCHANEN & JACQUE, PUBLISHERS

Port Washington, Wisconsin, U S A

1955

IN MEMORIAM

Had George Elder not built so well it is conceivable that with his passing the International Star Class Yacht Racing Association might have faced serious problems. That his untimely death only caused deep sorrow and regret is the greatest tribute that could be paid to him.

For a quarter of a century he labored so that the Star Class would be greater than any personality and on such a firm foundation that no one person could be considered as indispensible. He foresaw that eventually the original founders would pass from the picture, and as the Class approached the half century mark he well knew that many of its phases and many of its outstanding personalities would be only historical memories. He and we of the Star Class were fortunate in that George Elder never passed into history. He was vital, active and a guiding spirit to the end—witness this book which was his last great work for our Class, and which he completed save for the merest details just before he died.

It took the best part of a lifetime to create the greatest class of racing skippers in the world, to create a fraternal organization of thousands, knowing no national limitations or borders, guided by a spirit of comradeship that surmounts the barriers of countries, or of language, or of race, or of mountains, or of seas.

This book, and the thousands of friends all over the world, many who never met him, are all tributes to him. but his monument is the Star Class. Nothing I say can add one iota to it. Our little white sails that dot the seven seas of the world and its myriad of lakes, which can be seen racing in every clime and in far flung places at any season of the year, is the culmination of what his imagination envisaged. The sun never sets on the I.S.C.Y.R.A. This is the monument George Elder built. Verily it is not a mausoleum.

We are proud of George Waldron Elder—may he be proud of us! The spirit with which we race, the friendships we weld, and the fellowship of Star sailors the world over must be our continuing contribution. George Elder has made his.

Paul H. Smart
Executive President, I.S.C.Y.R.A.

DEDICATION

This book is dedicated to my wife Juanita It is she who urged me to write it, so that Star skippers of the future may have a permanent record, especially of the early years of the Class.

COMMODORE GEORGE W. ELDER
1893 to 1954

CONTENTS

CHAPTER

INTRODUCTION

THIS IS SIMPLY A STORY OF THE STAR CLASS, the most fabulous one-design in the annals of yacht racing. Posterity, therefore, is entitled to an authentic account of its development and achievements. The passing of George Corry, early in '44, made it dawn upon me gradually that I was the only one left who knew the facts from the inside looking out. I say this because I am the only remaining Star officer who has served in that capacity since the inception of the Stars first little local class association at the western end of Long Island Sound. There are no printed records of the first decade, hence I must depend entirely upon my memory. Oddly enough, the details of those very early years are indelibly engraved on my mind.

The Star is the common ancestor of all expanding one-designs. It paved the way, and classes with similar objectives later followed in its wake. Whether the countless thousands in these classes realize it or not, the Star's ancient history is in a sense that of their own organization. In the days of yore, when the huge regal racing yacht reigned supreme, the Star fought the small boat's battle and gained it recognition. It is actually largely responsible for the present small boat era. Those not interested in all this will probably find something in the following pages that may help them solve some problem of their own class organization. All of these organizations have been patterned after the Star's, naturally with some minor variations.

Since it has already been in print, there is no reason why I should not mention my personal contribution to the sport It so happens that I devised the Star's system of organization in 1916, although it was put on ice for six years. I claim no originality any more than I do to being an author. It was simply a matter of applying an old system to yacht racing but it worked. The results speak for themselves.

While common practice in other countries, in the United States very few yachting organizations have both a commodore and a president. In the Star class, commodoreships are bestowed upon those that have already performed a signal service. The president is the executive head. I mention this because of the many years that Pop Corry and I served side by side in these respective jobs. The late commodore's old friends, including myself, called him George. Hereinafter, however, I shall refer to him as "Pop", the nickname by which he became widely known.

I am fearful that I cannot portray in words the exuberant enthusiasm of those early Star owners. While I wrote the Star constitution and most of its subsequent rule changes, the Star would not be what it is today except for the whole-hearted support of those pioneers. The Star was their bible. So convinced were they of the righteousness of their cause that nothing was too much to ask of them. They met adversity with a grin and worked all the harder because of it.

Temporary waning of interest in one or two places means nothing and is to be expected now and then. The overall picture is what counts. The association has grown from five to some one hundred seventy odd fleets. As the old days merge into the new it becomes quite impossible to chronicle local activities and give credit where credit is due. I must content myself with thanking all those energetic Star officers for the part they played. Each and everyone of them was a necessary cog in the Star's ever spinning wheel of fame.

In recent years the panoramic view becomes so tremendous that I must refer to the Log and Starlights to refresh my memory and confine myself to covering outstanding incidents. For the most part that means radical rule changes and world's championships. Only in this book can the complete results of the latter be found under one cover. It would be practically impossible for anyone to work this out piecemeal by obtaining old Logs for the very good reason that many past issues have been exhausted. To the best of my knowledge there are only two entire sets in existence.

If the reader detects a slight similarity here and there to something he may have read before it is not plagiarism. All vest-pocket outlines of Star history, except for a few additions in 1951, were either written by me or from notes supplied by me. If I have inadvertently used some of the phrases of former star editors, I am sure that Jeff Davis, Charlie Lucke and Stan Ogilvy will forgive me.

No one must pick up this book under the misapprehension that it is some sort of manual on how to race or tune a Star While I have won more than my fair share of trophies in the past, I leave instructing to those better qualified in that department. Furthermore, I have no intention of writing an autobiography. My life, however, has been so closely interwoven with Star development that I must depend largely upon personal experiences and mention my own name frequently to make this a coherent narrative. Any theories or assumptions I may be tempted to indulge in are, of course, debatable, but the facts cited will be irrefutable.

Let me repeat that this is just a story of the Star's development. I aim to carry the reader through the evolution of yacht racing, from the dim past to the present, and try to show how the Star class has influenced that transformation throughout nearly half a century With the reader's indulgence, I shall strive to tell it with an open mind and without, I hope, being too trite.

CHAPTER I

MEET "POP" CORRY

"WAITER! HERE WAITER! . . . MORE COFFEE, MORE COFFEE."

This was supplemented by a visible signal—a long black arm being frantically waved to and fro.

Coffee pot in hand and with an absolutely blank expression the waiter shuffled by. He showed no indication of slowing down or altering his course. Being an efficient waiter he was a past master of the art of looking everywhere except in the direction of anyone who was trying to attract his attention. Out of the corner of his eye he caught a fleeting glance of that black arm, but it intruded upon the privacy of his thoughts. There was a sure thing in the third at Saratoga the next day. Should he bet his two bucks on the nose or to place? There was that damn arm again. There was something peculiar about it and the torso to which it was attached. He hesitated, took a second look and was lost. His curiosity got the better of him. At the risk of being unethical and a disgrace to his profession he decided that perhaps he had better serve that strange creature who had been bellowing for more coffee for the past half hour.

The strange creature turned out to be a coal black savage who, at first glance, appeared to be stark naked except for an abbreviated grass skirt tied about his middle. Closer inspection revealed the fact that he wore full length black tights and that his hands and face were covered with black makeup. The tights were not too snug a fit which gave one the impression that there might be a red flannel union suit beneath. Gold rimmed pince-nez, a big fat cigar and of all things, a high white starched collar completed the picture. Had the waiter known it, that collar was destined to become a trade mark identifying the wearer the world over. No one could ever have impersonated him because no one knew where to buy such a collar—the damn things had been out of style for about fifty years.

Having persuaded the waiter, much against the latter's will, to leave the coffee pot on the table, the cannibal king relaxed. He refilled the demi-tasse, tossed it off, and felt much better about life in general. Beside him sat the cannibal queen. Her wooly wig was a bit askew, but otherwise, except for the cigar and collar, her attire was the same. The occasion was a masquerade held in the pavilion of the Atlantic Yacht club, Sea Gate (Coney Island) N. Y. Mr. and Mrs. Cannibal had just been awarded first prize for the most grotesque costume. They richly deserved it. It would be difficult to imagine two more unsightly human beings. The king tossed off another demi-tasse. He was fairly bubbling over with good humor.

"Mother", he slapped his spouse on the thigh, "My gad mother, but you are the homeliest woman that I ever saw. Ha! Ha! Ha!"

"And you George", said the queen, eyeing the tip, which the king was pushing reluctantly towards the waiter, "are the meanest man that ever lived."

That was the first time I ever came in close contact with Mr. and Mrs. George Corry and it made a lasting impression. No one, as yet, called them "Pop" and "Ma", but I found out later that the press had already referred to him more than once as "The Father of the Star Class."

Atlantic Week, before World War I, was one of America's really great yachting classics. It did not draw as many entries as Larchmont or Marblehead, but that was compensated for in other ways. At that, quite a number of racing yachts from the Sound participated. The club provided two big sea-going tugs, which towed down from and back to the Sound, all who wished to attend, and many availed themselves of that courtesy. That was the way they did things in those days, when J. Stuart Blackton was commodore and Sir Thomas Lipton made that anchorage his headquarters for "teaing-up" the various "Shamrocks." It is difficult to believe now, but Gravesend Bay was then quite a popular rendezvous for large yachts. Its spectator fleet of steam yachts, large power boats and auxiliaries, was every bit the equal of Larchmont's. There were also other sizable clubs on the bay: The Marine & Field, Bensonhurst, Crescent Athletic, with a yachting division, and a number of smaller clubs. They had their own Y.R A., classes of their own and a number of classes in common with the clubs on the Sound. Combined, this resulted in turning lower New York bay, for one week of each year, into a scene of gay yachting activity.

Now do not confuse the foregoing with the deplorable attempts that were made some years later to revive this annual fixture, when the Atlantic Yacht club, in different hands, was not even a recognizable shadow of its former self. The era which I am talking about, and which few Star skippers of today remember, was in the early teens. The Star class was then new to the world of yachting. War clouds were begnining to gather over Europe, but in America life was carefree and gay, and no one as yet even suspected what horrors were in store. In those days, at Atlantic week, a guest's slightest suggestion was looked upon as a command. And do not think that the Star class, through its spokesman George Corry, did not have plenty of suggestions to offer. All I can

say is that anyone who attended those race weeks, and did
not have a good time, had no one but himself to blame.

The start and finish was off a high tower at the end of the
club dock. When finishing, all classes were required to pass
between Coney Island Point and a float called the "sea gate
mark." This forced them, on the home stretch, to sail for
about one hundred yards or so parallel to the shore. It made
for a better finish, from the point of view of the spectator,
and it also prevented the racing yachts from getting in among
those at anchor. Nearly thirty years later I almost suffered
what would have been my first and only disqualification in
the Star class as a result of an old race circular which mentioned the "sea gate mark." A scrub fleet committee was
conducting an elimination race and had handed out some of
these old circulars. Where they found them I have no idea.
They did not have the remotest idea of what the "sea gate
mark" was, never having seen it. Feeling that there should
be such a mark, they had taken it upon themselves to arbi-
trarily designate a white mooring buoy, way out in the middle
of the bay, as this mark. It made no sense at all. When I
tried to explain that there was no longer a "sea gate mark,"
they did not know what I was talking about. Finally I was
able to make them understand that this white buoy of theirs
was not described in the circular and they let me "withdraw"
instead of being disqualified. It was the same old story—
makeshift supplementary verbal instructions, given to some
and not to others. I could have won out on an appeal, but
what was the use.

As to the races in those grand old days of Atlantic Week—
well, it was different. You were not sent over the conventional
triangle, but given a series of buoys to round, which might
make a figure eight or most any fancy design. The tide was
cockeyed and ran like hell, but there was always a good
breeze. To locate a given buoy out around Ambrose Channel
was like trying to pick out a given fly on a well-filled piece
of fly paper. Once out in the channel you were apt to run
into almost anything from a submerged railroad tie, with a

spike in it, to an ocean liner. The more common obstructions, however, consisted of just good old healthy New York garbage, which you had to pick your way through or push off with a whisker pole—but it was interesting.

The race committee consisted of Sam Findlay, Doc Atkinson and good old John Brophy. I suppose that there were others officially on the R.C., but those were the old reliables, whose names remain engraved on one's memory. There was a trio in whose hands a stranger felt safe, and that is quite a statement to make, for in those days a visitor usually had to beat the race committee as well as his competitors. This is not meant as a reflection upon yacht racing. It was the trend of the times and true of every branch of sport. There was always a strong local prejudice against the visitor on general principles. A ball team that won was lucky to get out of another village with no greater casualty than being hit by a few pop bottles.

But let us get back to the masquerade—Atlantic week of 1914 was drawing to a close. We were seated at a large table over in one corner of the pavilion. By "we" I mean the Star crowd. Even in those nebulous days when there was not the vistage of an organization, Star folks gathered together. They felt even then that they were a different breed of cat from the rest and I am sure that the rest felt that way about them—they thought that we were crazy and still do. I was very new to it all. Names and faces did not as yet mean much to me, although Mr. Corry had introduced me to one or two Star owners that week as Mr. Alman of New London. My name was not Alman, nor did I come from New London. I was, however, flying a New Haven Y.C. burgee—so for Pop, as I was to learn later, that was pretty close. I cannot remember who else was at that table except Sig Adler. I knew him because his powerboat "Myjess" was anchored next to my yawl "Dawn II" and also flew a New Haven burgee. He was of the famous team of Adler & O'Brian. The latter was the skipper. He was an ice boat champ but only fair in a Star.

Corry, in addition to being a consistent winner in the

Star class, had made a habit of winning the masquerade prize. He was trying to tell us about the year before.

"Listen, let me tell you about mother. Listen! You, Adler, shut up," he gesticulated frantically. "Listen, will YOU PLEASE LISTEN . . ." "And when they gave mother the prize, they said, 'Take off your mask,' and she said, 'What do you mean? I'm not wearing a mask.'" It was an old bromide, but perhaps it really happened, because he told that story every year.

After that Mr. Corry settled down to talk Stars. That was what I had been waiting for. Being new to the Star class, I thought it best to adhere to the old principle of children being seen and not heard. I could not have been heard very well anyway, as I had a bad case of laryngitis. A drafty corner of an open air pavilion, with a northeast rain seeping in, every time the half-lowered awning flapped, was not the best place in the world to recuperate. Fortunately I did not have to make conversation, nor did anyone else. Mr. Corry was quite up to coping with that department single-handed. So I sipped old fashioneds and listened, with open mouth, to his words of wisdom—I did not know him as well as I did later. You will note that I was still thinking of him, most respectfully, as "Mr." Corry.

Seriously, there were many valuable hints, which we could have picked up, by paying more attention to what Mr. Corry had to say. He was one of the last exponents of the old rule of thumb school of skippering and those old fellows had a bag full of tricks, which any young skipper of today could use to advantage at times. There were things that they knew instinctively, which the aerodynamically minded brain trust has not even found a scientific answer for yet. When it's smooth sailing and one has plenty of time to figure out and apply one's text book knowledge, that's fine. When things begin to happen unexpectedly, however, then is the time when experience counts. It's then that a race can be won or lost by a decision that has to be made in the twinkling of an eye, and it's then that the old timer shines. He knows the answer. He does not know the reason for it, but he knows what to do and what the result will be.

To my mind George Corry was probably the greatest helmsman that ever raced in any class. Mind you, I did not say skipper, since that includes many other attributes. There is no skipper today, in any class, whose record is anywhere near as outstanding as was that of Mr. Corry during the early years of the Star class. Nor was his consistent winning confined to Stars. He did the same thing in the Bug class and in a couple of other small classes even before that. Now and then he skippered a larger yacht for some friend, a "P", "Q", "R", N.Y. thirty-foot, etc. and the result was the same. He told me once, and that was years ago, that he had won over one thousand prizes. He must, therefore, have had something on the ball. He knew very little about tuning a boat (we found that out later) and, for a good skipper, he did not keep his boat in what most of us would consider first class racing condition. He was, therefore, under a handicap to begin with. He took a boat as he found it, any boat, and he went out and won with it. He also told me once that he never read the rules, because they were just a matter of common sense and that he, therefore, knew them. When he was nearly eighty years old and had long since given up serious racing, he was loaned a Star, while a visitor, and damned if he did not win against the cream of our young skippers.

Strangely enough Mr. Corry reached the peak of his career while the Star class was still in its infancy. He was at his best in that year, 1914, when I first owned a Star. From then on he began to slip, because other Star skippers were not satisfied to go on sailing in the dark. They wanted to know the reason for things. They began hauling their boat out every week and took pride in having a perfect bottom. You heard the word "tune" much more frequently. It was not easy to tune a Star then. You could not shift your mast a fraction of an inch whenever you felt like it. It meant a half day's work to shift the mast position, but Star skippers kept working at it until they got their boats about as they wanted them This was something that Mr. Corry never did take the trouble to do.

In that year, 1914, Corry won Atlantic week with his "Little Dipper", Star No. 17. He did not then own No. 1, as some people think. It was ten years later that he acquired No. 1 and re-named it. Commander A. B. Fry, I believe, was second. He was usually second when Mr. Corry won. It had been the same in the Bug class. The commander always looked as if he had outgrown a Star and I oftened wondered how they ever got him in and out of a Bug without a shoe horn. He had a system all his own. While others tried to out sail or out guess Mr. Corry, the commander believed that useless, and just followed in the wake of the "Little Dipper." As a result he generally finished second. "Star Faraway" must hold the world's record for seconds.

Friday was to have been an off day. Some of the boys, however, intended to stay over until Saturday, anyway, for the Bensomhurst Regatta. Mr. Corry suggested a relay race between the sound and the sea. As I told you, Atlantic race committees were always open to suggestions. Just to show you how they co-operated on less than twenty-four hours' notice, they had on hand and ready to present, two sets of properly inscribed medals, by the time the said relay race was finished. Can you picture any race committee going to that much trouble today?

There may have been other relay races in yachting before or since, but if so I never heard of one. It was a publicity stunt, of course. Six new Stars had recently been delivered to Gravesend Bay and the press was all primed to give them a build-up. The new boats, however, refused to perform. Even Bill Inslee, reputed to be the most skillful tiller wiggler within smelling distance of the Coney Island hot dog stands, ended race week in about the middle. Seabury Lawrance, and no nicer guy ever lived, would have given us any sort of write-up we wanted, but the hands of the press were tied in those days. In an open regatta the big boats had to come first. They were owned by men whose names were something to

conjure with in financial circles. The Star was still just one
of many little classes. To play it up, you had to have a
good excuse. Mr. Corry had all that figured out. The relay
race would be something different. It would keep the boats
near home all the time and give the cameras plenty of
close-ups. There would be no other conflicting news that
Friday, hence the press could go to town. No matter which
team won, there would be a photo of Mr. Corry shaking hands
with the new owners and welcoming them into the Star
class. Just what his official position was no one knew, but
it was sort of taken for granted. The only thing that Mr. Corry
preferred seeing in the morning paper to a picture of a Star
was a picture of himself.

Now it so happened that I knew something about those
six new Stars. I was at New Haven a few weeks before when
they were launched. Irving Versoy let me sail two of them
on their maiden spin in Morris Cove. I had just traded an
Ike Smith Star for a Versoy Star, built the year before, but
I would not have accepted one of those new Gravesend boats
on a silver platter. They were the first Stars built with self-
bailing cockpits and I hope the last. I knew mighty little about
Stars then, but one touch of the helm was enough to tell me
that those boats were stiff, heavy and slow. They were old
apple crates. With all that extra weight and the water that
slushed around in the bilge, they could not be anything else.
Someone, of course, had an idea that a Star could not take
the rugged waters of Gravesend Bay. Someone has had the
same idea every year about some body of water, even little
ponds that you could spit across. The boats looked like
kayaks. The bright boy who thought up the idea has never
been identified. Like most people who go in for reforms
or safety measures, he overlooked a few things. One was
storage space. The whisker-pole had to be kept on deck,
being too long to fit in the cockpit. Once an anchor, cable and
two life belts, class requirements, were put in the cockpit.
There was no room left for the skipper or the crew. You
could not get any water out of the bilge until it was deep

enough to pump out, and in a flat bilged boat like a Star, in which the limber holes never work anyway, that meant that there was always a considerable weight of water to leeward. Needless to say, all those self-bailing cockpits came out before the season was over. I could have told them all this, but being a greenhorn, kept my mouth shut. It was still possible that they might prove their worth before Atlantic week was over. I had never sailed in those waters before.

The next morning, that is Friday morning, while I was at breakfast, I heard the club launch come panting alongside. I should have mentioned Charlie the launchman before. Charlie, with his handlebar mustachio, was as much of a fix-ture as the club house, the flag pole (A mast out of one of the famous America's Cup yachts) and the mint bed at its base. He ran that old naphtha launch from early morning to dawn the next morning, except when it caught fire—which was quite often. Some years later, when I was commodore of the Port Washington yacht club, we were able to acquire Charlie. He was probably the most famous launchman in yachting history. He remained at Port Washington until he died. On that day the club half masted its flag, so did the other clubs in the bay, and everyone in town went to his funeral. He had a host of friends, as he was never known to say a cross word to anyone. If he had, no one could have understood him. I had a paid hand of my own on the "Dawn II", one Olaf Hansen, who ran Charlie a close second, even to the mus-tachio. If I had to ask Charlie a question, I left it to Ole. When those two old squareheads started grunting at each other, it sounded like a pair of bull walruses, fighting over a fish, on an Arctic ice floe. Even the sea gulls began to screech and leave the bay.

Mr. Corry did not believe in signs, or perhaps he did. Being very yachty, we were flying the white meal pennant. Mr. Corry paid no attention to that but came aboard. He was in his morning regalia, a black and white checkered suit, high collar, black ascot tie and cigar, and a yachting cap. The latter was the only distinguishing mark between his business

attire and that which he wore at the club. I asked him if
he wanted a cup of coffee. That was a mistake, as I had
not had my second cup as yet and he finished up what was
left in the pot before I got it. The object of his visit was to
inform me that I was selected as one of the team of four to
represent the Sound. Why he picked on me I don't know.
Perhaps he thought it would impress New Haven, as the rest
were from the western end of the sound, but actually no one
knew me at New Haven except Jack, the bartender. He was
the one who got me into the club. To make matters worse, I
was to be anchor and sail the last leg against Inslee. I had
beaten him during the week, but a match race was another
matter. He waited for another pot of coffee to be brewed,
tossed off a couple of cups and left in a flurry of enthusiasm
and energy. You must not think of George Corry in those
days as an old gentleman. Far from it. I never saw such
a bundle of activity, but at that he was about fifty, although
he certainly did not look it.

I do not recall the exact batting order. Corry sailed the
first relay against "Half Moon", Chub. Corry won by a length
or so, high collar, cigar and sitting bolt upright as usual.
Cameras clicked and the most important part of the event
was over. Ray Findlay in No. 27 and Doc Atkinson in "Murad",
sailed the next two legs for Gravesend, but I am not sure in
what order. I cannot remember our second man—it might have
been Adler. Our third man was Commander Fry, but we
were a beaten team by then. Upon crossing the finish line,
a skipper had to pass or toss a flag to the next relay. The
course was short. A run to the sea gate mark and a beat
back to the club dock. Up to that point, the starting yacht
killed its headway on the line, boom eased to starboard and
the finishing one slipped under its stern from the weather
side. Commander Fry had other ideas. I still do not know
what they were. He bellowed at me to keep coming, so I did.
He tacked right in front of my bow, his crew tossing the flag
to mine. Then I got a perfect start. There was nothing on my
wind—why? because my boom swept his deck and took every-

thing with it, including Star Faraway's mast. It clipped it off as clean as a whistle. I looked back to see some three hundred pounds of indignant Naval officialdom giving his gob crew hell up Sixth street. It was all in a hopeless cause. Inslee, in "Shadow", No. 28, had several lengths lead. If there had been any appreciable distance to go, I believe I could have caught him, for No. 28, with its self-bailing cockpit, was an old crate. Bill Inslee, however, was some skipper and, although I gained plenty on the run down wind, it was no trick for him to keep me covered on that short beat home. I tried the few tricks I knew, like yelling to my crew that we were going about and not going. Inslee knew a damnsight more than I did, however. At that I almost got through him at the last moment. I sailed him in close to the dock, where the wind was a little tricky and I almost lost him. He won by one second. It was an inglorious finish. I felt very badly about the commander's mast, but could not see that it was my fault. I talked it over with Mr. Corry and he agreed with me.

And now we come to the GREATEST MOMENT in the life of every Star skipper—the WINNING OF HIS FIRST RACE. As previously explained, most everyone stayed over for the Bensonhurst Regatta. It was not part of race week but they gave good prizes. As a result they had a good entry list. That is something that yacht clubs do not understand today. They think that shooting a few guns and giving you a race is all that is required of them. They are very much mistaken. The character of the prizes determined a club's rating in a skipper's mind then and does now. I had been fighting laryngitis all week and it was winning. The question was whether I should take a taxi, go back to town and see a doctor, or take a shot at the Bensonhurst race. I should have gone ashore and got a circular, but figured I could pick one up from the Committee boat, if I decided to start. The start was about a mile away. We saw the other boats hoist sail and start over one by one. "Zete", my Star, No. 36, was astern of the "Dawn II." Ole had the sails bent on and was standing by. The temptation became too much to resist. I grabbed a quart of whiskey and started over. God, but it was hot and I had a fever.

I misfigured. The wind was light and by the time we got there, the race had started. It was too late to round up and ask for a circular. I shouted for the course and the committee shouted back. Neither I nor my crew, George Cochran, were sure as to what was said. It made no difference anyway. I would not be able to finish. He was a medical student and thought I was crazy to even attempt a start. All we had to do was follow the bunch and go where they went, as long as we could keep them in sight. "Just to make it interesting," I suggested, "let's take a drink each time we pass a boat."

It was pretty light going the first time around. We only passed two of the old apple crates and I had to cheat a bit. On the second round, the weather began to look bad. A squall was making up to the north and killing what wind there was. We passed a couple of more boats and did a bit more cheating There were no oilers aboard and Cochran told me that I would be crazy to get wet. The leaders were bucking a strong ebb tide and having one hell of a time getting around the outer buoy. Once they rounded it, they headed right for the Narrows and the squall. Whoever got it first would be the winner. At this point I felt so bad that I finally gave in and headed back toward the Atlantic Y.C. where the "Dawn II" was anchored. I was in hopes of making it before the squall hit and we were drenched. It was so black by that time that we could no longer see the rest of the Star fleet.

We were not fifty yards from the "Dawn II", my crew being already up on deck with a line in his hand, when things began to happen. The wind suddenly came in over Coney Island Point, a fine, stiff southwester. The finish line was only about a mile away. All I had to do was ease sheet and run for it. I yelled at Ole, as we went by, to start the motor and pick me up if it began to rain. The squall was breaking up The sun was getting low but there was still plenty of time before the time limit. The "Zete" went boiling across the

line and I got my first winner's gun. I'll say this much, I made
a good job of it. Looking towards the Narrows, I could see
a few little white dots on the skyline. Those were the other
Stars I have no idea when they finished. The sun had set
and we had finished dinner when Doc Atkinson sailed by and
said that he was second. It was difficult to tell how many
boats we passed on that last leg, but we played it safe and
finished the quart.

No story of Atlantic week of old would be complete, or
so I judged from what Mr. Corry told me, without mention
being made of its anti-climax, the Whitestone Regatta. The
Whitestone Yacht club was located somewhat to the east of
Hell Gate. It had been the custom of the yachts returning to
the Sound, after Atlantic week was over, to stop off and enter
its annual regatta. That, of course, was on a Sunday. Mr Corry
talked it up, but was not able to get many to promise to stop
off. The tugs agreed to drop off all who wished it, but they
would not remain and take them on to Larchmont and Manhasset Bay later. You cannot blame them. The tide was wrong
and they would have lost hours.

Mr. Corry persuaded me to tow his "Little Dipper", and
that was no trick at all for the "Dawn II." She had an old 4
cylinder Standard that could have towed a railroad float A
dozen or more Stars would have been a cinch. In fact in the
years to come, the "Dawn II" did that frequently. It became
the official tow boat from Manhasset Bay to points east, on
Long Island Sound, and return—that is for Stars, although we
often took along a couple of N.Y. 30's and the like.

We gave Whitestone a gun and waited. In perhaps twenty
minutes there was an answering boom from the club. The
tugs went by and did not even hesitate. We "must" Mr. Corry
told me, go ashore, since they were expecting us. If they were,
they had a strange way of showing it. I am very much afraid
that Mr Corry was thinking back to a custom that had died
out many years before. Some Whitestone official greeted us,
but you could see that he was ill at ease. It was like dropping
in on the maid's night out. The official acted like a husband

who had invited some friends to drop in, without having told his wife about it, on a Sunday afternoon, when she did not want to be bothered with visitors. All that slipped off Corry's back like water from a duck's. He took it for granted that there would be a race and those poor fellows got together somehow and held one.

It was the craziest race I ever did sail in. If you think the tides are bad in Lower New York Bay, then try racing off Whitestone. Aside from us, there was one other Star. I think it was No. 20. I do not know where it came from, nor was I ever able to find out later. It started with us, rounded the first mark and vanished. To this day, the official record on No 20 reads "Unknown." If there ever was a ghost ship in the Star class, that was it.

Whitestone had three old Bugs of its own. Poor little unkept things, I felt sorry for them. Even Mr. Corry, their champion for years, turned his back upon them and my Star "Zete" actually blushed. The "Zete" had never seen its poor relations before, nor had I. Anyway, off we went, or at least off went "Little Dipper." Corry knew the tides there and I did not. In a few minutes I could not even read his number. He had no crew and borrowed Olaf Hansen. I naturally thought he had won, but Ole had no intention of letting him get away with it—he said Corry hit a mark. Corry said that he did and so told the race committee. The committee, however, did not seem inclined to believe him. Even if he had hit a mark, they felt he should be credited with the race. It was my second win in two days and I did not feel that way about it We exchanged letters on the subject most of the winter and finally I received a little pewter cup, about two inches high.

There were two more years of the old time Atlantic weeks. Inslee, minus a self-bailing cockpit, had come into his own and won the next and Ed Willis won the following year. Still more Stars came down from the sound. There were boxing bouts, minstrel shows and masquerades. In the latter, Mr. Corry once more carried off the honors. This time he was an organ grinder and his crew, Billy Newman, who was only about four feet high, was the monkey. The way "Pop" treated that poor little guy was terrible. One morning he rounded up alongside my yawl, miscalculated and put a dent in her. It was his own fault, but "Pop" got so mad that he picked up a piece of rope with a knot at the end, and beat Billy over the head with it. That was the ancient and approved method of treating crews.

There is one other incident, that I feel is worthy of note. Adrian Iselin will remember this. He is the only active Star skipper left at this writing, who raced in those days In trying to get back across Ambrose Channel, we ran into a long tow, and I mean long. The barges had lengthened out to go to sea and I believe that tow reached back to the Narrows. It would have taken us the better part of an hour to pass. The hawsers were under water but no one knew how far or how long they would remain so. Iselin picked out, what appeared to be the middle of the line, and sailed over it I followed I looked back a moment later. One of the barges must have veered, for I saw that hawser lift clear off the water and shake itself. The next day the race committee made a rule against jumping tow lines, and rightfully so. There is some old saying about "Fools step in where angels fear to tread." There was no doubt in my mind as to the category in which Iselin and I belonged. If the rest of that gang, that were stuck out in the channel, on the other side of the tow, were angels, then the sounds that were wafted across the Bay was the strangest heavenly chorus I ever hope to hear.

I was destined to win the next Atlantic week, but not until after World War I. For four years there was no activity on the lower bay The Stars held together remarkably on the Sound, in fact they increased, and they were largely responsible for reviving yacht racing after the war. But not so at Gravesend. There, like many other places, yacht racing was almost completely wiped out. Atlantic week of 1920, however, was supposed to be a gala affair. The America's Cup race of 1914, postponed because of the war, was to be sailed that year between "Resolute" and "Shamrock IV." The latter, half way across the Atlantic when the war broke out in Europe, had been towed into Bermuda and had remained there for safe keeping ever since. Now she was anchored off the Atlantic Yacht club, which Sir Tom once again designated as his headquarters. Atlantic week was shifted to July, so it could be sailed on alternate days with the America's Cup races. The eyes of all the yachting world were on New York's lower bay again.

Quite a number of yachts came down from the Sound, but no Stars among them, except mine. That was the year George Corry was sick and, without him, there was no organization or enthusiasm. Mr. Corry was up on a ladder, mending something on the roof, slipped and fell on his head. Now you may not believe this and I will not vouch for its authenticity, but, George told me that his doctor told him that had it not been for his high collar, he would have broken his neck Because he was unable to race a Star that year, it broke his streak of consecutive years of racing. That is the only reason why I still hold the record of thirty-three consecutive years.

I expected to find some local Stars on Gravesend Bay, but there was only one—Murad, No. 24, owned by Doc Atkinson. The Doc was really quite upset. Before the series started, he took me aside and told me that he did not want to take any undue advantage of a visitor. If I preferred, I could race in the handicap division. He had worked out some sort of under-sized sail area for "Murad", which he claimed would make her outclass any Star. Of course, he would be busy with the committee and his son would sail the boat, which might offset that advantage a little—it was up to me. I elected to take a chance. Well, the Doc was right, except in reverse. I never won a Star series so easily in my life. I would be finishing the second round and the race, while "Murad" was no more than a couple of hundred yards ahead of me, starting the second round. Sir Tom gave a special prize for the Stars to sail for after Atlantic week was over. The Doc came to me again This time he wanted to know if I minded starting with the handicap division, a miscellaneous group of little craft, because his kid wanted a chance to win something. We were to count in both classes We did and I won both. It's queer what ideas people can get about rigging Stars in some special way for their local conditions. Will they ever learn?

That was really the end of Atlantic week, as we knew it. A number of years later a Star fleet was started on Gravesend Bay and a weak attempt was made to revive this old classic. The club, however, was in different hands. Things were not the same and, probably, the less said about that the better.

CHAPTER II

GENEALOGY OF THE STAR

HAVING MET THE STAR CLASS during an old fashioned Atlantic race week, I hope that the reader may have
gained something of the same impression of it as I did.
We must now delve into the dim past, for there is no point
in embarking upon a voyage without knowing from whence
you start. Those who have been in the Star class for some
time, probably know much of what is contained in this
chapter and they will have to bear with me. To others, however, the genealogy of the Star, which can be quite accurately
traced, and the circumstances and general conditions leading
up to the building of the first Stars, should prove to be of
considerable interest.

The hull is of humble origin but, nevertheless, of sturdy
pioneer stock. Its design is strictly North American and cannot be mistaken for anything else. When the first settlers were
able to obtain boards and gave up using log canoes, they
began to build little boats known as flatties. These flatties

---

FOOT NOTE
Data on the Star's hull and early one-design class activities, was furnished, in 1930, by the
late William P Stephens, acknowledged as the leading authority on American racing yachts
and the history of their design Genealogical data upon the rig was obtained from Earnest A
Ratsey He needs no other introduction, since his family has been the foremost sailmakers on
both sides of the Atlantic for many generations Such scanty information as the author has
of the Bug class, depends upon his memory of conversations with the late Commodore George
A Corry

became abundant along the North Atlantic coast from the Carolinas to and throughout New England. In these little flat bottom boats you find the first trace of what eventually led to the Star's design.

The Star's common ancestor was the New Haven Sharpie, which can be traced back to 1835. Although we blush to admit it, these sharpies were used primarily for oystering. They had two masts with leg-of-mutton sails, but no jib. Next came the Nonpareil Sharpie, built at Roslyn, Long Island, in 1880. It had a slight V bottom, another step toward the Star hull. All of these little boats, up to this point, had centerboards. The type was not considered especially adaptable for racing, nevertheless, several more or less unsuccessful attempts were made in that direction. There was the Mascot of 1879, a big lumbering craft with little speed. Then the Question, built in 1895, on whose performance I have no information. The Departure which appeared in 1896 was designed by William Gardner to beat the Newport 30's. It was able to do so in a breeze or with plenty of reaching, but not otherwise. The Departure has straight sides, a chine and a fin keel. It is the last connecting link, in an unbroken chain, from the primitive log canoe to the Bug class, the Star's immediate predecessor and prototype.

The rig, all four phases, which have been of European influence, is of more aristocratic lineage, that is to say rather of yacht than work boat derivation. There is no point in going into much detail of the genealogy of the rig, since it applies to all racing yachts Only the present phase, namely, *flexible spars*, originated in and were developed by the Star class Thus we have a new world hull and an old world rig, a truly international combination for a world-wide international class.

The Bug rig and first Star rig was the *sliding gunter*, presumably English. It consisted of a gaff (or yard) almost as long as the boom, which peaked up to more than half its own length above the top of the mast To give you some idea of the length of the gaff, it was about 3 feet longer than the present boom. It looked quite different from the average gaff rig of those days, which had a shorter gaff that set at perhaps a 30% angle to the mast. The first Stars had only one set of shrouds. The mainsail was laced to the gaff and the boom and the luff was lashed to old fashioned wooden mast hoops, which were supposed to slide up and down the mast but often jammed. Like the little East Side Kids, who used to be sewed up in their underclothes for the winter, the mainsail, once on, stayed on and in most instances for the entire season. After a rain you went aboard, took off the waterproof sail-cover and hoisted the drenched sail to dry. Within a week or so mildew began to appear and by the end of the season the sail was pretty black. It would have been difficult to beat any rule limiting the number of suits of sails allowed per season, had there been such a rule, because you could spot a new sail as easily as you can a substitute who has just gone into a football game on a muddy field. No one even thought of changing sails before a race. It was much too long a process.

In 1921 the *short Marconi* was made optional. Owners were rather skeptical about this, because an experiment a few years before on Star No. 46 proved a failure. The mast was the combined length of the old mast plus the distance the gaff had extended above it. Because good skippers had always kept the old gaff peaked up so high that it was practically parallel to the mast, the mainsail could be used on the short marconi by simply putting slides on the luff. The boom remained unchanged. The track and slide idea was so convenient that it was immediately applied to the boom also. From then on skippers began to own sails of different draft and bent them on just before a race. The rig varied considerably. Some used long wooden spreaders and others none at all. This rig was retained for nine or ten years, and in case of some fleets for even longer. The term *Marconi rig* is really a misnomer, although it has now come into pretty general use. When the first tall sticks appeared on the larger racing yachts, with several sets of spreaders and their complex systems of staying, it reminded people of a Marconi wireless station. Hence the name *Marconi*. The correct name is *Bermudian rig* It made its first appearance in Bermuda on a racing sloop in 1808 and that yacht is recorded as having easily beaten its rivals. Later it was used even on pilot boats in Bermuda, but more than a century elapsed before it began to gain favor among the racing yachtsmen of either continent.

The *tall Marconi* was made optional by the Star class in 1930. Enrique Conill had a long talk with the writer in January, 1929, at Havana. He was trying to develop the Star class in Europe, but reported that the European yachtsmen would not adopt any such antiquated rig as the Star still had Actually the *short Marconi,* with its long boom, was a bastard rig. The only excuse for it was to make it possible to use the same mainsail. Modernizing the rig had already been discussed, but economy in those days was the underlying thought that governed any proposed revision of the rules. It was obvious that the Star was beginning to look pretty seedy and out of date. Those intending to have new Stars built, both abroad and in America, did not own old mainsails and were not interested in that angle of it. Conill's arguments, however, were the deciding factor A tentative *tall Marconi* rig was demonstrated by Frank Robinson during the World's Championship at New Orleans in October of 1929. The mast was lengthened by almost five feet and the boom shortened, but the annual meeting, which adopted the rig in principle, insisted that the sail area remain the same. A committee consisting of Earnest Ratsey, Prescott Wilson, Frank Robinson and Larry Bainbridge worked out the new specifications. They are the same specifications that apply today This was the starting signal for the really worldwide development of the Star class on all continents. It made a remarkable difference in the boat's appearance, which can best be described in Commodore Corry's own words: "The Star now looks like a slim, graceful, young girl, instead of a fat dumpy little old woman."

Spar flexing is an operation. It was the fourth major phase in Star development, but it was no more a change of rig than the advent of the roller boom. By this I mean that it involved no change in the *tall Marconi* specifications, which were not even morally infringed upon. Spar diameters were slightly reduced, especially that of the boom. The latter was trimmed from about its mid-point to a bar across the center of the cockpit Spar diameters and method of rigging had always been optional. Only the length of spars and size of sails were regulated. This maintained uniformity in design, but gave the skipper enough leeway to use his ingenuity and this policy has been responsible for the continued improvement in Stars. *Flexible spars* can be credited to Walter von Hutschler. They originated in Germany in 1936, although von Hutschler claims that he was simply trying to lighten his rig and did not realize the advantage to which they could be put until he raced his "Pimm" in the 1937 World's Championships on Long Island Sound. Nevertheless several European Stars raced in the 1936 Olympics with booms that trimmed to the center of the cockpit. These included "Wannsee", the winning German entry, sailed by Dr. Bishoff. Leading skippers in the Americas began to experiment with *flexible spars* in 1938. This process opened up an entirely new field in *draft control*. It is the only completely new theory, of any real scientific value, connected with the aerodynamics of sail, which has been introduced since the Marconi rig. While this almost automatic method of *draft control*, by means of spars, may not be thoroughly perfected as yet, the theory is simple and fundamentally sound. For that reason, either in its present or some improved form, it will be eventually adopted by all racing yachts. But more about *flexible spars* later At the moment we are dealing with the general development of the Star's design, and this brings us up-to-date with regard to the rig.

Major dimensions of the Star's hull and its three rigs will be found at the end of this chapter. Those who desire greater detail, can obtain plans, or the specifications alone, from the International Star Class Yacht Racing Association.

One-design racing in the old days, or to be more exact, the adverse conditions surrounding this type of racing, had a very definite bearing upon the rules, policy and ultimate growth of the Star class. At this point, therefore, it would be advisable to briefly review the salient facts which affected the one-design yacht of the past. The dividing line between its ancient and modern history, was world war I. As we now look back, we can see that the first world war marked the end of an old era and the beginning of a new one. This was true, not only of one-design racing, but of yachting in general.

The first one-design yachts were the Water-Wags They began racing in the year 1878 on Dublin Bay, Ireland. The enterprising owners of these little boats, who were far ahead of their day, even had a class organization, known as the Water-Wag Association. It is too bad that they were unable to spread their idea further afield, since that might have saved about forty years in getting one-design racing organized on a sound basis.

An epidemic of one-design racing raged throughout the yachting world about the turn of the century, but it got off on the wrong foot. That, of course, was during the hey-day of the large racing yacht The activities of those majestic creatures, however, were confined to very few highly developed racing centers, localities where a number of prominent yacht clubs were clustered together within a comparatively small area In such centers, one-design classes had a name and sail emblem, and were included in the weekend open regattas, held by various clubs. Once you moved away from these centers, however, yacht clubs were widely separated. There was no inter-club racing and no large racing yachts were to be found in their anchorage, unless they were visitors. The one-design classes were smaller numerically, few carried any sail emblem and they were known only by the name of the club.

Every yacht club, large or small, had its own one-design class The smaller clubs, that were scattered throughout the world and constituted the great majority, were entirely de-

pendent upon their one-design class for such racing as they
had, plus, perhaps, a handicap class made up of miscellaneous
small boats. The idea seemed to be that each club must have
a distinctive one-design class of its own, a boat especially
designed for its particular weather conditions and different
from any other one-design class. In other words a one-design
class was considered a strictly local proposition and the
private property of a given club. That was fine for the
designers, but it isolated every group of small boat skippers
and prevented them, as well as the clubs, from having any
interests in common.

Most of these classes of little inexpensive cat boats, sloops
or knockabouts (a knockabout being a sloop without a bow-
sprit) consisted of from four to six boats. Of course there were
some larger classes of a dozen or more, but I am speaking
of the average little club. After the first flush of enthusiasm,
which seldom lasted beyond the first season, the class began
to break up. One skipper won most of the races, which was
natural enough, and the tail enders became disgusted and
sold their boats. They were frequently sold out of the club,
and then there would not be enough boats left to make a race.
As soon as one class died out, another was started. The average life of such little classes was two to three years. In the
established racing centers, their life span was a bit longer.
There, if a couple of boats were sold to a neighboring club,
it did not make too much difference, since most of the racing
was in open Saturday regattas. Even in such instances, however, unless the class was fairly large numerically, the boats
soon got into inactive hands.

There were also some one-design classes of large yachts,
such as the N.Y. 30's, 50's, and 40's. The first named held
together for many years. While these were New York Yacht
Club classes, nevertheless they enjoyed inter-club racing, since
their owners, in almost every instance, also belonged to other
clubs Furthermore, they had the support of all the prominent
clubs, which the little classes lacked. The little one-design
classes were constantly changing and difficult to keep track

of. There were so many of them, all of which had to be provided for in an open regatta, that several were started on the
same gun. There was one rule which held true in all cases,
every one-design class gradually began to dwindle after the
first year and in no case were new boats ever added to such
classes, until the Star came along. Before the Star, there was
no such thing as a growing one-design class.

The Bug class made its inauspicious debut, in the midst
of this chaotic jumble of small fry, in 1907, at the Western
end of Long Island Sound. It was a seventeen-foot knockabout,
the smallest keel boat of its day. The keel weighed one hundred fifty pounds and the boat cost one hundred forty dollars.
It has often been referred to as a Star in miniature, but
such was not quite the case. According to Francis Sweisguth,
while the design was very similar, it was not absolutely
identical

Very little of the Bug's history has been handed down,
for after all, it was only one among innumerable little classes
and did not attract much attention. Evidently they were
pretty seaworthy little fellows, for the New York Herald of
July 27, 1907, published a glowing account of a wind-swept
Sound, of lost masts and split sails, and stated that the Bugs
were the only class to finish without a casualty. The Big
Bug, sailed by George Corry, won that race. Again in 1909,
when the Larchmont Yacht Club cancelled its regatta, because of a northeasterly gale, four Bugs sailed the course,
with double reefed mainsails and no jibs; Corry winning and
Donald Cowl finishing second. While several of the Bug
owners sailed for the first couple of years in Stars, the two
just mentioned and Commander A. B. Fry, were the only
ones whose names made Star history. The Bug was also
one of the very few classes that actually started as an inter-
club class, rather than becoming one later as a result of boats
being sold into other clubs.

There was one interesting story about the Bugs, which
George Corry was fond of telling. It seems that some of the
owners became fed up with his winning so constantly while

his shadow, Commander Fry, placed second. Then for a time Pop was beaten by boats which he had experienced no trouble with before and could not remember having seen in the race. Race committees also began to notice that more Bugs finished than had started. What happened was that some of the Bugs sailed over to the Long Island shore or lurked behind Execution Light, depending upon the course, until all the miscellaneous small fry began to round the mark. Then they would sail out and mingle in the parade, making sure that no Bug had yet rounded. The race committee, of course, gave a gun to each new sail emblem that crossed the line. It might have jotted down the number of boats that started, but it did not have a list of the numbers on their sails, that is not until Pop smelled a rat and put a stop to this.

You may think that the above is a pretty tall tale, but I am not so sure that it is. I raced in those days myself and can tell you that the idea was to win, no matter how. A smart trick, if you could get away with it, was something to even brag about, that is after the time limit for filing a protest had expired. The general feeling seemed to be that rules were written to be beaten, if you were clever enough to do it. For example, I doubt if there was a skipper who did not, at one time or another, haul out his boat secretly in the dead of night, before some important race, and apply potlead to the bottom. It was believed to be against the rules, but the laugh was on them Not so long ago, Yachting published an article about having looked back over all available old racing rules and having found no rule against the use of graphite on a boat's bottom. In spite of this, I know of cases where race committees, of small clubs, disqualified yachts for having done that, so sure were they that it was against the rules. You can scarcely blame them, for there was no standard code of rules in those days. A race committee of one of the isolated little clubs was lucky if it had an old year book of some larger club to refer to I know that I raced cat boats for two years before I ever saw a rule book of any kind. If we did get our hands on one, we assumed it to be a syllabus and not the complete text.

If you really want to hear a tall tale, also told by George Corry, here it is. Before the day of the Bug, when he was sailing a Swamscot Dory, a race was arranged from Cow Bay (now Manhasset Bay) to Hempstead Harbor, the next bay to the east. This was a free for all, open to all the little centerboard boats. No rules, other than right-of-way were to apply. That meant that you did not have to round any given buoys but cut corners as you pleased. The first in was to be the winner. Since there were no power boats, the question of getting a tow was not considered. Immediately after crossing the starting line, one of the entries sailed back to the club and beached his boat. The crew went overboard and carried it to a farm wagon, which was waiting. Passing through the village of Port Washington, they picked up a little German band that was playing in front of a saloon. It was only a short distance overland to Hempstead Harbor. When they reached there they launched the boat, stepped the mast, and, as there was no crew limit, crowded the four piece German band aboard. It almost sank the boat, but the weather was light and they only had a short distance to go. With the band playing "There'll Be A Hot Time In The Old Town Tonight," they crossed the finish line. Having complied with all the conditions of the race, the triumphal procession started home, with the cup, before the first sail was sighted in the mouth of Hempstead Harbor It was just as well, for fists had been known to fly after a race for much less provocation, especially when Baymen (professionals) were allowed in the boats. My only comment on this yarn is that George Corry was always known to be a pious, temperate and truthful gentleman.

Getting back to the Bug class, after four years, the owners decided that the boats were too small, too wet and much too uncomfortable. Anyone who has ever raced a Star can well imagine what it must have been like in a six foot shorter boat, for two persons to handle themselves in a proportionately smaller cockpit. In all other respects the owners liked their boats and believed that a slightly larger boat of the same design would be ideal—and in this they were right It has been generally believed that George Corry was the first to suggest that the lines of the Bug be extended. That may be true, as he was the ring leader of that group. If we are to stick to the known facts, however, there is no proof of it In discussing the matter, he always said "we" From that one might assume that it was a natural conclusion reached by the majority of the owners Commander Fry had every reason to think of it first He was a man of such ample girth, that he must have suffered more discomfort sailing a Bug than any of the others. Be that as it may, a committee was appointed, consisting of George Corry, A B. Fry, Thornton Smith and William G. Newman, to take this matter up with William Gardner. That was done in the early fall of 1910, and thus the Star was born.

Because George Corry, in later years, became known as the "Father of the Stars," numerous false rumors have been spread about his early activities. He accomplished enough for the Star class, as it was, without the need of any mythical buildup, to further prove his right to the foregoing title. To keep the records straight, let us correct these rumors. More than once I have seen it in print that he designed the Star. While it is understandable that some uninitiated reporter may have assumed this, I happen to know that quite a number of people believe it, as I come across one every now and then. He was not a naval architect and could not have designed any boat. One ambitious Log editor, amplified upon my data, in an effort to show that George Corry was responsible for the Bug class, since he had always felt that a flat bottom boat with a fin keel would be popular He may have thought that, but William Gardner incorporated that principle in the Departure, which was built eleven years before the Bug class. Nor did our former commodore name the Star. He himself admitted that he wanted it called the Big Bug class. One shudders at the thought, for under such a handicap, no class could hope to attain international dignity or respect. Stuyvesant Wainright, of the American Yacht Club, suggested the name Star, although he never owned one of the boats. What George Corry did, once the project was launched, was to promote the Star class. He did practically all of the committee's work. He was the one who went out and found the original twenty-two owners. He possessed the rare attribute of being able to impart his own enthusiasm to others, and this he continued to do for the Star class as long as he lived.

The Star and the Bug also were designed by William Gardner, all other theories to the contrary notwithstanding. Curtis D. Mabry was the draftsman, who put the Bug on paper, although Francis Sweisguth had something to do with that also. The latter was the draftsman assigned to extending the Bug lines into those of the Star. William Gardner supervised the work in each case, but even if he never touched pencil to paper, the others were in his employ and he was the chief designer. He took far more interest in the Star than most people realize. He lived in Port Washington at the time and was a personal friend of George Corry. On an average of twice a week these two went over to Ike Smith's shop and watched the first Stars being built. They did this in the evening on their return from work. I have that information from the taxi driver who drove them from the station to Smith's shop and who still drives me down the Island now and then when I go on a fishing trip.

William Gardner was a very meek self-conscious little man. For that reason it was always very difficult for us to get him to attend Star functions. He had the mistaken idea that he was only invited for the purpose of astounding us with some new ideas about yacht design That we just wanted him there for himself never seemed to occur to him. Throughout dinner he was always too nervous to eat. Once he was through with his brief speech, however, he would relax, light a cigar, and tell very interesting things to those who were near enough to hear him. If we had only thought of just asking him questions, it would have been much easier for him and more interesting for all, as he was a man who never felt at home in a crowd.

Ike Smith of Port Washington built twenty-two Stars during the winter of 1910-11. Half of these boats went as a unit to the American Yacht Club of Rye, and the rest were sold to members of various clubs at the western end of the Sound. They cost $260.00 each. Here again I must correct a false impression. They were not the only first Stars built, as Green Brothers of Chelsea, Mass., built eleven Stars that same winter. These Green Brothers boats were built for members of the Nahant Dory Club and were originally known as Nahant Bugs. It was not until ten years later that we discovered they were Stars. That is why Ike Smith was credited with building the first Stars, instead of having to share that questionable honor with another firm. Why William Gardner never told George Corry about this, is difficult to understand, as they saw each other almost daily on the train. He may not even have known that Star plans and not Bug plans were sold to Nahant, for his was a large and busy office at that time. The Nahant Bugs, in spite of their name, had a Star emblem on the sail. They raced at Marblehead Week each year. Yachtsmen from the Sound went there in larger yachts and still no one noticed that there were Stars up there. It only goes to show how disorganized small boat racing was at that time. The Nahant Stars had duplicate numbers to those on the Sound, hence when this group joined the association, they had to be given new numbers, which were not in keeping with the year the boats were built.

The first Star race was held by the Harlem Yacht Club on May 30, 1911, off Execution Light, at the western end of Long Island Sound. The order of finish was as follows:

No. 17	*Little Dipper*	G. A. Corry	3:13:52
No. 11	*Twinkle*	A. B. Alley	3.16.56
No. 19	*Snake*	F. S Richards	3:19:37
No. 7	*Ceti*	R G. Browne	3:22:40
°	*Gold Bug*	H. K. Landis	3:26:16

* NOTE—Except in the summary, published by the New York Herald, the following day, Star records do not reveal either a boat or owner of this name. No reason is given why the rest of the 22 new Stars did not start.

George Corry's winning streak continued throughout 1911. He won 10 out of 12 starts and the Sound championship. Larchmont Race Week, however, went to Twinkle. Corry and Alley are the only two names that figured in Star history thereafter, although it was Jack Alley, the son of A B, who sailed Twinkle from that point on. There is no record of who won the first race later that summer at Nahant, but A. S. Johnson and the Motley brothers were the most consistent winners. I did race against A. B. Alley during a Larchmont Week, some years later, when he was substituting in one race for his son. He was way back and never bothered to round the last mark—Scotch Caps. He probably did not intend to cross the finish line in entering Larchmont harbor, but he did and his time was taken. He beat about 10 boats that were ahead of him, as a result of this, but no one protested. No one liked to protest unless they had a chance to win some silverware because of the hostile attitude of most race committees. One who protested was always made to feel like a very poor sport, no matter how just his cause.

The family tree had two other branches, the Indian class and the Fish class, both of which withered without bearing fruit. The Indian was a glorified Bug. Sponsored by a Mr. Carpenter, about a dozen of these boats started racing at Ossining, on the Hudson, in 1909. Some claim that they were Bugs, except for the sail emblem, the profile of an Indian chief, with feathered headdress. I question this, for two reasons. I have seen plenty of Bugs and a couple of Indians, but not together. I never mistook a Bug for a Star, but I did the Indian, at first glance. It impressed me as being a step nearer to a Star. That was too long ago for me to remember whether this was due to the hull or the rig, but there was something different Then too, I know the tendency of Gardner's office to make some changes in plans or specifications, upon the least provocation. Remember that clubs, at that time, wanted a special class of their own, designed for their particular conditions Unless the designer made some changes, he would hardly feel entitled to his fee. There have been a number of Fish classes, but the one I refer to was a twenty-eight foot Star. There were four or five of these boats built for owners at Port Washington, N. Y , in 1913 Ed Willis, who later became a famous Star skipper, won all the races. The Fish, with a Dolphin as a sail emblem, suffered the common fate of all one-design classes of half a dozen boats or less. It lasted less than two years. Star lines, extended to that size, made a very box-like clumsy-looking boat.

It will be seen from the foregoing that the Star hit the happy medium of this type of design. Larger boats did not look yachty and smaller ones were much too cramped for comfort The reason that the Star has been able to keep modern in appearance is that its hull design is unique A Star is a Star and looked upon as such. No comparison is drawn between its hull design and that of other boats, hence the hull can never be out of date, nor need the Star fear competition in other boats of similar design, as it has been tried in both larger and smaller yachts and proved to be a failure.

The age of fittings really began in 1924, when Rhody, sailed by Comstock and Gidley, of Providence, appeared at the Internationals (now called World's Championship) with enough hardware on the boat to sink a small battleship. Those fittings were very heavy, but accomplished much the same purpose of most of the fittings now in use. At least they supplied the idea from which lighter and more efficient fittings were later developed. The Rhody Runner, for example, was the first self locking backstay device. It consisted of a track and a latch, which fell over the end of it. The tension of the stay was adjusted by a small turnbuckle or a lanyard This, and a number of other Rhody fittings, were introduced by Walter C. (Jack) Wood, also of Providence, who was the first manufacturer of special Star fittings. Hence Providence, R. I., was the birthplace of Star appliances.

The original gaff rigged Stars had only a few very simple fittings—a stern traveller, half a dozen cleats and a metal strap, with just one hole drilled in it, which served as a chain plate. Those who used backstays (they were optional) usually had a small block and tackle at the end of the stay, which hooked into a ring bolt on deck and you then trimmed and fastened to a cleat. No one ever thought of setting the backstay, when going to windward, to keep the jibstay taut. Those short masts were heavy and substantial and, in fact, a backstay was really not necessary running down wind, unless it was blowing half a gale.

When the short Marconi came into vogue, regular chainplates, with a cross piece having a number of holes in it, became necessary to take care of the two sets of shrouds. That is when Star owners first began to become fitting minded. The first mast raker was nothing but two threaded bronze rods, held in place by brackets. To shift the mast, you unscrewed one, pushed the mast fore or aft and tightened the other. It meant crawling in under the deck. Then came a partner, a flat bronze plate, with a hole in it for the mast. At each corner was about a four inch slot, through which it was bolted to the deck. You loosened the four wing-nuts, pushed the mast to the desired position and then tightened them. While all this took time, it did give those who possessed that sixth sense of tune, an opportunity to exercise it. It was a vast improvement over former conditions. Then came the tall Marconi and finally flexible spars. The latter brought into use all sorts of fittings. I will not attempt to describe them, for every builder and a number of hardware firms, each had their own line of special Star fittings. Everything on a Star was adjustable and almost everything could be controlled from the cockpit, while under way. The fitting craze reached its peak in 1939 and 1940. There were so many things to fool with that unless you really knew what you were doing, you usually got into trouble. Since World War Two, the tendency has been to again eliminate all but essential fittings.

Each phase of Star development resulted in a number of old timers, and I mean good skippers, fading out of the picture. They did not leave the class, but their names no longer appeared among the winners New and unfamiliar

GENERAL DIMENSIONS, given for quick comparison

Hull Specifications	Gardner's	Original Assn.	Present Assn.
Length overall	Max. 22'8"	22'7½"	22'8½"
Beam at deck	Min. 5'7½"	5'8¼"	5'8¼"
Water line (approx.)	15'5"	15'6"	15'6"
Draft (approx.)	3'4"	3'4"	3'4"
Keel weight (max)	860 lbs.	900 lbs.	900 lbs.

Spars and Sails	Sliding Gunter	Short Marconi	Tall Marconi
Mast, deck to sheave	18'5"	27'0"	31'9"
Boom	18'4½"	18'4½"	14'7"
Gaff (Or Yard)	17'6½"	none	none
Mainsail Luff	7'4"	24'11'	30'6"
Mainsail Leech	28'6"	28'10"	30'6"
Mainsail Foot	18'4½"	18'4½"	14'7"
Jib Luff	17'9"	18'4"	20'6"
Jib Leech	15'3"	15'7"	17'10"
Jib Foot	7'8"	7'7"	7'2"

FOOT NOTE
No major change has been made in the *hull*, since it was originally designed in 1911 Gardner's specifications, in almost every instance read — "Not over" or "Not under" a given dimension, which was not always the one shown on the plans This led to some boats being built of somewhat greater beam and shorter length, than shown on the plans When the association gained control of the specifications, it specified the standard dimension, as per plan, and adopted a table of limitations, to cover over and under tolerances allowed The overall measurement, originally to the stem, was later changed to a theoretical point "A", which is the intersection of the sides of the deck prolonged until they intersect That was necessary to prevent blunt-nosed boats from being built, to gain length but keep within the rules The original *keel weight* was due to an error Ike Smith, who made the first keel pattern, evidently did not know that he should have used a shrink rule The pattern was true to plan but the casting was slightly smaller No one, including William Gardner, realized this The weight of the first keels were accepted as standard Later, when keel patterns were made by regular pattern makers, it was found that a casting, that conformed to plan, was about forty pounds heavier In the case of the *mast*, the measurement is now taken from point "B", which is the true deck, disregarding the crown Spars now govern the *luff* and *foot* of the *mainsail* There is also an across sail measurement that governs draft and roach

names, of younger men, came into the limelight. Of course,
there were exceptions. A few skippers, like Adrian Iselin, took
each step in stride, and did not seem to experience any particular difficulty. Many veterans, however, could not keep pace
with this. It may not have been noticed in any given locality,
where it applied to only one or two. To anyone like myself,
who was in a posiiton to see the class as a whole, it was
very obvious. Each step forward meant that the skipper
required additional knowledge of tune. The rule of thumb
skipper, by trial and error, had learned to get the most out
of his boat. He was accomplishing the same thing as those
who had greater knowledge of tune, but did not know the
reason why. When a change of rig occurred, he was lost and
did not know what to do. In other words, it was just a
question of being unable to teach an old dog new tricks.

Strangely enough, the first affected by this was George
Corry himself. That was even before there was a change of
rig. In 1915 it was found that Star keels were too far forward.
The better skippers shifted their keel about two and one-half
inches aft. That made a lot of difference. The boats pointed
higher, were more responsive to the helm and no longer
wallowed in a knockdown Star owners became much more
condition conscious. I do not say tune conscious, because,
with everything in a fixed position, it was almost impossible
to tune a boat properly. They did, however, begin to haul
their boats out every week, to keep them light, and rivaled
each other in maintaining a perfect bottom finish. For one
of his enthusiasm and experience, it was astounding how little
attention George Corry paid to the condition of his Star. He
slapped on a new coat of paint in the spring and pulled it
up, over one tide, alongside the dock, now and then to scrub
the bottom. That was all. As I have already stated, he was
one of the best helmsmen that ever lived, but in 1916, for
the reasons given, he ceased to be the undisputed champion
of the Star class. He freely admitted that he knew little about
tune and this was proven in 1924, when he bought No. 1,
Taurus, from Bill Inslee. That boat had won two Interna-

tionals For a short period George was his old self again, winning races. Then gradually he kept slipping back to where he had been before. He just could not keep the boat in proper tune and condition. Only under exceptional weather conditions did he win, now and then, as result of experience.

The short Marconi was not a very drastic change and did not affect the veterans too much, plus the fact that competition then had not developed to too great an extent. The tall Marconi was a more radical departure and some never did learn to master it. Flexible spars, however, took the greatest toll They required some knowledge of sails and aerodynamics. A new generation, of the airplane age, knew something about such things. The old fellows did not. Father Time, quite naturally, slows up all Star skippers eventually. This last innovation, however, was just one too many for the great majority of them.

CHAPTER III

FIRST FEW YEARS

AND

STAR CLASS ASSOCIATION OF AMERICA

BACK IN THE HORSE AND BUGGY DAYS, when beer was five cents a glass, the Star class sailed its maiden race at the western end of Long Island Sound. Little one-designs were then as plentiful as fleas on a dog's back. They came and went without fanfare, unnoticed by the public and usually unrecorded by the Press. That is probably why the doings of the Nahant Stars are veiled in obscurity. Those eleven New England Stars, which the owners may not have even known to be Stars, began racing a little later in that same summer of 1911. They played no part, however, in the early history of the class. The growth and development of the class took place on Long Island Sound and its western end has often been spoken of as "The cradle of the Star."

Half of the original twenty-two Stars were owned on one side of the Sound and half on the other. While it has been lost sight of, the Star actually started off as an inter-club class, a rarity indeed among small one-designs of that era. Nothing of moment happened during the first three years, according to Pop Corry, except the American Yacht Club fire. It was reported that its entire fleet of eleven Stars were destroyed. That is incorrect. It is true that American Yacht Club members no longer participated in Star races, after the fire, but nearly all of the boats were salvaged and found their way to other clubs. This I can state with authority, as I did not join the Star class until a couple of years after the fire, yet I have myself seen all of the original Ike Smith Stars, except numbers 7 and 13. The fact is that both of these boats are recorded as having owners, so it is entirely possible that none were lost.

The story of those early years can be told in about two words—Pop Corry. He did not win every race, but the lion's share of them. For example, his Little Dipper, No. 17, won four of the first five Star championships of Long Island Sound. Up until 1915 might well be called the Corry age, for as a skipper, he easily outranked anyone else in the class. If the Star was not news, Pop was. He took the fancy of the yachting scribes and they usually managed to work in a line or two about him. If he did not win you might read, for instance, that due to adverse conditions he was only able to place third among the Stars, but not a word about who finished first and second. You might find out by looking at the summaries and again you might not. The Stars were among the last to start and the order of finish of the little classes was the first thing to be deleted, if the summaries took up too much space.

I can contribute quite a few facts from memory about the fourth unorganized year. This is partially due to the fact that I was aware of what was going on in 1914, but not entirely so. The class had more than doubled, there were many new owners and those fellows were beginning to feel their oats. They demanded recognition and obtained some, but not much. Pop was still king pin. He was not yet being called Pop, but the press had already begun to refer to him as the "Father of the Stars."

Perhaps this is the best place to tell about how I happened to become connected with the Star class, in whose interest I was destined to devote innumerable hours of work for the better part of my life. Gerry Ford, the yacht broker was responsible. I wanted an inexpensive little one-design boat to tow around behind the yawl and race here and there. He sold me the Comet, No. 14, which was one of the original Smith Stars. Incidentally, it was also one of those erroneously reported lost in the American Y.C. fire. The former owner, Jack McMahon, of South Norwalk, later became better-known as a Star crew.

I already belonged to the New Haven Yacht Club. It was a nice little club and a very convenient place to stop off, cash a check and have a good meal, when cruising up and down the Sound. The Comet needed conditioning and I took it there to have the work done. Unbeknown to me, in 1913 and 1914, Morris Cove boasted of a very active group of Versoy built Stars. They were too far from the western end of the Sound to enter any championship regattas, but did send a few Stars to Larchmont Race Week. Here again I have been unable to obtain any record of local results. Like most isolated one-design classes, interest soon waned and the Morris Cove group disbanded.

The first thing I did was order a new suit of sails from Christ Bottger. Yes, this was the same Chris Bottger who measured sails for the 1952 U.S. Star Olympic trials. Chris brought those sails to New Haven himself and fitted them on the Comet's spars. My bill amounted to thirty six dollars including his railroad fare from New York and return, as well as his time for an entire day . . . Star owners of the present day please note.

New Haven had a big harbor, which provided an excellent twice-around triangle, starting and finishing at the club. I sailed my first Star race there on July 4, 1914. With George Cochran, who became my regular crew for several years, the Comet stepped out into the lead and steadily kept increasing it. That was probably due to the new sails. On the last leg, a beat, we must have been half a mile ahead of the second boat. I do not know its number For that matter I did not know any of those Star skippers or the names of their boats. In fact the only person whom I knew at the club was Jack, the bartender. The second Star tacked inshore and so did I. It was the orthodox thing to do. The only trouble was that I did not know the local waters. Where the second boat tacked, there was plenty of water inshore. Within about two hundred yards of the finish there was not. I sailed the Comet right into a mud flat and we remained there until a launch was sent to tow us off. It taught me a valuable lesson. Thereafter, when racing in unfamiliar waters, I always studied the chart very carefully. That was the first and the last time I ever raced the Comet.

Several days later Irving Versoy informed me that the owner of No. 36 was willing to swap Stars, if I added $50.00, each to keep his own sails. I still think it was a good trade. I got a boat that was two years younger and much more substantially built. It was a more expensive Star and, with new sails, I was all equipped for less than it cost the original owners to buy their Ike Smith boats. No. 36 was renamed Zete. It took a little time to put the boat in proper shape and get the numbers changed on the sails. As a result I missed Larchmont week. We were ready, however, to go to Gravesend Bay. On the way we stopped at New Rochelle to enter a Sound championship race. Adrain Iselin, sailing the Snapper, No. 33, just did nose Zete out of third place. That was big league competition, however, and I was more than satisfied. What happened during the following week at the Atlantic Y.C. has already been related in chapter one.

It is safe to say, with all due modesty, that I had more general boating knowledge than the average new Star owner. Mind you, I said boating knowledge, not racing experience. There is a decided difference, a fact that I was to learn very quickly.

I owned and lived aboard my own boat, practically the entire year, since I was a kid of twelve. While other youngsters were sweating over textbooks, I was gunning and fishing, back in the days when both fish and game were plentiful.

It may not have been too conducive to study, but, with a little tutoring, I managed to enter college at the average age. I raced cats on the Peconic for a couple of years and won the season's championship. At the time I bought the Comet, I was the proud owner of a sixty-foot auxiliary yawl. While there had been a lapse of five years since my small boat racing, I kept the yawl on the Sound during the summer months and learned a lot about rules and procedure from personal observation. It did not take me too long to adjust myself to the racing game, but in those early days Star racing had not reached the highly developed science of today.

I do not wish to bore the reader with my presonal background, but am doing so for a reason. To this very day there are fellows, that can scarcely sail a boat in and out of a harbor, who believe, if they buy an expensive Star, the rest depends entirely upon the boat. You simply cannot make them realize that yacht racing requires ability the same as any other sport They would not expect, just because they could buy a Stradivarius, to become the world's foremost violinist. Yet they seem to look upon yacht racing in a different light and if they do not win, blame the boat. Out of the hundreds who try the sport, only a very few ever attain a degree of efficiency that enables them to win a World's Championship, or even a District Championship. This is especially true of the Star Class, into which has been crammed the cream of the world's small boat talent.

To return to our story, we raced the Zete for the rest of 1914, although I cannot recall the results, and remained in Manhasset Bay for a few weeks after the season ended. It was during that period that we made the first move toward forming the Star Class Association of America. It was an impressive name, but actually only a little loose-knit class organization. All of its members were on the Sound and the majority in Manhasset Bay. Dues were one dollar and class rules scarcely filled a normal mimeographed sheet. Four Star owners at Toledo, on Lake Erie, enrolled the following year, which justified the last two words in the association's name.

Pop, of course, was elected president. Credit for forming the Star Class Association of America and starting the ball rolling, however, goes to Allen Walker, its first secretary. Allen never set the world on fire as a Star skipper. He was even subject to mal de mer and withdrew from a number of races. On the other hand he was a good organizer and a bundle of energy. From the very beginning, therefore, our most efficient officer was a mediocre skipper. That has usually been true and is not difficult to understand. One who cannot become famous by winning, can gain recognition and respect by the work he does. Furthermore, being of the rank and file himself, he can see the picture more clearly and the needs of the class as a whole. The expert is more apt to devote his time to his boat and his thoughts to his personal problems. Naturally there have been exceptions, but generally speaking our best officers have been enthusiastic Star skippers of mediocre racing ability.

Buck Hyde was made treasurer, although his Star was still under construction, and I was named vice-president. The other officers were men in their forties, while I was at least twenty years younger. Even in those days towing was an important consideration Mornings were calm and the afternoon southerly (which no longer reaches the Sound) never put in an appearance much before starting time. During the closing weekends of 1914, the Dawn II had taken a number of Manhasset Bay Stars to and from Sound regattas. Someone must have figured that she might become a sort of unofficial towboat and was right. My election was due to the Dawn II. During the teens the old yawl never left or returned to the Bay on Saturdays without having a string of Stars astern. She became so well known to Star owners, west of Execution, that a brief summary of her own exploits seems to be in order.

Her racing number was N 2. During the twelve years I owned the Dawn II, she won three of the four events in which I entered her. All three were of an entirely different character. I made the mistake of entering one of the Larch-

mont Week races. That was before I had a Star. At that time
I always had a full crew (in more ways than one). consisting
mostly of fraternity brothers. With her flat sails, the yawl
was becalmed a short distance from the start, while class after
class passed us. That was the first time I ever saw Stars
in action. The last class to sail by were the Bayside Butter-
flies, a sort of glorified bedpan, with the sail area of an
umbrella. That was just a little too much to take. We started
the engine and went back into the harbor.

That same week she won Larchmont's illuminating contest. We picked up a lot of red, white and blue one hundred
ten volt lights, wiring and all, for one dollar fifty cents The
man who was taking down some street decorations even threw
in a number of Japanese lanterns. The lights were connected
to the dynamo, while the engine was left running. It was too
much of a load and they kept flaring up and growing dim. It
was unintentional, but effective. At the inspection hour, we
hoisted a string of giant sparklers (also second hand) and a
quartet, beneath a lantern bordered awning, completed the
tableau. But there was no inspection. The boys got mad and
the songs less refined. We went ashore and located the commodore watching a movie. He admitted that he had forgotten
all about the contest. The other entries were all big steam
yachts, adorned with a burgee or private signal in colored
lights, which must have cost a pretty penny. A choice between
them would have been difficult. We pointed out that our
display was different. The commodore saw an out and
grabbed it. He took us into the bar and formally presented us
with first prize. He was a good guy and a fine host. When
he learned that our efforts had cost less than four dollars,
he thought it a huge joke and a splendid excuse for an all-
night celebration.

Some years later, N 2 won a bona fide sailing race.
It was a squadron run from New Haven to New London,
held by the Seawanaka Corinthian Y.C. We were headed
east anyway and entered. It was so thick that you could
not see two lengths ahead, but there was a nice little fog

breeze dead ahead. No attempt was made to point. We sailed a compass course for a buoy we felt sure we could make and sighted it as per schedule. Then we tacked for one on the opposite shore and the same thing happened. It may have been luck or my efforts at dead reckoning. A vicious squall hit us at dusk and we went boiling towards New London in pitch dark. It dropped out and shifted to a light northerly, when we were in sight of the committee's red flares. It was almost impossible to make any headway against the current coming out of the Thames and we did not finish until after 1:30 a. m. The results showed that the Dawn II had won in the class for L, M and N yawls and ketches. Why? Because all the rest were lost in the fog and never finished. A big black ketch, the Windward, was among them. It boasted of never having been beaten in its class before.

The old yawl's last exploit, believe it or not, was to win a powerboat race. It also started from New Haven and our entry was again impromptu. We were given a handicap, based upon our engine, but told we had no chance. All the other entries were cabin cruisers, mostly small Elcos. An easter had kicked up a sea during the night and was still blowing hard. When those little cruisers stuck their noses outside the breakwater, they were tossed around like corks. A gust would hit their high cabins and drive them back half the distance they had gained. With our low trunk cabin, flush deck and heavy duty forty h p. Standard, we ploughed through it at our regular nine and one-half knots. Of course we won We had dinner at the club and were back aboard getting ready to turn in when the first cruiser finished. I have tried a lot of different kinds of competition from marathon running to checkers. I can honestly say, however, that I have never experienced anything as uninteresting as a race between cabin cruisers. And so ends the saga of the good ship Dawn II, which has already taken up too much space in what is supposed to be a story of the Star class.

In 1915 the character of Star racing underwent a change. Pop Corry was still recognized as the leading skipper, but his

supremacy was being challenged by Willis, Hyde and me.
We were always well up and now and then one of us would
beat him. He won the Sound Championshiip, but lost Larchmont Week to Willis. Port Washington Y.C. Star owners were
becoming condition conscious. They bought a hand winch
and steel cable. Every Sunday night their Stars were floated
into cradles, at high water, and rolled up on a sloping beach
to the north of the club, when the tide went out. They were
kept dry and light during the week, while their bottoms were
continually worked on, and launched Friday night. This
was a must, and if the tide was at an inconvenient hour,
alarm clocks were set Pop could have paid his share and
joined us, but he never paid much attention to the condition
of his boat. He felt that to tie her up to the Manhasset Bay
Y.C. dock for one tide and rub off the bottom was enough.
This, I believe, accounts more than anything else for his
eventual downfall.

We learned that year that Star keels were too far forward and shifted them about two and one-half inches aft.
The boats no longer wallowed, but stepped right up to windward in a breeze Tuning was still very difficult. As yet the
various parts of a Star were not movable. You had to be
absolutely sure of what you were doing before you tried it.
Moving the mast a little fore or aft meant cutting a larger hole
in the deck. Ed Willis was one of the all time greats. His
sixth sense of tune was more highly developed than that of anyone else. He was always glad to help the Star owners of his
own club. The showing of Port Washington Y.C. Stars, in the
early teens, was due as much to his advice as to their condition.

Pop finished the 1915 season in a blaze of glory, by
winning the first Captain's Island race, just beating Bill
Inslee. It started and finished in Manhasset Bay and the
course, exclusive of tacking, was about forty miles. It provided both Bay and Sound sailing. Since you could leave
Execution Light on either hand and sail on either the north
or south shore of the Sound, one had to be a good guesser
of wind, weather and tide.

I donated the first cup. While eligible for daily prizes (there were always five) the conditions provided that my points would not count. Willis retired the cup in three years. While I took two seconds, it did not affect the points and enabled him to win sooner than he would have otherwise. A group of Manhasset Bay Y.C. members gave us the second Captain's Island Cup, which Colin Ratsey, of the Solent, eventually won. J. Rulon Miller, of the Chesapeake, presented us with the third cup, a perpetual one, which is still being raced for. The Captain's Island race is the oldest strictly-Star event in existence. It was not even interrupted for either world war.

During the last war, yachts were not allowed to cross the channel, near Execution Light. This led to a change in the Western L.I.S. fleet's territory. The event is now being held off Larchmont, over a regular Sound course, which goes to Captain's Island. It is longer than average, but eliminates all the original characteristics of this classic and attracts very few outside entries. True, Manhasset Bay is now overcrowded, but that was one of the intended hazards The conditions were devised by me and approved of by the first winner, the late Commodore Corry. It was a grueling contest, with all the elements of luck that go with Bay racing, but that was what attracted outside entries. I am quite sure that one of the original clubs, if properly approached, would hold the event for old times sake. If not, the fleet could hold it, starting and finishing in Manhasset Bay. That would restore its original character, which Roulon Miller sought to perpetuate.

The first Atlantic Coast Star Smoker was held at Mouquin's, on Sixth Avenue, New York City. It was famous for its red wine and that was what most of the boys drank. That smoker has been held every year since 1915 and I have attended every one up to 1952.

Allen Walker, a member of the U.S. Chamber of Commerce, arranged for a demonstration of the first trans-continental telephone. Earphones were at each place. We heard the various connections being made, the roar of the Pacific surf and then Pop talked to the commodore of the San Francisco Y.C. He challenged him to have California build a Star and race us for the championship of the U.S.A. Both laughed. No one realized that within a decade it would actually happen.

Bill McHugh was the impromptu toastmaster. He was sort of a rough diamond forerunner of "Lash" Nelson. Bill "wrasseled" the head waiter, the hat check girl and several others with success. Later he tackled a New York cop, but lost that bout.

During that same year of 1915, we held a meeting of the Star Class Association of America, at which I submitted a graphic chart of a proposed method of organization. Probably because of the Dawn II, they did not laugh at me, but probably thought I was slightly touched in the head. I was given a polite brush off and the organization chart was pigeonholed for another six years.

There were a couple of personal incidents, which I recall from 1915, that may give the reader an idea of the conditions that then prevailed. I cannot, for example, forget winning the twenty-fifth Anniversary Regatta of the Stamford Y.C. I cannot forget because I see the prize every day. It is a sterling silver pitcher, of Plymouth design, which was worth about one hundred dollars even at that time. Stamford was a long trip and very few of the western boys went Commander Fry, with his navy launch and professional crew, however, did. We figured that he was the only one who had a chance of beating us. There were quite a few entries, but they were from what is now the Central L.I.S. Fleet. None were very good, except McHugh, although we had not yet learned to take him too seriously.

Cochran started an argument with the commander, just before the preparatory signal. I do not recall what it was about, but the idea was to make him mad and it did. He did not notice the signals or look at his watch. As soon as the preparatory came down, we headed casually for the line.

We took an almost perfect start at the stakeboat, while the commander was still sputtering away at Cochran. It was only then that he realized the Stars were starting. It gave us a lead of a good one hundred yards, and winning after that was easy. At that time anything was fair in love or yacht racing, if you could get away with it.

Then there was a race held by some little club off Captain's Island. It was not Indian Harbor and I cannot recall its name. The big yachts were sent off to the east, but the little fellows were given a special course around Great and Little Captain's Island. The start was rather confused. All the entries started to the eastward, as the big yachts had done, except Charlie Davis, sailing Neptune, and me. We went to the west. It was a very dangerous course for a keel boat, as it took us among many unbuoyed rocks. Charlie Davis was a very fine skipper, with lots of experience. He did not sail a Star too often. If he had, he would have made a name for himself. I simply followed in his wake. If he hit anything, I figured I might be able to keep clear. I do not mean that I could have beaten him, because I probably could not have done so. He was the one who protested. The circular read "Around Great and Little Captain's Island." No reverse course signal had been displayed. The others all sailed around Little Captain's Island first. They were all disqualified. Davis was first and I was second.

A somewhat similar incident happened, probably in 1924 or 1925, which I had better relate while I have it mind. Cochran was practicing medicine and I had no regular crew. I wanted to enter the annual regatta of the American Y.C., which was always held on July 3. A week of phoning produced no results, so I took the club steward, a fellow named Quail, who had always wanted to sail in a race. He was late in getting away and we must have been ten minutes from the line when we cast off from our tow. Just as we crossed I said, "Ease the sheet," and the whole mainsail came down, most of it in the water. A great laugh went up from the committee boat. We managed to get the slides back on the mast and the sail up. By that time the rest were almost out of sight, but we were over the line and had to go on. I was about to round the buoy, which the others had rounded, when I happened to see the Little Dipper coming from the opposite direction. We sailed toward it and Pop yelled, "Reverse course." Having nothing to lose, I sailed all the way over to the other mark. By the time we finished, everyone had gone home. Pop was right, however. The red flag had been up. All the others, except Pop and I were disqualified.

An amusing thing happened in 1915, which might have ended very seriously. On the first Sunday of Race Week, Pop sailed the Little Dipper over to Larchmont. He was attired in a black and white checked suit, wore the usual high collar and black stock tie and a straw hat. It was an off day, but the harbor was full of large yachts. He tipped his hat or waved to those he knew. In passing Dawn II, he asked if we could keep an eye on his Star until he returned the next day, as he was having lunch at the club and had a ride home. Then he headed for the Zete, which was anchored as close to shore as possible, to get out of the traffic. Pop was alone. He shot up into the wind and, when his boat had lost headway, rushed forward and gave the anchor a mighty heave. He did not notice, however, that one foot was in the center of the coiled cable. Suddenly Pop followed the anchor. Somehow he managed to grab the bow and hang on, yelling for help.

It so happened that we had a small boat tied to the stern. Cochran and I jumped in and reached him in no time. What we saw was so funny, however, that all we could do was laugh and were unable to row further. Only his head was above water. The straw hat was jammed down over his eyes, so he could not see, a soggy cigar was still in his mouth and he was bellowing harder than ever. By that time other row boats were around, but they were also resting on their oars and laughing. Finally it dawned on us that something was really wrong. We managed to retrieve Pop and the anchor. The cable was wound around his ankle so tightly that he could never have removed it under water. The weight of the anchor had been pulling him down and his grip on the bow was weakening. When we got him aboard and out of his wet clothes, we found that his shin had been cut from knee to ankle. On the way back to Port Washington, he sat in the galley and drank hot coffee. The next day, after a doctor had fixed him up, he was as good as new.

There was a Ladies Race at Atlantic Week that year. Mom Corry was the skipper and Pop was the crew. The Little Dipper was leading and Pop was tending the mainsheet,, in a puffy wind, on a reach. It got away from him. He had forgotten to tie a knot at the end. Before he could grab it, the sheet had run through the blocks. When we passed them, Pop was trying to pick up a loose end of the sheet with the whisker-pole. The air was blue and what his skipper said cannot be repeated. I do not remember who won, but it was not the Little Dipper.

Star races conducted by the Seawanaka Corinthian Y.C. were always my nemesis. It was a long trip up to Oyster Bay and most of us would have been better off had we remained at home. My first experience was against a rather large field of Stars. The Dawn II had towed up quite a number, while others picked up tows of their own. Indian Harbor was holding some sort of a special race on the same day. One of its stakeboats was placed in close proximity to the one we were to round. Both, if I recall correctly, displayed white shapes. In any event the description in our race circular could have applied to either. We passed the Indian Harbor stakeboat first and all the Stars rounded it and all of them were disqualified for sailing the wrong course. I believe that I have stated elsewhere that I was never disqualified in a Star race Technically that is an error, as the Zete was included in that wholesale disqualification. I feel I can be excused for not counting it. That race should have been ruled "no contest." The precedent has been established in numerous cases, where the instructions were confusing. Little one-designs, in those days, were only tolerated, however, and were supposed to consider themselves lucky to even be included in a regatta.

The next time I raced off Oyster Bay was almost as bad. We were started in such light air that a lot of the large yachts were unable to stem the tide and a number of them anchored Then we were hit by one of the worst squalls I have ever seen. We tried to keep going under the jib, but it was blown to ribbons. We tried to anchor, but it would not hold and were almost swamped. Finally we managed to lash the jaws of the gaff to the boom and tie a stop around the sail. With about four feet of sail, we were able to maintain headway. It was as black as night and we had no idea where we were or in what direction we were sailing. Fearing that we might go aground, we kept sailing back and forth over the same bottom, insofar as we could tell. After about half an hour it began to get light again. There was the good old Dawn II, not a hundred yards away. For that matter, we were about that distance from the line. I can tell you that we were mighty glad to take a line and be towed back to the harbor and so were many others.

We learned later that evening that one Star had finished. It was handled by a couple of youngsters, who had never figured much in Star racing before. It was so black during the squall that I doubt if they could have seen the mark had they passed within five feet of it. Once it was over, there was an almost flat calm. No one could understand how that Star could have possibly completed the course within the time limit. On the other hand we had no proof that it had not done so. No one protested and it was awarded the race. The rest received D.N.F.'s, which did not help their percentages in the Sound Championship. It was quite a number of years before any of the good boys, from the western end of the Sound, attempted to enter a Seawanaka Corinthian regatta again.

Ed Willis was the outstanding Star skipper of 1916. Buck Hyde won the Sound Championship and Adrian Iselin took Larchmont Week. Willis, however, won the majority of the races, including Atlantic Week and the Captain's Island race. Those were the four important Star events of that period.

Perhaps the one thing that can best be remembered about that season is that we caught up with and passed Pop Corry. Under unusual conditions, such as a fog, bad squall or even in a Captain's Island Race, his years of experience still counted. Over an ordinary afternoon triangle, however, he could no longer place and, from then on, kept falling back more and more.

Prizes were prizes in those days. There were only about twenty-two Sound Championships, held on Saturdays and holidays. The clubs that were able to get on the schedule made their annual regattas memorable affairs. A third daily, for the lowly Star class, was better than the average series trophy of today. A few clubs mailed you orders on a well-known silversmith. The great majority, however, selected their own prizes and sent them to you. They arrived usually during November. Opening the packages was exciting and sort of a premature Christmas.

The Zete did not win too many firsts that year, but 1916 contributed more prizes to the trophy cabinet than any other. The inscriptions on quite a number of them were for two or more races held by the same club. Actually the Zete placed in over seventy-five per cent of her starts. Doing away with the daily third was a minor tragedy. While it did not mean much to the really good skipper, it represented a year's effort to the little fellow. If it was not for the mediocre and poor skipper, there would be very few yachting entries indeed. The inscription, not the intrinsic value, was what mattered. A cheap medal or brass ash tray, inscribed with the club's initials, place and year, would be good enough and could be bought, even today for around one dollar and fifty cents. Is it not worth that to encourage the rank and file, who make yacht racing possible?

I still boil with indignation over a lengthy speech made by a delegate from a small club, to the Y.R.A. of L.I.S. He spoke of racing skippers as "mug hunters." That is about the most unfair characterization of a racing skipper I can think of. What was really in his mind was that the small clubs could not afford prizes of equal value to the large ones, and therefore, that no prizes should be given. This happened some years after the first world war and resulted in pennants being given for a couple of years. No one wanted those dust collectors, or knew what to do with them, and most clubs then discontinued the practice of giving any form of daily prize for an individual race.

Tennis, golf and athletic clubs, etcetera, always give prizes for the open events they conduct in such sports. Why should the yacht club be immune? If it is now supported by members who are not interested in sailing, then let it call itself a country or social club or whatever it is. Who has a better right to be a mug hunter than your racing skipper? He has become the chief contributor to the club's prize fund. Is he not entitled to some sort of mememto, when he himself pays for it? The trouble is that, in some localities there are more yacht clubs than there are racing skippers to distribute among them. People join those clubs because they are yacht clubs Well then, let them also contribute to the fund for sailing prizes or call the club by its correct name, whatever that may be.

CHAPTER IV

WORLD WAR I

AND

THE LATE TEENS

A RACING YACHT was an extravagant luxury, a million-aire's hobby, which could well be dispensed with in times of strife. To the public the very word yacht meant grandeur. We were living in the age of the great racing yacht and its professional crew. Even the owners of those majestic crea-tions did not consider a cheap little boat a yacht. Yacht racing was unpatriotic and was discontinued while the United States participated in World War One.

On Sundays, in 1917 and 1918, Stars sailed inter-club races on Manhasset and Little Neck Bays. The Port Washing-ton, Manhasset Bay and Bayside Yacht clubs each held a Sunday series and the Star Class Association of America gave inexpensive series prizes for the over-all result. Nevertheless, there were some conscientious objectors. They would have preferred, I suppose, to have had those ineligible for service spend Sunday afternoons at a movie or in a speakeasy.

Prohibition had descended upon us in the guise of a war measure to conserve grain. I went to a couple of caba-rets (they were not called night clubs then) just before the lid was clamped down. They were crowded, but otherwise normal. No one took it seriously. Long lines waited in front of wholesale grocers and the like, on the final night, with baby carriages, wash tubs and most anything to help them carry bottles home. It was a huge joke and could not last for more than a month or two, but they were wrong. We were on the eve of a long arid period of bathtub gin and racketeers, when even the usually abstemious delighted in circumventing an unpopular and unenforceable law.

In those so-called dry years, I visited a lot of clubs in various parts of the country. It seemed to me that more alcohol was consumed then than at any time before or since. Lockers were well stocked, mostly with bottles of synthetic Bacardi. If you gave one to the bartender and ordered half a dozen cocktails, knowing that only one-third would be used, it was the last time you ever saw that bottle. It was too general a practice to have been a coincidence, but no one cared. If you ran short there were ways and means of replenishing your supply, provided you were known and had the price. Legitimate clubs were not molested and that sense of security was worth putting up with a minor racket.

During the two war years there was only one open regatta on the Sound. It was held by the Indian Harbor Y.C. for the benefit of the Red Cross. A five dollar entry fee was charged as a means of raising money. This is mentioned because entry fees are quite common in some localities but, to the best of my knowledge, that was the only one ever charged for a yacht race on the Sound. Against a field of about eight Stars, Bill McHugh won the silver medal for first and I took the bronze one for second. Only a handful of comparatively small yachts, of miscellaneous classes put in an appearance. The answer is simple—there were none in commission. It could not have been a very profitable experiment as it was never repeated.

In the meantime the number of Stars at the western end of the Sound kept increasing. New Stars have been built every year since the class started, but in 1918 it was a pretty close shave. Only two were produced that year. However, it was enough to keep our record intact. The increase, in what later became the Western L.I.S. Fleet, was caused by Stars from nearby places, where all racing had ceased, being brought there by new owners. Some went to the clubs on the Bays that were holding Sunday races and others were distributed along the clubs on the north shore of the Sound. Quite a few of the latter came over on Sundays for the inter-club events.

The greatest influx was of Versoy built Stars from New Haven The best known of these was sailed by Pingree and VanWinkle Van, who was never a ninternational officer, played quite an important role in local affairs and still is an associate member. Bill Inslee brought the Shadow from Gravesend to Bayside. Previously there had only been a single Star, No. 1, that came out of Little Neck Bay, but during the war the Bayside Y.C. group grew rapidly. Of course there were Stars by other builders than Versoy and many new names. They did not mean much then, although many among them became famous in Star circles later.

The Rocky River Dry Docks built sixteen Stars for Rochester in 1917. The Star Log shows that the Rochester Boat Works built those boats, but I know that the original lot was built at Rocky River. They probably did some racing during the war, but, like Nahant, Rochester remained an outlaw group for a couple of years after the I S.C Y.R A was formed and their early races are not recorded. Those boats had two inches more beam than the average Star. It was perfectly legal, as Gardner's specifications read, " . . . no narrower than . . . " That additional beam was intentional and supposed to produce a boat better suited to conditions on Lake Ontario. This is a good example of why our original limitations had to be so liberal. Actually they proved to be slow Stars in any locality.

There were also some Stars on Lake Erie, some at Toledo and a few at Cleveland, that may have raced in the war years. Their owners were members of the Star Class Association of America, but no effort was made at that time to keep records. Al Wakefield joined the Cleveland group in 1918. He had been an international Star officer of high rank for quite a number of years and is still an active skipper. Al is the only one, who may, in recent years, have eclipsed my record of thirty-three consecutive years of Star racing. He cannot remember whether he skipped a couple of seasons or not and the records do not show it one way or the other.

Most of us were too busy with war work, during those two years of Sunday racing, to remember about them. I know that I was. Only two incidents are clear in my mind. In one race hailstones fell with such force that it was impossible to keep your hand on the tiller. All one could do was crawl under the deck and let the boat take care of itself. All the Stars went aground. None were damaged, but it was already late in the evening and no one was able to push off and finish before the sundown time limit. Races were not scheduled for every Sunday. On open dates we held impromptu ones. I cashed in some United Cigar Store coupons and provided prizes for one such event. It was won by Buck Hyde. Port Washington Y.C. Stars, with Inslee added, continued to dominate. I evidently placed in some of the inter-club series, according to the inscription on a few of my trophies. Pop won the 1917 Captain's Island race and Ed Willis took the honors in 1918. I am sorry, but that is about all I can remember about that hazy and hectic period.

Mars finally sheathed his sword and departed from this terrestial sphere to hibernate for another quarter of a century. The return of peace found racing to be in a very precarious state. None of the really big fellows, and only a few of the semi-large yachts, had been put back in commission. The innumerable little one-designs throughout the country had been wiped out. Only one or two scattered remnants of those pre-war classes were left and they had nothing to race against. The Star Class was the only exception, it was bigger and better than ever.

The early Sound regattas of 1919 were sad affairs indeed. Aside from the Stars, no more than two of a kind started on any gun. A N.Y. 40, two 30's and a large handicap boat, for instance, would race together on time allowance. The press did its best. It gave the corrected time of the mixed or special class, the elapsed time of the two 30's and listed the other two boats as having won a sail-over. This was repeated down along the line, where miscellaneous one-designs and handicap boats, of about the same size, raced against each other. At first glance the summaries were impressive. If you read them carefully, however, you could see that the same names were repeated and that, except for the Stars, the total starters did not amount to more than about fifteen. Twenty-six Stars were in Larchmont Race Week, which was by far the largest class. By that time the Victories, another Gardner product, were racing and several reasonably large yachts had joined in. That relieved the tension somewhat. A total of thirty-two Stars competed in the Sound Championship that season. The fact is, that if the Stars had been subtracted from any of those open regattas, there would have been mighty few entries left.

The foregoing, mind you, refers to conditions at the western end of Long Island Sound, which was then the mecca of yachting. Elsewhere things were very much worse Places that had been quite well established in racing did not have any yachts with which to even hold a token regatta, in an effort to revive interest in the sport. In such places the fate of the game hung in the balance for nearly a decade. Had the Star not led the way to an era of organized small one-design racing, there might easily have been no yacht racing to speak of today.

In one respect, all this may have been a blessing in disguise. The rocking chair owner was a thing of the past. No longer did very rich men feel that their social prestige demanded that they own a large racing yacht. No longer did they sit around the club and sip highballs, while their professional crews were trying to win silverware for them. The larger yachts, which had a short revival on the Sound, were being skippered by Corinthians, usually their owners.

They had a skeleton crew of pros, to keep the yacht in shape, but the majority of the racing crew consisted of amateur friends. Only those who really loved yacht racing were connected with it. The old theory about a professional skipper being better than a good Corinthian had been exploded. That influence extended even to the few remaining races for the America's Cup. The skipper and afterguard became Corinthians and the size of the yacht was reduced, until owning even a small one became too great an expense and the famous Cup was put away in moth balls, perhaps never to be raced for again.

That first peace time season was probably Willis' best. He won every major Star series, except Larchmont Week, which was won by Inslee. It was also the last year in which the Port Washington Y.C group, generally speaking, dominated Star racing on the Sound. After that the balance of power shifted to the boys from Bayside, at least for a time.

Perhaps the most important development in 1919 was the creation of a "B" division. That eventually led to the Novice (green star) Championships, which are now being held by most Districts of the Star class. The "B" division was in no sense a junior proposition. It included all, whose combined average the year before, had been fifty per cent or less. It was optional. If any skipper felt that being rated "B" was a reflection, he could elect to race with "A" only. In like manner, the officials of the class could rate any dark horse as an "A", if they felt his showing in some other class made him ineligible as a "B." Both divisions started together on the same gun. A separate score was kept of the "B" group, regardless of how many "A" entries finished among them. Hence a "B" skipper could win both an "A" and a "B" daily prize. This applied to Sunday Star racing only, but it increased interest tremendously.

Another interesting thing happened in 1919. Donald Cowl put the first short Marconi on the Mara, Star No. 46. The rig was designed by Gardner himself. The Mara was not allowed to enter any open races with it. A lot of scrub races, however, were held in Manhasset Bay. All the good boys raced No. 46 It had very wide spreaders and a steam bent hollow mast. The result was a rank failure. No one was able to place much better than last with that boat and the Marconi rig was temporarily ruled out.

A professional, as crew, was allowed by the old association and carried over as a fleet option by the new one, but professional crews were barred from any form of inter-fleet competition. Pop put through the original rule for the sake of his friend Commander Fry. The old commander was the racing brains of his Star, but was not spry enough to do any heavy work and was dependent upon his regular pro crew. The ostensible purpose of the rule was to ease the minds of parents who wanted their children to race a Star. This was absurd. The Star has always been a class for adults and the competition too highly developed for the average kid. I know of less than a dozen child skippers in the past forty years. Only one of them had a pro crew for a couple of seasons, hence the professional crew has played a very minor role indeed in Star racing. I refer, of course, to the old type of dyed in the wool bayman, once held in high esteem. Most of them only had a scanty knowledge of the more common rules and believed in ignoring them, if smart enough to get away with it. They were not a good influence as a regular racing companion. No longer does anyone take advantage of this option and, like all obsolete rules, it should be weeded out of the book.

The first division "B" championship was won by a real junior, Gordon Curry. At the time he was a fat little boy, with a shrill voice that could be heard all over the Bay. His crew was a youngster of about the same age, Fred Richards, and my how those kids could eat! We made the mistake of once asking them aboard the Dawn II for a slice of cake. It was a large cake, that had never been cut. Between them they finished it in a few moments. One grew up to be a tackle at Harvard and the other to tip the scales at about two hundred and thirty pounds.

In 1920 the balance of power shifted from the Port Washington Y.C. to the Bayside Y.C. Star group. Gordon Curry's Acquilla ended the season by winning the Captain's Island race. I won a two boat attempt to revive Atlantic week, which has already been related. Otherwise, Bayside took all the honors. Inslee, who was sailing No. 1, the Taurus, won the Sound Championship. Ben Linkfield took Larchmont Race Week. Ben is the only Star sailor that I ever heard of who became an expert skipper in middle life. In that respect he stands alone. He was good, make no mistake about that. If I recall correctly, Fred Teeves also came into the picture for the first time by winning the division "B" championship. I do not remember who won all the individual races, but the Bayside boys won the lion's share of them.

"Buts" Whiting, who owned Star No. 2, was a great hand for trying innovations. He tried an airplane wing as a rigid sail. To go about, the wing had to be turned end for end over a short mast. He also tried to incorporate the parachute spinnaker idea with a hole in the mainsail There were a hundred odd flaps, about two inches in diameter, cut in a semicircle and wired, so as to open when running before the wind. He was allowed to race with that sail, but it never worked. "Buts" was chairman of the Larchmont R.C. for a time and introduced new courses. The first leg was to a buoy off Execution. It applied to all classes. The idea was to separate the yachts, by giving them a short beat, and avoid a jam at the first mark. It was discontinued the next season.

I am not apt to forget Larchmont's spring regatta that year. I had a newly launched Smith Star, the Saturn. Most of my belongings were on the Dawn II, which had not yet reached Port Washington. Nevertheless, we sailed her over to Larchmont and started. The leg to Execution was a reach that day and a squall was making up in the Southwest. It turned black as night and broke just as the Stars rounded. I caught a fleeting glimpse of a couple of long tows out in the channel that had put up their running lights. Then the rain came down in sheets and obliterated everything. The rain and wind stopped as suddenly as it had begun, but left a dense fog over the water. I never saw anything quite like that before or since. It became light overhead but you could not see fifty feet. We must have sailed around in a circle for a long time. Finally we almost hit a buoy and tied up to it. It was the same buoy we had rounded three hours before. We knew where we were and stayed there. Except for the cry of a few gulls, we did not hear a sound that afternoon. Execution never blew its fog signal. We had no oilers, dry smokes nor anything, but a pint of whiskey, which we polished off. Pretty soon a cruiser loomed up out of the fog. It was also lost, but offered to take us aboard and tow the Saturn to Bayside. The fog did not lift until the moon came up that night.

In taking it for granted that none of the Stars finished, I was mistaken. It seems that Canis Minor, with Charlie Davis at the helm and Sig Adler as crew, was the first yacht in any class to cross the line. They swore that they sailed the course. I believe them, as that sort of thing has often happened, but the R.C. thought it impossible that Canis Minor had finished before all the larger yachts and refused to award it the race. Little Dipper crossed half an hour or so later, but several large yachts finished ahead of her. That satisfied the R.C and Pop won. I did not hear about all this until the following morning. When I saw Pop, I asked him how he managed to locate that second mark in the fog.

"Well, I actually did not see it," he admitted. "I hailed a Victory to leeward. They told me they had hailed another yacht to leeward of them, which had spoken to still another that had rounded So you see I must have rounded also." I did not see and asked him how long after the alleged rounding, by the unknown yacht, did this hailing business take place. "By gad," he replied, "I never asked."

I let it go at that. Winning had become a rarity for Pop, who honestly believed he had sailed the course. Perhaps he had and perhaps he had never come within a mile of passing that second mark on the required side. It was one of those things that no one, including himself, could ever prove. His claim to the race was just as valid as the handful of other Stars, that finally found the line. That is one reason why we have always had an official at every mark in a Star World's Championship.

Pop inedvertently talked himself into another first during Larchmont Week. A light fluky wind had brought the yachts astern up to the leaders and left them there. A bunch of yachts, from different classes, crossed the line at about the same time. Their mainsails were held out, to catch what there was of a following zephyr. It must have been very difficult for the R.C. to spot the numbers. Bill Inslee and I were crossing quite near the committee boat. His bow may have been just overlapping my stern and the distance between the hulls laterally was no more than a foot. I know he was behind, as I had to turn my head completely around to talk to him. We had seen the Little Dipper at the stakeboat end of the line, where Pop could harden his wind, and were wondering whether he could beat us. Passing under the white flag, we had a good view of the line and agreed that Pop had not yet crossed. As soon as he had a chance, Pop sailed over to the committee boat and yelled, "I guess I won." After quite a pause, a voice answered, "Yes, Mr. Corry, I guess you did."

The summaries the next morning credited Pop with first, Inslee with second and I was placed eighth. Probably my boat had been cut off from view entirely by another sail and the R.C had not noticed my number until later. I rushed ashore, phoned Inslee and asked him to sail over to the R.C. with me that afternoon and explain that I had beaten him. He said that angle might have been deceptive. Deceptive my foot! His boat could not have crossed ahead of mine unless we had been drifting over the line stern first. I called his attention to the fact that the fourth Star had not even been in that bunch that crossed together and asked him how five Stars could have possibly squeezed in between us. He stuck to the deceptive angle theory. I have never forgiven him for that. Pop had not seen either of us and my case was hopeless. To argue with an R.C. in those days was like trying to argue with a baseball umpire once he had made his decision.

But race committees are human and the best of them can make mistakes. Larchmont is supposed to have a pretty efficient R.C., yet I saw it start the Stars one minute too soon I must have knocked off the end of a cigarette, which had burned its way into the kapok of a life vest that I was seated on. I noticed that it was getting rather warm and, believing that we had a minute to spare, we went about putting out the smoldering mess. I heard a signal, looked up and saw the Stars had started. All the others agreed that the gun was a minute fast, but the R.C. time is always official, even when wrong. That is one thing you cannot protest. If you could, any skipper whose watch was a few seconds fast or slow, could protest a race.

The Star's evolution from a cheap little one-design to a racing machine actually began in 1921. Notwithstanding its failure two years before, the use of the short Marconi was again made optional. Star skippers were beginning to think. To eliminate the overlapping gaff would reduce weight aloft and should make the boat faster. A still more important consideration was that sails could be changed in a few minutes and taken off entirely between races. Sail specifications were unchanged, so all one had to do was get a track mast and sew slides on the hoist of an old sail. Hollow and steam bent masts were barred, but the diameter and rig were optional. Most Stars already had some crude fittings that made a certain amount of tuning possible.

The good skippers, who did not start off with a Marconi, changed to it before 1921 was over. There were all sorts of rigs: wide wooden spreaders, short metal ones and some even had two pairs of them. The rigging method also differed Bill Inslee and Ben Linkfield, both with wide spreaders, finshed Larchmont week in a tie for first. Inslee, however, won the Captain's Island race and Atlantic week. There were

only two Stars left on Gravesend Bay, Murad and Ray Findlay's Meteor. For that matter there were only a few yachts
in any class on the lower bay, but there was quite an inva-
sion from the Sound that year. That was the last of the old
Atlantic weeks ever held. I believe that Carl Searing won the
"B" Championship, making it a clean sweep for Bayside,
except for the Sound Championship.

The Saturn did not change to the Marconi rig until
mid-season. It was the only Star of the lot that used it without
any spreaders at all. My mast was light and, while I did not
realize it at the time, believe it incorporated some of the
advantages of the flexible rig. After an inauspicious start,
the Saturn really began to go. The season ended in my winning
the Sound Championship. I just got in under the wire, as that
event was still considered top honors in Star racing. While Ben
Linkfield won the next three consecutive years, with Maia and
Maia II, he was just one year too late. After 1921 the Star
class had its own World's Championship, which was quickly
followed by the Mid-Winters and several District Championships. The Sound Championship became an event of local
significance only. Ernest Ratsey, sailing Irex III, won in
1925 and 1926, then I repeated. It did not amount to much
in Star circles, but that medal probably represents the closest
percentage series ever won. Pop was second and Duncan
Sterling third, but it was necessary to go into the fourth deci-
mal to determine the order of finish.

There is another incident connected with the early Star
era that deserves mention. On September 25, 1921, the Indian
Harbor Y.C. held a team race for the small one-design
championship of the Sound. The Stars were represented by
a boat from each prominent club—Willis, of Port Washington (who won); Curry, of Manhasset Bay, Inslee, of Bayside,
and Ratsey of Larchmont. It was blowing half a gale and
conditions could not have been more adverse against larger
and round bilged boats. Two of the Stars were reefed. The
results were: Stars forty-two points, Stanford O.D. thirty-two
points, Indian Harbor O.D. fourteen points and the Sea-

wanhaka Fish two points. Going back to 1916, the Stars defeated the "X" class, on Gravesend Bay fourteen to seven, winning the Barstow Cup. Up-to-date Stars have never been defeated in any sort of competition against other small one-design classes. In races for the Child's Cup, where they have raced with spinnakers, on their rating time allowance, they have been beaten.

The first Marconi rig facilitated tune. It brought with it the sliding partner and mast raker, so that the position and rake of the mast could be changed quite quickly. Those fittings, however, had not yet been perfected to the point where this could be done underway. Turnbuckles became an important consideration. The old frozen turnbuckle had to be replaced with one that locked, as any change in the mast changed the tension of the shrouds. The position of the latter might also have to be adjusted. That meant chain plates with a number of holes so the turnbuckles could be moved. Backstays still had to be fastened to a cleat by hand. Track and slide spars included an outhaul and a downhaul. The tension of the bolt ropes could be governed, even while racing, and a sail could be made to set properly for the first time.

Those who knew something about tune, even by trial and error, had a great advantage. A skipper also had to know what a sail should look like, in order to keep it that way. The old fellows, who depended entirely upon helmsmanship to win, did not fare so well. The change was not as drastic as the two that were to follow, but it took its toll. A number of the old timers could no longer win and new names came into the limelight. For the most part, however, the good Star skippers were able to weather that first change without much trouble.

Aside from trying to master the intricacies of the short Marconi, 1921 turned out to be a pretty busy year for me. At the annual meeting I had again introduced my pet scheme of forming an international association. More to keep me quiet than anything else, I was appointed as a committee of

one to arrange a match race between the best Star on Lake
Erie and the best one on the Sound. No one really thought
it could be done. Why it would cost almost as much to ship
a Star from the Lakes to the Sound and back as it would
cost to build a new one. Only Pop was carried away with
the idea. "The Lakes versus the Sound. My gad, just think
of the publicity," he shouted, "I'll get Seabury Lawrence
to spread it all over the sporting page of the Herald."

From that point on I am afraid that I exceeded the
authority vested in me. I first contacted the Lake Erie boys,
who already belonged to the association we had, although
it had nothing to offer them. Then I located half a dozen
or so Star owners, who raced on the Detroit River and Lake
St. Clair and called themselves the Detroit Star club, or
something like that. Eugene Bussy was their key man and a
most enthusiastic one. I found that five Stars were being
raced at Black Point, which is at the extreme easterly end of
the Sound and only a couple of miles from New London. They
did not even have a club, which accounts for the original rule
about a member having to belong to a recognized club, if any,
existed in the locality. There was also a Star group being
formed on Narragansett Bay. They already had three Stars,
bought from Nahant. That was how we first learned that a
Nahant Bug and a Star was one and the same thing. The
Narragansett Bay owners also established the precedent that
a minimum fleet must consist of three Stars. I explained my
idea of starting a parent association and holding an annual
championship. They were all for it and pledged their whole-
hearted support.

With Star owners at Nahant (which is near Marblehead)
and at Rochester it was a different story. A few answered
in a vague sort of way, but you could see that they were not
interested. Some large yachts were being raced in their
vicinity and they suffered from the same inferiority complex
as my own group on the western end of the Sound The latter
had become the most highly developed racing center in existence. The yachts were not as large or as plentiful as before

the war, but semi-large yacht racing was enjoying a temporary
revival. A Star was just a cheap little one-design and Star
owners had become reconciled to their ignominious status.
The Star was a fine little boat for local racing, but that was
about as far as it went. They just could not visualize any
small one-design being successfully developed on a widespread
scale. Their yachting horizon was limited. They knew that
yachts were being raced in some other places, but it was
too far away to amount to much It is difficult to understand
such a frame of mind today, but conditions were very different then.

Everyone lost sight of the hundreds of small clubs
that were scattered all over the United States. The fact is
they did not know about them. I refer to clubs that were
off the beaten path of the large yacht and had never come
under its influence. The great majority of them before the war
had a handful of little one-designs, which had been designed
and built for their private use. Those classes were gone and
racing activities were at a standstill. The Star offered them
something they had never enjoyed before—a chance to compete on an equal footing with any locality. The real problem
was to tell those clubs our story. We did not know then how
to reach them, nor would the yachting publications stick out
their necks by printing propaganda for any given class.

I have been speaking of the United States only, because
early Star development was confined to it. Europe must have
been hit as hard by world war one, but it had its I.Y.R.U.,
an established parent body. Few people over here had ever
heard of the I.Y.R.U. The N.A.Y.R.U. did not yet exist and we
actually had no uniform code of rules. Many of the small
clubs I have mentioned did not even belong to one of our
regional Y.R.A.'s, none of which had any connection with
the rest An effort was once made to unite them. I forget the
name of the organization, but it never got to first base.

The moment my own group of Star owners on the Sound
heard that four other localities were anxious to form an association and hold an annual championship, their entire attitude

changed. If some were still skeptical, they kept it to themselves. No one could ask for more co-operation than I received.
Had it not been for their untiring effort, we could never
have held our first few championships and I doubt if there
would be a Star class today.

An organization meeting had been arranged and I spent
the closing weeks of 1921 drawing up a tentative constitution
and set of by-laws. It was not as easy as it sounds. There
was no precedent to follow and I had to do the work at home
on an old invisible Remington typewriter. It was a grand
old machine. You could have hit it with a sledge hammer
and it would have come up smiling and unharmed. I must
have re-written both documents at least half a dozen times
before they satisfied me. The delegates to that meeting would
only have about half a day to transact their business. I was
asking them to adopt my plan and it was up to me to put
something concrete before them. If I was able to cover the
essential requirements of the proposed association, then they
could make whatever changes they saw fit and there was a
good chance that the business could be completed at one
session.

CHAPTER V

THE BIRTH OF A GIANT

FIVE STAR LOCALITIES, that became Fleets before the day was over, were represented at the meeting which launched the Star Class Yacht Racing Association. It was held at the Hotel Astor in New York City on January 20, 1922. The charter fleets, in order of size, were Western Long Island Sound, Lake Erie, Detroit River, Eastern Long Island Sound and Narragansett Bay. Each fleet was entitled to as many votes as it had Stars, owned by different members in good standing. That rule still applies. Western L.I.S. commanded more votes than all the others put together and continued to hold the balance of voting power for several years. Everything ran smoothly. There was the same undercurrent of levity and goodfellowship that has marked all subsequent Star meetings.

The constitution and by-laws were read and adopted almost verbatim. Ben Linkfield, retiring treasurer, suggested that our units be called fleets. It was more fitting than the term chapter, which I had originally used. I cannot recall any other changes. The western end of the Sound was selected as the scene of the first championship, because of the size and seniority of its fleet. The delegates also voted to publish a yearbook, to be known as "The Log of the Star Class" In addition to the constitution and by-laws, it was to contain a register of all Stars.

George A. Corry was elected president and Henry Watterson, of Cleveland, vice-president. I was made secretary-in-chief, the fancy title being to distinguish me from fleet secretaries. Charles Burlingham, of Black Point, became the first treasurer. We then elected three executive members. Together with the four major officers, that constituted an executive committee of seven, who were in charge of association policy, appeals, etcetera. The three elected were Jack Wood, of Narragansett Bay; Jack Miller, of Detroit River and Bill McHugh. It will be noted that the elective officers were distributed among the charter fleets insofar as possible. It was already known that Bill McHugh intended to form a Central Long Island Sound Fleet and he did so within a couple of months. It began with four boats. By the mid thirties it had a total of eighty-one, a single Star more than its western neighbor, and became the largest fleet in the association.

The old association turned its bank balance over to the newly formed one. It amounted to the large sum of fifty-nine dollars and some cents. That was all the working capital it had to start with. The most recent balance sheet shows the net worth of the I.S.C.Y.R.A. to be about $15,000.00. Its chief source of income has been derived from dues, which were only a little more than nominal. There have never been any assessments, contributions, or bonded indebtedness to offset a deficit. Perpetual trophies, including the present World's Championship one, have never been listed as an asset, since they were procured by donations I wonder how many other yachting organizations existing through so many critical years can match that record.

Approximately thirty-five attended the organization meeting. Following it they dined at the Astor. While it was not mentioned, everyone seemed to sense that a new page had been written in yachting history, one that was destined to alter the future of the sport. That you may know we knew what we were doing from the start, let me quote, in part, from an editorial in the first Log:

> "It is conceded that the future of yacht racing rests with the small one-design classes . . . The first step is to select a boat that meets the requirements of the majority; then for the clubs to build such boats and make intersectional and international competition possible . . . "

After dinner Sig Adler took the visitors and a few locals to an artists's dance in Greenwich Village. And that is the story of the founding of the I.S.C.Y.R.A.

Aside from the Captain's Island race, which I happened to win in 1922, Sound racing had lost its significance, insofar as the Star Class, as a whole, was concerned. The Ratsey brothers had grown up and Ernest, sailing Irex III, won a lot of races, including Larchmont week. Arthur Knapp, then a promising young skipper, had his Star, Southern Cross, cut in half by a steamer, while waiting for a start at Seawanhaka. Atlantic week had folded up. I was too occupied with the affairs of the association to remember much else.

We were obliged to hold a National Championship and publish a yearbook, although we had no funds for either. Pop Corry, with the help of the old timers, handled the former and made a fine job of it. The Bayside, Port Washington and Manhasset Bay yacht clubs were inveigled into holding a race and throwing a party the night thereof Bayside's vaudeville, Port Washington's stag smoker and Manhasset's farewell dinner dance, featuring the presentation of prizes, became fixtures for a number of years.

Due to Pop's influence, Horace Boucher presented a perpetual trophy. It was a half model of a Star under sail. The plaque on which it was mounted must been three feet high. Pop and Charlie Davis concocted a special prize for the winning skipper. The latter made an exquisite little thing, a tiny Star listed close-hauled, sailing on greenish opaque glass. It was enclosed in a glass case no more than a foot long It was far more valuable than the perpetual trophy. Pop was the best salesman I ever knew. He could convince any powerboat owner, after talking a few moments, that we were actually doing him a great favor in allowing his boat to be used as a tender for one of the visitors. As yet there were no associate members, but I managed to get the New England Boat Works to offer, as a prize for the winning crew, a half interest in a new Star. Harry Reeve, who won it, sold his share at a good price and is probably the only Star crew that ever made money out of a Star championship.

All the business details of the association, however, were heaped upon my shoulders. With some help, I sold eight hundred dollars worth of advertising space in the Log. Printing was not too expensive then. It paid for the Log, its mailing and we had enough over for three National Championship medals. They were heavy medals of gold, silver and bronze, about two inches in diameter, with a raised Star sailing toward you. They were better than any Olympic medal I ever saw, but am afraid that they were not appreciated.

The most tedious job connected with that first Log was the register. A questionnaire had to be sent to every owner, with a self-addressed stamped envelope enclosed, otherwise no one would reply. Many of the Stars had been in existence for twelve seasons and had had several owners. After the original answer, I had the long drawn out task of tracing all the former owners. Nahant and Rochester, which eventually became two of our most loyal fleets, caused the most trouble at first. These owners were not inclined to answer at all. All their Stars had to be given new numbers, as both groups were numbered from one up and the members of the old association, on the Sound, were given priority That accounts for the jumbled dates among the first hundred Stars in the register It was at that time that I started the first volume of a permanent register It was a ledger, with one page devoted to the history of every Star. There are now over a dozen volumes.

If I thought I was busy before, I was just beginning to learn the meaning of the word. We had no forms that first year. Everything had to be typewritten, even the original charters. There were many questions that the executive committee had to decide. Each meant seven copies of a lengthy letter and a vote sheet. I was flooded with correspondence. Some eventually resulted in new fleets, but the majority, of course, did not A few commodores misunderstood our aims and ordered me to stop contacting their club members. Later they became our best friends. Toward the end of the year, I drew up many of the forms now in use. It had become obvious that the association must be run automatically on some system of forms, otherwise no one man could do the detail work. It was fortunate that I was on the sick list for a couple of years We had no money to pay for the work and anyone engaged in business could not have devoted his entire time to it. The old Remington was kept going day and night.

Two serious mistakes had been made. Dues were continued at one dollar, which was not enough to cover our normal expenses. We had also failed to state how fleets should choose their entries. That first year it was done by selection committees. That is how the term eliminations came into use. From then on entries were selected as the result of a series of trial races.

Western Long Island Sound had its three most promising condidates, Ratsey, Inslee and Linkfield, sail a number of short races. Any advantage gained by a wind shift was not to count Ratsey won the majority of the races that first day and Linkfield was eliminated. Inslee had his mainsail re-cut overnight and, on the following day, easily won every race. He was unanimously named.

Even before that first championship, the association started to grow. A fleet was formed at Los Angeles and sent an entry. In fact we had a total of nine fleets before the year was over, with several more forming.

Bill Inslee made a clean sweep of the 1922 National Championship. Number one, the Taurus, was never even seriously threatened It was simply a question of who would be runner-up. The only exciting moment was toward the end of the final race Lake Erie's Fejo was second, with California's Three Star right astern Both were running free. Weston pulled the old fake luff and got away with it. While the Schweitzer brothers, without looking behind, were still trimming in, Ben eased sheets, broke through Fejo's lee and took second in both the race and the series. The Schweitzers made another mistake. To quench their thirst, when at home, they had always dipped a tin cup in the lake. They tried the same thing in the opening race, without realizing that the Sound was salt water. Having had several cups, they did not feel too well that first evening.

From the point of view of the association, the event could not have been more satisfactory. The three major sections of the United States, the Atlantic coast, Pacific coast and Great Lakes had placed in order named. All the entries had won one or more daily club prizes, except Eastern L.I.S. The entertainments were crowded every evening. Inslee's victory had been a foregone conclusion from the start The locals, who constituted the great majority of those present, gave all the visiting contestants a rousing ovation Had a visitor won, it might have been different. People were still very narrow minded, especially in regard to intersectional yacht racing. If the local boy was beaten, they were inclined to take it as a personal affront and attribute it to almost anything, except that the best skipper had won.

That first championship was an opening wedge to the many international Star events that were to follow. Being a national championship, it is not included among the summaries in the back of this book, Nevertheless, it was of historic importance and the complete results should be a matter of record:

Yacht & Fleet	Skipper & Crew	Club	Daily Place			Pts
Taurus	W L Inslee	Bayside	1	1	1	18
Western L I S	Harry Reeve					
Three Star	B P Weston	California	3	4	2	12
Southern California	Owen Churchill					
Fejo	J P Schweitzer	Cleveland	4	3	4	10
Lake Erie	F W Schweitzer					
South Wind	W J McHugh	South Norwalk	2	*	3	9
Central L I S	R Comstock					
Brownie	G H Armitage	Washington Park	6	2	5	8
Narragansett Bay	W H Gidley					
Tara	B N Heminway	Black Point	5	5	6	5
Eastern L I S	W Staughton					

* Disabled

At that time it was much harder to win the Western L I S. eliminations than the Championship Any one of a dozen in that fleet could have won the title during the first five years. There were other good Star skippers elsewhere but they were under a handicap. They did not have enough local competition to extend them to the limit New to the class, they were forced to race on strange waters against a veteran of about ten years of Star experience. Gradually the fleets improved and closed the gap. The same is true today There is no case on record of anyone comparatively new to the class winning a world's title It takes a certain amount of big league experience to pick up the tricks of the trade To get the most out of a Star requires a technique all its own, which cannot be acquired overnight, not even by the best of skippers in another class.

The second annual meeting was also held in New York City, in January of that year, but was very poorly attended. Only nearby local fleets sent delegates The rest were represented by proxy About the only business transacted was to place the word "international" before the association's original name. That was made possible by the English Bay fleet of British Columbia. Another small Canadian fleet was being formed at Victoria. The fact is that the championship was already was being called the "Internationals." The title of the event was not officially changed to World's Championship until a number of years later. While international in character, the event has always been for the inter-fleet championship of the Star class. No restriction has ever been placed upon the number of separate fleets, in a given country, that could send entries. It became obvious that a winter meeting in New York City would not serve the purpose The date was changed to the period of the Internationals. That is why there were two I S C Y R.A annual meetings in 1923.

Bill Inslee won his international title in 1923, but he did not have things all his own way The second race was the first windward and leeward course the Stars ever sailed. Harry Wylie, of English Bay, took advantage of the rule which made a local crew optional. He selected Ernest Ratsey

Harry was the first to loom up out of the heavy fog and win, thereby becoming the first Star outside of the United States ever to win an international race. On the final day, Inslee was last at the first mark. The second leg was a broad reach, but no one paid any attention to him. He went far to leeward, lee-bowed the tide, hardened his wind to round the mark first and won by a good margin. British Columbia placed second in the series and Ralph Walton, of Central Lake Erie (there was then a Western Lake Erie), was third.

There was also an Australian entry that year. Ernest Walker sailed a chartered Star, renamed Kangaroo, to represent the New South Wales fleet. He did not materially affect the point score, which was lucky, as that Fleet never materialized. It taught us never to accept an entry from a pledged fleet thereafter Pop was so enthused over the international aspect of the event that he wanted Howard Curry's Japanese butler to also sail a chartered Star and represent a proposed fleet in Japan We turned thumbs down on that.

A disgraceful thing happened at the smoker on the night that Wylie won. Harry was feeling no pain, when the daily prizes were being presented His empty plate pushed aside, he was enjoying a restful snooze, head pillowed on his folded arms. The announcement that he was the winner was greeted by cheers intermingled with boos. A shower of uneaten rolls was tossed at the recumbent figure. Perhaps that was done playfully, but some inebriated fool tore down the Canadian flag from the wall behind the speaker's table. He was immediately ejected and the flag replaced. A lot of outsiders crashed the gate at those early entertainments. He must have been one of them, as I never saw the fellow before and would have recognized him if he had belonged to the Star class or the host club, of which I was then commodore. I mention the incident only to show that I was not exaggerating about the feeling against anyone who beat the local entry in those days.

The annual meeting, held during the period of the Internationals, accomplished quite a lot Ben Weston was elected vice-president and Bill Gidley, of Narragansett Bay, treasurer. The most important thing was to change the International to a five race series. The boys from a distance felt that it was asking too much of them to make such a trip for only three races. Harry Wylie wanted a news publication and Ernest Ratsey named it Starlights. Miller, of Detroit, became the first editor Bulletins were to be issued now and then and contained in a loose-leaf folder, on which was a beautiful picture of twenty-five Stars starting at Larchmont. Members could get all this for fifty cents. It's a minor matter, but a milestone in Star history.

Pop was becoming a problem. He had several typewritten pages of new business to place before the meeting, but could not keep his mind on the agenda. Who wanted ham and who wanted cheese sandwiches to take out on the morrow? Then he interrupted things again to explain about the spectator boats. When urged to please get down to business, he would laugh and say, "Before I forget I must tell you about . . . ", and he would drift off into an endless story of some race sailed in his youth Pop was simply not interested in rules or business. It was all a gala affair to him, at which everyone must have a good time. The night was hot and nearly two hours were spent with practically nothing accomplished.

Bill Gidley left the room. A few moments later the club steward opened the door and said there was a long distance phone call for Mr. Corry. Pop dashed off and I took the chair. Watterson was absent and Weston not yet elected Skipping the reasons, I read the proposed resolutions Almost before I was through with each everyone yelled, "Yes, read the next." By the time an indignant and puzzled Pop returned, all the business had been transacted. He had spent a long time arguing with the regular and then the chief operator who could find no trace of any such call. Bill told me later that he had left the receiver off the hook and a dollar tip to the steward had taken care of the rest.

Bill Gidley was really responsible for the Narragansett Bay fleet. He bought Stars and sold them on easy terms to young fellows, who otherwise could never have afforded one.

That quiet old New Englander had a heart of gold and a head on his shoulders. He is gone now, but will always be remembered for his unselfish efforts in behalf of the Star class.

Jack Robinson was the sensation of 1924 He had sailed Stars on the Sound for a number of years, but had never even been a threat in the "B" division. He not only won the "B" Championship (from which he was automatically disqualified), but the eliminations and carried his streak right through to the Internationals. Arthur Knapp was his crew in the last named event, which certainly did him no harm. The Little Bear was found to be seven inches too short and a false bow had to be added. Yes, there were limitations by that time, but they were not published. It was Jack's first and last big year, but no matter what he did in 1924 he gained by it.

Let me give you an example. A flock of Stars were sailing the reverse course at Larchmont. They had rounded Scotch Cap and were drifitng along on the last leg, sheets eased. The Little Bear was about twentieth and far behind the leaders. A big triple-decked houseboat came barging through the almost becalmed Stars. A davit caught Little Bear's shroud. After a vain attempt to free her, Jack and crew jumped for the guardrail and hung on, as the Star was being sucked under. Half full of water and listed, Little Bear broke clear of herself. They dove in and swam back to the Star. The houseboat never slackened speed. Whoever was at the helm should have been prosecuted, but nothing was done about it. The Star had been dragged almost to the finish line. With wet sails and still bailing, Jack placed third. Even being run down helped Jack that season.

Bill Inslee left the Sound and joined a new fleet on Gravesend Bay. To return to the waters whence he came, seemed like a perfectly natural act, but it caused much malicious gossip. The rooters that accompanied Bill and his new Star Sonny to the Internationals were so sure that he would win for the third time, that their attitude only made things worse. Pop had bought the Taurus and renamed it Little Dipper. He felt that he should be the owner of Star

No. 1. For a time Pop did very well with the boat, but he could not keep it in tune and gradually fell back.

In order to hold five races, it was necessary to seek the help of two clubs on the north shore of the Sound, Larchmont and New Rochelle. Both had efficient R.C.'s, but they were used to running open regattas. They believed in starting on time whether anyone was there or not The fact that the home fleet was responsible for getting distant entries to the line on time did not much interest them, nor would they act on a violation reported by a Star mark or course official Larchmont insisted on starting off its breakwater. The race had to be held in the morning, not to conflict with an open regatta that afternoon. The Stars were sent over a special course. The wind was light and they were finishing as the large yachts were starting. The latter, unaware that an international race was in progress, yelled at the Stars to keep out of the restricted area and those on the Stars had a few choice words to say in reply There was a lot of confusion but the Stars were strung out and no position was affected Only a few Star members attended the entertainments given by those two clubs. After returning to Manhasset Bay, no one felt like crossing the Sound again.

A sequence of black Thursdays started that year. A tropical storm from the south with violent rain and wind squalls was the order of the day. At the attention signal Bill Inslee bent on his mainsail, started to hoist it, lowered it again and went back aboard his tender. No one ever knew the reason for his withdrawal. It was said that the crew was ill, but that was only a rumor. Certainly Bill did not mind bad weather.

Comstock and Gidley won the race, in the worst blow of the week, and gave Narragansett Bay second place in the series. With his most dangerous opponent eliminated, Jack was content to keep clear of everyone and bring the Little Bear back in one piece. At that he finished second to win the championship. Ben Weston took third honors for California.

The Star roster had jumped to twenty-seven fleets and with Cuba, New Zealand and Hawaii, the class had really become international. A gold star on the mainsail officially became the emblem of the champion and was retained by the skipper. A pair of these gold stars were presented to Jack Robinson at the final banquet and various sailmakers continued the practice for a long time. It was decided at the annual meeting, held in the Manhasset Bay Y.C, that the Boucher half model was not a suitable perpetual trophy anymore. As Bill Inslee had won it two out of three times, it was presented to him. Pop undertook the task of obtaining funds, by subscription, for a large silver cup. Sam Pirie, Woodie's father, was the largest individual contributor He stipulated that no race should be held on Sunday, but Pop managed to get around that somehow.

A lot of things happened at the annual meeting. Starlights was to become a printed monthly publication and included in the dues, which were already five dollars Stakeboats were to be used as marks instead of buoys and courses sailed twice around. A race circular was to be printed by the association and the accounting for rule emphasized It must be remembered that a different club was holding every race and that the nearest starting line was about five miles from the anchorage. There had to be standard signals and courses and we could not take the chance of some race being started, which a visitor was unable to reach through no fault of his own. To sail twice around would also tend to limit any advantage gained from local knowledge and wind hunting. I agreed to take care of all this.

Six districts were established and, according to my original scheme, each was to be under the supervision of a district secretary. He was supposed to be a connecting link between the association and the district, but for a number of years that officer was only a fifth wheel to the cart. Fleet secretaries ignored him and continued to transact their business directly with the association. In fact the district secretary did not really come into his own until the members voted by ballot. Then voting for that officer was restricted to members within the district. Before that district secretaries were elected by the delegates to the annual meeting, who often did not know enough about strictly local district conditions to select the proper person.

What could we do with Pop Corry? He knew practically nothing about the organization, parliamentary procedure and seemed incapable of conducting a meeting. The old timers understood the situation, but the many new delegates, who had made a long trip to discuss business matters, were annoyed by the sort of horseplay, which had characterized our annual meetings. I believe it was Ray Schauer that came up with the answer. Create the office of commodore, especially for Pop's benefit. It would be a promotion, but would keep him out of executive matters. It was not the sort of thing that could be brought up at an open meeting and had to be planned several days before. It was done and Pop was elected. He did not like it at first. He thought he was being sidetracked and his feelings were hurt. After sleeping over it, however, he changed his mind. He was the number one member of the Manhasset Bay Y C., had started it on a barge in Little Neck Bay, but had never been a commodore. The job fitted him like a glove. In that capacity he became a great asset to the association and, as I have said before, no one will ever be able to fill his shoes.

I became president and Tim Parkman, the one association minded member of Gravesend Bay, was elected secretary-in-chief These changes necessitated a lot of amendments. The more important were to confer powers upon the president that had previously been vested in the secretary-in-chief. At first we had been forced to write the constitution around the officers we had, instead of electing officers with the qualifications for the respective jobs.

The Ace, sailed by Adrian Iselin and Ed Willis, qualified for and won the 1925 Internationals. Phillips gave English Bay runner-up honors and third place went to Schauer, of Southern California. By this time there were more fleets on the Pacific coast, but the original one did not change its name to Los Angeles Harbor until the following year.

The fourth race was between Iselin and a five hour time limit, which then applied. Ace just did manage to win, as the

sun was sinking in the west. On one of the days it blew, the
Ace finished ninth. Many felt that a shorter time limit would
have cancelled a couple of races and that the result might
have been different. I doubt it. Iselin and Willis, at that
time, were the best combination in the Star class. Ace was
second on the other windy day and, I believe, would have
won regardless of conditions. Nevertheless, we changed the
time limit to three and one-half hours and it has so remained. With a very light air, provided it is steady, a standard
Star championship course can be sailed in that time. This
has been proven over a period of twenty-eight years.

It was a period replete with notable incidents. Iselin,
winning the Pandora trophy, had the most far-reaching effect.
It was presented by Commodore Vance, of the Port Washington Y.C , for the highest score made in the last three races
by entries representing fleets on the Atlantic seaboard That
was the first Star district and it became the first District
Championship. Such championships are now held in almost
every district in the association. The Pacific coast claims to
have held such a championship as far back as 1923, but
that is impossible. There were no districts at that time. As
a matter of fact, the event in question was an open one for
all classes on the Pacific coast and did not meet the requirements of a Star District Championship.

Any skepticism about the international aspect of the event
was dispelled. M. deSena, who brought his Star up from
Havana, could not speak a word of English. Earl Blouin,
Talita's Cajun skipper, could, but no one could understand
him. The new vice-president, who served for five years, came
with the New Orleans boys. He acted as delegate and chaperon combined—and what a chaperon Prentice Edrington
turned out to be. Far-off Hawaii was entered. We saw and
heard (with emphasis on the latter) Herb Dowsett for the
first time. He was and still is the leading Star spirit around
Honolulu. Prentice, of course, was no shrinking violet. He
answered to the nickname of "Noisy" for a a time.

Joe Jessop, a California entry, brought his Star from
San Diego Bay. While at anchor, mainsail flapping in the

breeze, the boom hit his crew in the head and knocked him overboard When Sykes did not come up, Joe dived for him and managed to get the unconscious Sykes back aboard the Windward and revive him. That was almost a fatal accident. There might have been another In a light air race, Blouin slipped and fell in, while fussing with the outhaul He claimed that he could not swim a stroke, but he learned mighty fast. He covered the twenty yards that separated him from Talita in nothing flat.

It was a year in which many things happened for the first time. Lake Otsego, of the little inland lake fleets, was the first of such fleets to enter the Internationals. It was represented by Bill Hyde, who sailed the Cooperstown It was a shame that Colonel Wait did not make it that year. For two years he had represented Eastern L.I.S. and "Waiting for Wait" became a byword. Sometimes one added, "He may finish with the help of the Lord," Lord being the name of his crew Yes, the colonel would have found a worthy opponent for last place in Bill Hyde They were two of the nicest and most popular fellows imaginable, but in championship competition they sure were babes in the woods. The following is almost unbelievable, yet it actually happened.

Bill Hyde missed one race because of a luncheon date in the city. On a rainy morning, he boarded the Cooperstown with an umbrella and wearing galoshes Sailing a windward and leeward course, he was half a lap behind on the second leg. He met the other boats, again tacking for the weather mark. Evidently Bill decided that he was not doing too well because he had his sail out. In any event he strapped her down and sailed Cooperstown downwind close-hauled for the last half of that leg Nor did the crew Brewster fail to contribute, as a delegate at the annual meeting He suggested that one of the title races be a sort of novelty Women's bathing suits were to be placed on a float and numbered. The entries should sail a short course, anchor, skipper and crew swim to the float, put on the bathing suits, swim back to their boats and sail to the finish line. It had been tried on his local waters and created a lot of interest. The heck of it was that he was perfectly serious and it was introduced as a motion and voted down.

Sampson Smith was a charter member of Lake Otsego. Through his efforts many other little lake fleets were started and eventually combined into the Twelfth District, one of the largest in the association. Oh Sam, what a skipper you must have been in 1925 to have been beaten in your eliminations! But don't worry, you have more than atoned for it since. Aside from winning the District Championship five times. Sam is the only small fresh water lake skipper that ever won a silver star and made a real showing in the World's Championship. He knew his class rules and for years was one of our most able major association officers.

As per schedule, a printed Starlights appeared in January, 1925, and not a single monthly issue was skipped for nineteen years. During the second world war, due to lack of material, only seven or eight issues were published for a couple of years, until the regular monthly schedule was again resumed. Starlights has been one of the chief mediums of keeping the Star membership united. "Little Star Boat Of Mine," words and music by Nell Jacobsen, came out that year. It was a simple, catchy little tune, that became the theme song of the Star class for a number of years. One of the printed score sheets is on file at the central office. It is the only original tune especially written for the Stars and should be revived.

Another thing done at the annual meeting was to create an international race committee. It was quite similar to the one we have today. All major association officers, present and eligible, by reason of not being contestants, plus as many district officers, as had to be elected, constituted an I.R.C. of five. It was not supposed to run races or have anything to do with rules of right-of-way. It was given jurisdiction over class rules and regulations only and required to have at least one member aboard the committee boat, to act as an observer and advise the R.C. about class requirements. The Star class was again lucky, as the I.R.C. was forced to act the following year.

Everyone was getting fed up with having the Internationals constantly on the Sound and interest was starting to lag Other fleets had developed to the point where they could now hold the event. It was voted that the Internationals could not be held on the waters of any given fleet for more than three consecutive years. Then, if not won outright by a challenger, it would go to the fleet having the greatest aggregate points in those three years. The rule was changed several times, until the present rotating system was finally perfected.

The defender of a Star championship (primarily the skipper) is the entry representing the fleet that last won the title in question. In other words the fleet defends, regardless of who represents it or where the event is held. If not represented, then there is no defender. People were not yet accustomed to the idea in 1926, at least not as applied to yachting, and being the defender was looked upon as sort of an empty honor, since the Internationals had to leave the western end of the Sound.

I was sailing 343 that year, my first Iscyra. It was built the previous winter by Joe and Tom Parkman, Tim's father and uncle respectively. Tim, our secretary-in-chief, was a young lawyer and not connected with his father's boat business. The name Iscyra, suggested by Herb Dowsett, is the initials of the association and seven of the fifteen Stars I have owned were so named.

Iscyra won the home eliminations hands down. It was still more difficult to win than the Internationals, as there were the normal number of entries in all but the last two races. Due to a postponement, they were held as a double header. Having already qualified, I did not have to enter either. Ed Willis, the potential runner-up, would have to put about a dozen boats between us to top Iscyra's percentage. The series, to all intent and purpose, was over. There were no daily prizes and the races did not count for anything else. In those days, the boys did not race without an incentive. I just went along to see what would happen. One other Star showed up in the morning and Ed and I were the only starters in the afternoon. Perhaps he had to sail one more race to qualify, I cannot remember. Otherwise those two races were a farce. He won both and I just followed leisurely over the course, to wind it up.

With three firsts, Rhody won the Internationals easily, It was a popular victory and far better than if the event had gone to Narragansett Bay on the aggregate point system Swing Starring gave Central L I.S. second place and Harry Fisher, of San Diego Bay was third. With two Cuban entries, one representing Cienfuegos and three from California, it gave us a total of sixteen.

Stainless steel rigging was not yet in use. Iscyra had been hauled to dry out and we found that the shrouds had rusted through just above the turnbuckles and had to be renewed. That meant stretching the wire and tuning all over again. I came down with the gout and could not do it alone. My crew, Ray Finlay, was one of the best, but he had to work late right up to the first day of the series. He had a brood of kids that could not be left home alone so he was forced to help his wife wash and dress them every morning so they could come along. I had to conduct the annual meeting and attend to a lot of advance details. To tell the truth it did not worry me and I never gave a thought to the boat. I was suffering from the overconfidence of most Sound skippers. I thought that I could take care of all this while racing—but I was very much mistaken.

The foregoing is not an alibi. I might have done better, but am sure I would not have won—the gap had been bridged. It is mentioned to illustrate a point. Many of our fleets have made the mistake of electing a skipper, who brought a title to their waters, to some important local job. The intent was to confer an honor upon him, but actually it hurt both his chances and theirs. It's the old story. Executive work and racing ability are separate and distinct and cannot be combined at the same time. No one can win a major championship unless he devotes his entire attention to his boat, both before and during the races. Star records will bear me out in this.

A distant skipper could still use a local Star, if he desired. The theory was that racing a boat, with which he was not familiar, placed him at a disadvantage. Harry Fisher took advantage of the option. Ernest Ratsey, who was willing to do anything to cooperate, put his Irex III in tip top shape and brought it over to Port Washington for San Diego's use. Harry took one look at Irex III and said something to the effect that he would just as leave bend his sails on the club float. Irex III had won at Havana and was also Sound champion that year. Many thought it the best conditioned and fastest Star on the Sound. Everyone, of course, is entitled to his own opinion and eventually Harry was able to obtain another Star.

That incident brought to light several defects in the chartering rule In the first place skippers, who had gone to the expense of shipping their Stars a long distance, began to ask why they should continue doing so, if a fellow could bring his sails and race a local boat, which had not been subjected to the rigors of a lengthy trip and was already in perfect condition. A new fleet, which did not yet know too much about tuning a Star, gained by using a local one. We already had more distant entries than there were Stars in some of our smaller fleets. Suppose all distant entries requested local boats of such a fleet, it would not have enough to go around. The chief objection to the rule was the bad blood it caused. Fortunately very few had ever availed themselves of this option If there were two, however, the fellow who did the worst would claim favoritism. No owner likes to loan his Star any more so than his tooth brush. "Charter" was a technical term. It involved the passing of a mythical dollar. Hence the use of chartered Stars was barred from then on. An exception, however, could be made in extraordinary cases, such as a yacht being damaged beyond repair.

The first race of the Internationals, held by the Bayside Y.C. is worthy of mention. Ernest Ratsey had presented me with the lightest weight duck sail I have ever seen. There was not a cloud in the sky and we decided to give it a try. The R.C. made a mistake and gave us a gun on the lower. I was almost on the line and got quite a start on the others. The first leg was to leeward and Iscyra ghosted away. Then it began to breeze up. When we hauled on the wind that sail just collapsed. I was lucky to be able to finish ahead of two boats. If it had stayed light, Iscyra would have gone into a very big lead, but I doubt if we could have finished within the three and one-half hour time limit. The moral is, do not use light weight ghosting sails in a championship.

Now we come to the all important incident of 1926, which affected the method of holding all future Internationals. The New York Y.C. had agreed to hold one of the races, replacing New Rochelle on the schedule. It was considered a big feather in our cap. Pop and I had a long talk with Edmund Lang, then commodore of Manhasset Bay Y.C., and a member of the New York Y C race committee. He wanted to be sure that our I R.C. would not reverse their decision on right-of-way rules. We assured him that the I.R.C. had no such power, but explained that it did have jurisdiction, on appeal, over class rules or procedure. An I.R.C. member, however, would be on the committee boat just to make sure that nothing went wrong That was fully agreed to and should be remembered, in the light of what happened.

It started to blow the night before and kept increasing. The east wind had an unobstructed sweep of nearly two hundred miles. By starting time it was blowing fifty-six miles per hour (weather bureau) and was accompanied by a cold driving rain. The seas were sharpened and curling, as it was blowing against an ebbing tide. The Stars started out at the appointed hour behind their tenders, mostly small cruisers and auxiliaries. When they rounded Gangway, these could not buck the wind and sea and headed for the sheltered waters of Crescent Cove, so the crews could bend on sails. The two marker yachts could not take it and were there also, having turned their marks over to John Atwater, course official, and the Mongoose. She came in a little later with the two marks, anchored them and Johnny circled about with a megaphone. He had tried to place a mark, but it would not hold, nor would the Mongoose. He did not think there could be a race, but instructed us to wait there until he went back to the committee boat and found out what the R.C. wanted to do. When he returned he told us that three Stars were already racing, although there was no mark. He had reported that twelve entries were awaiting instructions, he said, but no one paid any attention to him.

What actually happened was this: a large steam yacht (presumably Fred Bedford's) had managed to tow four Stars to the line The R.C. gave the signals and three of those Stars started, with double reefed mainsails and no jibs. They were Bill Inslee, Vic Darlinson and Floyd Clancy, who finally finished in the order named. The fourth, Starring and Bedford, used better judgment and did not attempt it. Our two I.R.C. representatives aboard the committee boat, Prentice Edrington and Tim Parkman, went below and partook of champagne and an elaborate buffet lunch, which no one else seemed interested in. They claimed to have called the R.C.'s attention to the fact that it could not start a race without marks or all the entries being accounted for, but were told that the responsibility of placing marks was that of the Star class and that the race would start regardless of who was missing. Pop Corry was largely to blame for what followed. He was aboard a drifting Coast Guard boat and had no authority over the course sailed. It was perhaps a mile and one-half from the line, when Inslee approached. Pop signaled him to round the Coast Guard. The second time around, the Coast Guard boat had drifted to within less than a mile of the line and was rounded again.

The R.C. insisted that it was a race insofar as it was concerned and that it would present the daily prizes to the three who sailed. A notice was posted and the R.C. went home. When the skippers and crews, who had followed instructions and waited in the cove, saw this, hell broke loose. When efforts to reach the R C by phone failed, they got together and protested the race, for gross violation of class rules It was not sailed around specified marks, the marks used were drifting, the course was about half the required distance, the attention signal was given with twelve entries unaccounted for and the R.C. would not heed the report of the Star course official or the advice of the I.R.C. representatives aboard. After about half an hour's debate, the I.R.C. announced that the protest was sustained and the race thrown out. Too many cooks spoil the broth and it was simply an unfortunate misunderstanding as to who had authority over what.

On the following day the Manhasset Bay R.C. used its head and established a course to the west of Execution Light. The wind moderated a little and Rhody won, just about clinching the title. After that race Bill Inslee went home and, to the best of my knowledge, never sailed a Star again.

One more race had to be sailed, but there was no club to conduct it. The I.R.C. did so, using a Coast Guard boat as a committee boat. It was a dark fall day and still blowing pretty hard. We were sent to the east over a windward and leeward course. The weather mark, which still displayed a black shape, was easy to find, as a Coast Guard searchlight was kept on the metal cone above the shape. By that time I had Iscyra going again and won. The daily prizes were presented by the I.S.C.Y.R.A. Comstock and Gidley sailed to an easy third and took the series.

At the final banquet, the New York Y.C. presented its prizes to the three skippers who had sailed in its race. Feeling was running pretty high, but those three skippers deserved something for bringing their Stars back in one piece. Since then many races have been cancelled for half a gale, much less a full one. Nobody stopped to think about the accidents, which might have happened, if all the entries had been able to start.

That unfortunate race, however, made one point very clear. There cannot be two heads to any given enterprise. At the second session of the meeting, the duties of the I.R.C. were extended to cover the actual conduct of all World's Championship races and decide all protests.

A few yacht clubs objected to this at first. They felt that if their name was in any way connected with a Star World's Championship race, it should be sailed over the club's courses and under its own method, or not at all. This was the dawn of a new era, however, and they soon began to realize that the championship races of a world-wide class must be conducted according to a uniform system and that only those versed in regulations of the said class could be expected to enforce them properly. In fact I believe they soon welcomed shifting the responsibility to our shoulders. From then on clubs could play host to an international event without risking criticism that was bound to follow any unintentional mistake, or having a decision of theirs overruled.

At that time we were only measuring Stars entered in the Internationals. Adrian Iselin's suggestion that all Stars be measured and that a certificate become mandatory, to enter any Star race, was approved. This mde it necessary to develop a new department. We already had a chief measurer in Fred Teeves, but he had to appoint certified measurers in every Star locality. Their job, for which they were entitled to a fee, was to take the physical measurements only and submit them to Teeves, who would apply the allowed variations, granting or refusing the certificate. While those variations existed, they had not as yet been made public. It was a gigantic task, since around five hundred Stars already existed, nor was it possible to fully complete it during the first year.

Those first five years, when the Internationals were held on the Sound really amounted to an experimental period. We were floundering around in the dark and making many radical rule changes. Others followed, of course, but generally speaking they were of minor importance. From time to time our rules have been amplified, more or less to plug loopholes that had been discovered in existing ones. Practically all of the fundamental rules, the rules around which the Star class has been built, were adopted during those first five experimental years on the Sound.

CHAPTER VI

HAVANA AHOY!

Havana, Paris of the Caribbean, basking beneath the glory of azure blue skies and fanned by the soft tropical breezes from the Gulf, beginning in January, 1926, became annual winter rendezvous for Star skippers. For the first couple of years and, without any good reason, this winter classic was spoken of as "les petite Internationals." Henceforth it assumed its rightful title of "Mid-Winter Championship."

It is difficult to find adequate words to describe the gracious hospitality and good sportsmanship of the Cuban yachtsman. No effort is spared in providing entertainment and looking after the comforts of the visitor. Your Cuban skipper, when he loses takes it with a smile and, if he wins, he modestly attributes it to a stroke of good luck. That first year must have stretched the good nature of our hosts almost to the breaking point. Coming from an arid region of ice, snow and bath tub gin, into a Utopia, where a man could order any drink he could think of, did not help to preserve decorum among the visitors from the States. At that time we did not know each other too well. We were looked upon as "crazy Americans" and certainly acted the part. That we were ever invited again, considering the many things that happened that year, is surprising.

The prizes made our eyes bulge. The Cup of Cuba, for the Mid-Winter Championship, is the largest sterling silver cup I have ever seen. Ernest Ratsey, its first winner, has a photograph of his young son sitting in it, and all you can see is the boy's head. The national crest of Cuba was on every trophy, as the government sponsored the event. In those days we went by rail to Key West and took the ferry across the gulf. And how some of those old steamers rolled! When the steamer docked, Rafael Posso—who does not look a day older now than he did then—came aboard. All contestants were asked to step forward and, while the tourists awaited their turn, we were whisked through the customs. After being photographed by a battery of cameras, we were driven to our hotel or to the yacht club, where those going stag were quartered "for free" in the dormitory. And what a gorgeous club the Havana Yacht Club is! Then came those first few nights of sampling wines and cordials, the taste of which we had almost forgotten.

What many people do not know, is that the first Bacardi Cup was not for an open series, but the international team race. My own experience, in connection therewith, was not too pleasant. We only knew of three U.S. skippers, who were taking their boats to Havana. A fourth was needed to make up the team. I had sold my Star and my first Iscyra was being built. I did not have a Star at the time, but an American, George Elliott Patterson, who lived in Havana, offered to loan me his. I, therefore, volunteered to go down and make up the team. There had been some talk about Bill Inslee going. My mother was in Florida and I intended to spend about a week with her, before continuing to Havana. Before leaving New York, I phoned Bill just to be sure. I explained that Prentice Edrington, of New Orleans, would be my crew and that neither of us wished to make the trip, unless we could sail in at least one race. Bill assured me that his business was such that he could not possibly go himself.

The first person I saw, on reaching the Havana Yacht Club, was no other than Bill Inslee. "It's too bad, Bill," I said, "if you had known that you could come down sooner, you could have been on the team." "Oh! I'm going to be on the team," he informed me. He argued that his record entitled him to be on the team and that he had his own boat. That was true enough, but neither Edrington nor I would have made the trip, if he had not stated definitely that he could not do so. The Cubans settled the matter by increasing the team to five. Al Buckley, from Narragansett Bay, had also put in an appearance without advising anyone, but he did not wish to be on the team. Prentice and I took out Patterson's Star, the Cygnet, in the first tune-up race, just to see how she went. What a boat. The mast had a forward hook, that we could not get out. She had the old bulkheads, fore and aft, and leaked like a sieve. On each leg downwind, I was obliged to stand and hold the tiller in a vertical position, while Prentice removed the hatch and bailed eight or nine pails of water out from under aft. The tiller had about a three-inch play in it. When we reached our mooring, in the Almendares river—where the boat house is located, about two miles from the yacht club—we decided not to sail her again before the team race, for fear that she would fall apart and we would not get into the event after all. In Havana, each visitor is allocated one of the club sailors, who looks after his boat, hauls it out, polishes the bottom or does any work you wish. We turned the Cygnet over to our boy with instructions to try to locate the leak and fix the tiller.

The Bacardi Cup was a beautiful thing, far more elaborate and expensive than those presented in subsequent years for the open series. What to do with it, if we won, was a problem, since each skipper was from a different club. This was also true, to some degree, of the Cuban team, which was made up of skippers from both Havana and Cienfuegos. Before the race we drew lots to see who would have permanent possession of the cup. And who do you suppose won?—Bill Inslee. The others were each to get a pair of very fine binoculars, in a leather case, surmounted with the crest of Cuba in solid gold. Those were the four original individual prizes. It was because of this complication about what to do with a team race cup, that henceforth it was presented for an open series.

While the team race was the last event of the week, 1 might as well complete the story at this point. The U.S. team won by a score of thirty-nine to fifteen, but the entire team almost fouled out. All five U.S. boats reached the windward mark in a bunch. We had just eased sheets and started downwind when the five Cuban boats, closed hauled, loomed up right in front of us. There seemed to be no space to get through. In some way Ratsey, Hayward and Inslee managed to do so, but Bedford and I were forced to make a complete circle and head back toward the mark to keep clear. The Cygnet was not leaking too much, but the tiller got loose again and it was almost impossible to put her about. At that, only one Cuban beat us.

The Cygnet vanished in the 1928 hurricane. Several years later a gang of workmen who were digging near the bank about three miles up the Almendares river unearthed the transom. This was the only piece of the good ship that was ever found.

Commodore Corry arrived a couple of days after the rest. That evening, everyone had their own private little dinner parties arranged. The tables were set up, with the usual floral decorations, on the veranda of the Havana Yacht Club, overlooking the moonlight beach and sparkling waters of the gulf. When Pop learned of this, he said that it would not do at all. Star members must eat at the same table. The tables were dismantled, taken inside (where it was much warmer) and rearranged as one long table. Many objected, as they had already carefully selected their menu and the wines to go with it and were entertaining guests. Once Pop made up his mind to do something, however, all objections were overruled. He had not yet learned that, while you might order at seven o'clock, no one ever sat down to eat before ten or later. He fussed and fumed and looked at his watch. Then he did something I never saw him do before or since, he had cocktails. Some Cuban member told him that a Presidente was a lady's drink and he probably thought that meant a soft drink. It tastes sweet and harmless, but has a kick like a mule. At long last the crowd assembled. Everyone was at that long table except four men, wearing business suits, who were seated at a small table in a far corner of the room. The commodore took his rightful place at the head of the table and his chest swelled with pride. There must have been seventy or eighty Star members present. He even made a couple of impromptu speeches, which did not make too much sense—the Presidentes were working. All went well, however, until dinner was over and a waiter handed him the check. Pop turned scarlet, choked over his coffee and tried to explain to the waiter, who could not speak English, that he was not going to pay for the whole gang, but individual checks should be made out for everyone. Then the captain came over. He could speak some English. What the commodore wanted could not be done. He no longer remembered what each person had been served. No, the check could not be divided by the number of people there. Some had ordered little and others a rather expensive meal, with wine. He would, however, talk with the manager and see what, if anything, could be done. Within a few minutes the captain was back. Everything had been taken care of. The check was paid. Who paid it? The commodore of the Cienfuegos Yacht Club. Which was he? Pop could not remember having met him. Why he was one of the four gentlemen seated at the little table over in the corner, the only four people that Pop had not invited to join the Star party.

Before getting off the subject of Presidentes, I recall a remark once made by Miguel (Mike) Riva. A Star skipper and at one time commodore of the Havana Yacht Club, Mike represented Havana in the 1929 World's Championship at New Orleans and was always very popular. He said, as if it was a problem which caused him great concern—"Somehow or other I cannot seem to drink more than 14 Presidentes before my dinner." I can sympathize with him. For some reason I cannot drink seventeen martinis before my dinner—I tried it once. Mike was a famous swordsman. I understand that he once challenged Patterson. It is too bad the latter did not take him up—then I would never have had to sail the Cygnet. Miguel Riva later became Cuba's minister to England, where he died.

Let us get back to the trials and tribulations of Commodore Corry. Breakfasts were served upstairs to the inmates of the dormitory. Pop told me one day that it was a shame how our boys from the States cussed at those nice Cuban waiters. He, Pop, was always first up. There was always plenty of coffee, he said, and all the food he could possibly eat. Come to find out, breakfasts were ordered by the others the night before, but not by Pop. What he had been doing was eating the breakfasts ordered by the rest. Of course, the waiters, who could not understand English, did not know what the boys were complaining about.

Quite late one night, Prentice Edrington and Gordon Curry, who was crewing for Al Buckley, returned to the club in a taxi. They did not make a price with the driver, which you are supposed to do. They considered the fare he demanded out of reason, which it probably was, and paid him what they had been paying before. The enraged taxi driver returned to the club with two gendarmes, who started to search for the culprits. Pop was sleeping in the first room they entered. He was dumped unceremoniously out of bed upon the marble floor before the taxi driver would admit that he was not one of the offenders. One of the club members intervened at that point.

Since Pop, Prentice and I were the ranking officers of the association, we were asked to assist the race committee in conducting its first championship. Off we went in a private yacht, a fifty-foot cruiser, belonging to one of the club members. The start and finish, in those days, was off the Maine Monument, so that the public might see the races. There was great interest, especially that first year. The sea wall, which borders the Malecon, was lined with spectators. It was a natural grandstand, since most of the course kept the yachts near shore. Naturally it was a fine day, for otherwise seas would have been breaking over the wall. On such days, even cars can only be driven on the in shore side of the Malecon, if at all. We were a little late in starting out and all the competing yachts were waiting for us, but the cruiser kept right on going toward Havana harbor. Inquiries revealed the fact that there was no ice aboard. The owner of the cruiser must go and get some, as he could not properly entertain his guests without having ice in their drinks. Prentice exploded. "Did you all ever hear," he shouted, "of a race committee in a civilized country postponing a race, because they have no ice for their drinks?" When we docked in Havana harbor, we were politely requested to go ashore. The owner decided that his country had been called uncivilized. There we were, stranded in Havana, eight miles from the yacht club, and with no means of communicating with the contestants, who had already been kept waiting almost an hour. If you ask me, we were in the middle of a hell of a fix.

Luckily a vessel of the Cuban navy, I believe her name was the Yara, was tied up at the same dock and under a full head of steam. It only took Possito a few minutes to arrange matters and we moved aboard. Our troubles had just begun. The Yara was a big heavy ship, of extensive beam and a towering superstructure, topped off by a spacious bridge, which we shared with the officers. The first shock came upon reaching the line, when the commanding officer informed us that he could not anchor. He was perfectly right, but not understanding conditions, we thought it unreasonable. A rather shoal ledge runs out one hundred and fifty yards or so from the shore and then the bottom takes a sudden drop to a depth of about half a mile. This has always made it very difficult to establish courses at Havana A wind shift was eminent. Quite a swell was already rolling in from the gulf. While a small yacht could have anchored at the edge of the ledge, the Yara, with her draft and scope of chain necessary to hold her in a stiff onshore breeze, would have swung on the rocks. The commanding officer, however, assured us he could hold her in a fixed position. That we doubted, with such a swell under the stern of this big unmanageable craft, to say nothing of the Gulf Stream set. Whoever he was, he deserves a lot of credit for doing as well as he did.

The Tower of Babel had nothing on us. Orders were given in English, translated in Spanish to the officer in charge, who repeated them to some sailor. Everyone tried to out-shout the other. From our lofty bridge, we had a fine birds-eye view of the situation, but it was like running a race from the top of the Statue of Liberty. The gun was on the lower deck and the visible signals were being hoisted on a yard somewhere behind us. To synchronize these signals with the clock was some job. We finally worked it out by having an officer on the lower deck watch a handkerchief which was dropped when it was time to fire. Commodore Corry was seated on the deck of the bridge, over in a corner, as far from us as he could get. I can see him still, in his white turtle neck sweater, with a red star number one on it, a cigar in his mouth and an amused twinkle in his eye. I went over and said, "George, why not give us a hand?" "Me," he replied, "I'll have nothing to do with any such mad house business as this." He would not even look at the start, being fearful of what he might see—and he would have seen plenty.

Some of the yachts were working into position from the committee boat end of the line. About thirty seconds before the start we saw that the Yara was drifting down on them and cutting off the little air they had. The skippers began to shout at us to move the committee boat. "Who in hell ever heard of moving the committee boat," Prentice shouted back. Technically he may have been correct, but if the committee boat fouls a racing yacht, what then? The Yara could not be moved sideways, so we backed her up. That gave these skippers a little better start than they were entitled to, so those at the other end of the line told us what they thought of us. Up to this point, the club's little signal cannon had been used. The officer on the lower deck, however, did not feel that it was suitable for such a momentous occasion as the start, so he had a blank charge put in the swivel gun, which must have been a five pounder, and which was trained across the line. Inslee made a perfect start, right under our bow. The concussion almost capsized him. The wad hit his sail and made a black spot fully two feet in diameter. Bill was almost stone deaf for a couple of days.

Not to be outdone by the lower deck, a junior officer on the bridge thought it might be a good idea to salute the visitors with a long blast of the siren. That would have been a recall. Prentice saw what was about to happen and saved the day. The young officer's hand was already reaching for the whistle cord. There was no time to argue with him through an interpreter. Employing football tactics, Prentice threw a block, preventing contact between hand and cord by a split second We had visions of "Peaceful Prentice" spending the rest of his days in a dungeon under Morro Castle, for assaulting an officer of the navy. It took a deal of explaining to avert an international crises, but it was managed and all hands were good friends again. Needless to say, they did not use the Yara again. A club launch became the committee boat. Pop's policy struck me as being a pretty good one. Let Possito run his own ding busted championship. I viewed the next two races from a taxi cab, driving back and forth along the Malecon. It was much more restful.

Ernest Ratsey's name is the first to appear on the Cup of Cuba With his father George, as crew, he took two firsts and a second, to win the Mid-Winter title by a safe margin of four points. His Irex was nosed out by inches in the last race, giving Jim Hayward of New Orleans, for whom Peter Donez tended jib sheets, runner-up by a single point over Bill Inslee and Fred Bedford, who tied for third place. That was the only exciting incident in an otherwise cut and dried series, the outcome of which was never in doubt. Al Buckley was next, followed by Tolo Pons and Filippe Silva, representing Havana and Cienfuegos respectively.

The Havana Yacht Club has always been the scene of the final banquet, except for the first couple of years. Then it was held by the Vedado Tennis Club, to which quite a number of the Havana fleet belonged at the time. It was the initial appearance of Havana's fair sex. They were seated at small tables at one end of the room, while the yachtsmen occupied a horseshoe table at the other end. This may have been a local custom, since those were still the days of the duenna, when women were not allowed in a bar and a lady could not venture upon the street without a male escort. Perhaps they just felt that the ladies were not interested in yachting. This was obviously the case. When the after dinner speaking began, the gals must have been discussing Paris fashions, or something, for you never heard such an incessant chatter. Whether the speeches were in Spanish or English, some could not understand, but that made no difference, as you could not hear what was being said anyway. Even the magnificence of Pop's full dress commodore regalia made no impression. He tried to talk against this clamor for about ten minutes, then sank back into his chair, with a gesture of resignation, admitting defeat for the only time in his career. Now, of course, all that has changed. The ladies of Havana are ardent Star fans and take an active part in all our social affairs. Outstanding among them is Luisa de Cardenas, Charlie's charming wife. While raising four husky lads, to perpetuate the de Cardenas name in Star circles of the future, she found time to attend more major Championships than any other Star wife. No big event would be complete without her. She deserves an "Oscar," or something, for her unequalled enthusiasm. Sometimes she gets a bit mixed up in her English and orders a "scotch and whiskey," or writes to tell us that young Carlos "bit" her husband in a race, which is quite "understoodable."

There is usually an aftermath to all championships. The Ratseys carried off enough watches to open a jewelry shop. Can you imagine watches worth around one hundred and fifty dollars as daily prizes? We went part of the way home together. When we boarded the train at Key West we were not in the same car. A part of the train, including Ratsey's car, pulled out of the station. We were told that it was going only to the switch yard and would return shortly. It never did, but went on as section one. The porter got some of our luggage mixed. The conquering heroes arrived in New York, in a driving snow storm, wearing white flannels and straw hats.

They had my share of liquor. No, we did not smuggle it in.
Every taxi driver had a price list. You could order what you
wanted. He would dash up to town and bring it back in a
two dollar suit case.

The Mid-Winter Championship is the only silver star event
which is held at the same place each year. No such exclusive
franchise can be granted today. The reason should be explained. At that time, Cuba was the only place having Star
fleets where an event could be held in winter. Of course
there was New Zealand and Hawaii, but they were too far
away to draw much of an annual entry. We did have some
fleets where the climate was such that off season events could
be held, but they copied the northern customs at that time
and their clubs went out of commission during the winter
months The Mid-Winters have now become a fixture, established for over twenty years. To some extent the same holds
true of the Spring Championship, which started eight years
later. Fleets are constantly requesting the privilege of holding
an annual silver star event. With one hundred seventy odd
fleets in the association, there would not be enough weeks
in the year to make that possible. Silver stars would not be
worth ten cents a dozen and they would all be cutting each
other's throat and have no entries. Aside from that, today
we have district championships so that almost every fleet,
if it can win, has an opportunity to hold a championship.

There is not sufficient space to give a detailed account
of each championship series, for the cup of Cuba, or the
accompanying open Bacardi series. A list of the winners of the
Mid-Winter title will be found at the end of this chapter. I
will, however, relate such highlights as I can remember. If
I elaborate more upon the years when I was present, it is
because I know what happened then. For other years I must
depend upon hearsay, which is none too reliable. That an
entire chapter is devoted to this silver star championship
is because, next to the World's Championship, it is the oldest
international Star series and, therefore, rich in tradition and
fond memories.

The winter classic follows a pretty set pattern. The races are held in the morning and usually enjoy a moderate breeze and no sea—just a gentle ground swell. You start at the beginning of the northeast trade which is light, but increases gradually to twelve or fifteen miles before the race is over. Special mention is made of this, because some people may have gained a false impression about Havana racing, from having seen photos of the gigantic seas and read of the rugged going, which was encountered during the 1946 World's Championship That event was held in November, when weather conditions are different than in late January. Sometimes, during the Mid-Winters, there is an off-shore breeze. In the old days, when the races were sailed off the Malecon, this was very tricky, the wind being deflected by the buildings and city streets. If such a wind does not veer back into the northeast, as I understand it, that is a danger signal and heralds the coming of a norther. These northers last for two or three days, blow up to eighty miles or more and all racing is suspended. The majority of the Mid-Winters have been subject to such an interruption, but the schedule allows for it. I do not mean to say that there have never been any rough days. There have, but they have either been in the afternoon races of double-headers, due to a postponement, or in the morning after a norther, when the wind has subsided but not the sea.

There are some who prefer the Mid-Winters to the World's Championship, because it is not such a serious business. They get in their racing, but also enjoy an ideal winter's vacation. You are back at your mooring by about one o'clock and have the entire afternoon and night to play. There are the horse races, the casino and many excellent cafes. You can play golf at the country club, go fishing or just sun yourself on the beach. You are a good eight miles from the city and in no way mixed up with the tourists and get an entirely different view of the real Havana Stars can be shipped from New York or New Orleans under a special rate, which is very reasonable, nor are the hotel rates high for Star members. You are not subjected to the pettty nuisances of getting a pass-

port or a lot of shots, which usually applies, when leaving the
States for another country. I have only one complaint—the
gamecocks. There always seems to be one of those dern birds
parked beneath your window. They start crowing their challenge to the gamecock world at midnight and keep it up
until sunrise.

Peaceful Prentice liked Havana so well, that he brought
his own Star down there in 1927. The Sparkler, with beautiful
red sails (which were the envy of a flock of semi-tame fla-
mingos) defeated Ernest Ratsey by one point, for the Cup of
Cuba. Edrington was able to sew a gold star over the silver star
the following year. He was a much better skipper than most
people realized and did much to make the New Orleans fleet
known in the Star class. Adrian Iselin, sailing Ace, won the
Bacardi Cup. This was the first time that it was raced for
as an open series. Incidently, this is not a perpetual trophy. A
new Bacardi Cup is presented each year. At that time, only one
entry from each fleet was allowed in the Mid-Winters. Iselin
and Jack Robinson, both former world's champions, went
down for the open event only. These two, plus Ratsey and
Edrington, qualified for the U.S. team. As crew, Jack had
Jack Dalton (of the U.S.A.). After the team race, Jack Robinson wanted to protest another U.S. teammate for not giving
him room at a mark. That's one for the scrap book.

The next year, Frank Robinson, from the Peconic, and
Tim Parkman, our hard-working international secretary from
Gravesend Bay, tied. Frank won the sail-off. Competition became so equal and ties so numerous that sail-offs began to
disrupt departure schedules and prize presentations. A few
years later, the association adopted a rule to correct this
condition. It was very simple and I wonder why more organizations do not use it. The entry that finishes ahead of the
other in the most races, automatically becomes the winner.
Since our championships must consist of an odd number
of races, the possibility of a sail-off is practically nil It could
happen in the case of a dead heat, or, the still more remote
chance that there might be as many entries tied as there are
races in the series and that they finished in reverse, with

respect to each other in each race. Had the present rule existed in 1928, Tim Parkman would have been the winner. J. E. Gorrin, of Havana, defeated Ratsey by two points, in a field of eighteen starters, to win the Pan American series. While this has been lost sight of, throughout the years, Gorrin is the first Cuban to win an international Star event.

New Orleans was represented by Earl Blouin, a Cajun, with the reputation of being about the most profane gentleman in the south. He sailed in Sinkin Susie, although the word "Stinking" was usually substituted, as it sounded more euphonious. Earl brought wire with him, for a complete new set of shrouds, which he bent on at Havana. Darkness, however, overtook him before the job was quite finished. The next morning he gave his crew a pair of wire cutters and sent him down to the boat with instructions to trim off the loose strands of wire above the splices. The crew, in his desire to please, cut all four shrouds off above the turnbuckles, so that there was nothing to support the mast. The gang waited on the dock to see the fireworks and perhaps add a few choice words to their own vocabulary, if they could understand what Earl said, which was not too easy—or they might witness a murder. When he arrived, Blouin surveyed the damage, hands on hip, and then said in a soft voice, "My friend, I do not know what in the world to say to you." For once he was nonplused and could not find adequate words with which to express his feelings.

Fred Bedford won the title the next year and romped away with the Bacardi series. He won the hard way. Colleen leaked so badly that his captain, whom he brought with him, was obliged to stay up and pump all night, to keep the boat from sinking at its mooring. Bill McHugh bailed continually throughout each race. He did this with a dipper lashed to the end of a long pole so he could keep on bailing while lying on the weather rail. Bill said his right arm was so tired that he was forced to drink with his left. The restraining influence of his skipper was probably a greater handicap than that sore arm, but Bill may have felt that a more tangible excuse was necessary to account for his exemplary behavior. It was a memorable year for me, as I almost won the Cup of Cuba, and would have, probably with a clean sweep, except for a comedy of errors, in which I had a strong supporting cast.

We were on a broad reach, with one more mark to round, then just a short run home. Enrique Conill was out in front He only had a couple of points and I would have been glad to see him win that race. Bedford was my concern. I had a nice lead over him and was ahead in the point score. Unfortunately Iscyra II was rapidly overtaking Enrique's Talita I could have driven under his lee and been inside boat on the jibe. It was the thing to do, if I was trying to beat him and he should have realized it. It would have meant, however, that he would have camped on my stern all the way to the finish, and might have slowed me up enough for the Colleen to overhaul me. I wanted him to round first and go on about his business that I might keep my wind clear. Then Bedford never could have caught me, on that short run. So I edged up to windward, expecting to see Enrique bear off for the mark, which was getting close. Instead, he began to work windward also. He kept looking back at me through that damned monocle of his, which to say the least was disconcerting and an alibi in itself. I motioned to him, but he did not grasp my meaning and I doubt if he does to this day. I had just decided to give it up and drive for the mark, and so told my crew, Jack Robinson, when the latter yelled, "Luff quick." I did so instinctively. I believe that any skipper would have done the same. I thought that Jack had seen a log or something in the water, if I thought at all Enrique luffed sharply, European fashion, dead into the eye of the wind. I had no choice but to respond, Iscyra II having shot forward enough to have a slight overlap. There we both lay in irons, while the rest sailed past us. He lost the race and I lost the series by one point, in spite of having two firsts. It does not always pay to think too far ahead In that split second none of us did our cause any good, Enrique, Jack or I.

Having a gold star skipper as crew has both its advantages and disadvantages The mast in Jack's Little Bear was undersized, hence his boom was closer to the deck than that of other Stars. From this he believed in the theory that one's boom should be as low as possible, even in light air. Mine was up to the top of the goose-neck. We were in the lead, but Jack tried to persuade me to lower it. I said no but he attempted it of his own accord. The halyard got away from him and a good two feet of slides came off the track. With his feet braced, Jack was trying to get the sail up again. "Jesus," he said, "I can't do it.' How we ever got that sail up again I still do not know.

Jack, who had never crewed before, was complaining that he barked his knuckles, because my cleats were too close to the deck. He wanted to put a block of wood under each cleat The afternoon, when he got that bright idea, I was going to the race track. He told me to go ahead and that he would attend to it. On my way home, I stopped at the Vedado Tennis Club, where the boat was hauled out. There was not a cleat on the boat Jack and the Williams brothers were asleep in the baseball grandstand, but Jack finally heard me shouting and came over. He showed me the little blocks he had cut out. Why, I asked, had he not finished the job. The bolts, he said, were not long enough. Then put the cleats back on the deck, I suggested. "Can't" said Jack, "I threw the old bolts overboard." Jack was obliged to get up at five o'clock the next morning and go into Havana in search of bolts. The only ones he could find were the same length as those he threw away—so the cleats went back on the deck.

There was just one other incident which I cannot resist relating One night we were eating some sort of Cuban dish—rice, with a lot of things in it, covered with a rich yellow sauce. At the bottom of it all was a little octopus, about the size of a silver dollar. When Jack uncovered his baby octopus, he let out a blood curdling scream, dashed from the table and it was the last we saw of him that night.

Just to be consistent, before leaving I also made a grave social error The only inscription upon daily prizes was the crest of Cuba. It was not a bad idea, as it gave the committee sufficient leeway to see that winners got what they really wanted. Since I did not win the series, I was taken aside and asked which two of the three daily firsts I would prefer. I picked a watch, for dress occasions, and an onyx and silver bureau set. The piece de resistance, however, was a dozen cut crystal wine glasses with a silver base which must have been a foot in height. I would have liked them but did not see how I could get them home unbroken. I was too stupid to take the hint, when asked if I was sure I did not want the wine glasses. Later that evening, when the trophies were given out, I learned that those glasses were a special prize presented by the president of Cuba. It must have looked as if I did not think much of their president's trophy. That was about the last year of fabulous prizes. They still give very fine ones, better than you get elsewhere, but the daily prizes for those first half dozen years had no equal in yachting or any other sport.

Colin Ratsey still is the only skipper representing a European fleet to have won the Cup of Cuba. This is not surprising, since Colin was at the peak of his Star career in the early thirties. Next in '31, came the Atkin brothers and de Cardenas won the Bacardi cup. The latter was hailed as Cuba's first major triumph, but it was not, as de Sena won a three race series against twice as many entries a few years before. It was also de Sena who drew first blood in a World's Championship. His record at home and abroad entitles him to much more recognition than he ever received I believe that '31 was the last year the races were held off the Malecon. I too was there that year, although as far as the racing was concerned I might as well have stayed home One day a norther was not only expected, but you could see it coming. A long black cloud, with curling pink jellyfish-like tentacles beneath it, stretched across the northern horizon. Those who were weather wise said it would not hit until late afternoon. George Patterson and I refused to sail down to the Maine monument. We were called yellow, but they started us off the mouth of the river and the norther struck five minutes after the last boat got back to its mooring. If we had not had our way, it would have been a repetition of 1928, when a howling norther hit in the middle of the race. The yachts scurried for Havana harbor, under jib only Tim Parkman made it under full sail, in a wind estimated at eighty miles an hour (probably over-estimated) with no greater casualty than a couple of broken battens. It would be foolish for anyone to attempt to get back to the Alamendares river, for within a few minutes it would be impossible to cross the bar. The Malecon course is very dangerous under such conditions, because of large concrete blocks which extend out from the sea wall. If a boat was washed up on that lee shore, those aboard would be dashed to pieces before they could reach the sea wall, even assuming that someone was there with a rope to haul them up.

From this point on, we must skip quickly over the years. While the Mid-Winters have lost none of their glamor, the event has become more conventional. Everyone, of course, comes back with a story to tell, but that is true of any Star championship. The wild crazy days of yore are over. This may have been due to the same crowd, a more sedate group (with some exceptions, such as Sam Smith) going down every year, or the repeal of prohibition in the States may have had something to do with it. The story, however, is not finished. There are a few more incidents to relate.

The Sea Wolf dinner, was at one time quite an affair. The room was littered with old rusty anchors, pieces of rope and other marine debris. The boss Sea Wolf, whatever his title may have been, sat at the head of the table in a chair at least fourteen feet high. It was mostly a red wine jamboree Like other stag affairs, it has been abandoned. Today there are too many members of the fair sex that attend championships, and they object. Then there is the Bomba, a quaint Cuban custom. You are given a tall glass, containing about a pint of red wine. I do not know the words to the Bomba, but it has something to do with killing you, if you do not toss off the wine without taking a breath. They keep up the chant until you have gulped it down. Then everyone cheers, slaps you on the back and tells you that you are a real man after all and a worthy companion. That, at least, is the jist of it.

One morning, while out for a tune up spin on the Gulf, Adrian Iselin bumped into a whale shark They are supposed to be perfectly harmless playful little fellows, about sixty feet in length. When the Ace disturbed the whale shark's morning nap, it flipped its tail some twenty feet out of the water Adrian beat it back to the Alamendares as quickly as he could get there—do you blame him? It evidently was not too gentle a bump, as Adrian claims that, when the Ace was hauled out, there were scales on her keel.

From 1932 on, skippers formed the habit of winning the Mid-Winters two years in a row. They were, in order named: Harkness Edwards, Adrian Iselin, Harold Halsted, Harry Nye and Woodie Pirie. Only twice was this cycle broken. Once by Pirie in 1937, which makes him the only skipper who has won the event three times. In 1942, Charlie de Cardenas was the winner. That was fortunate, as the cup remained in Havana, where it belonged, during the six year intermission caused by the war. That series of '42 was risky business. Four U.S. Stars were shipped down from New York and returned safely, although German submarines were playing havoc with shipping along the North Atlantic coast. The sinkings became so numerous, about that time, that the Spring Championship at Nassau had to be called off. In this respect we always have been very lucky. All entries in the 1939 World's Championship, held in Germany, when the war first started, reached their home ports safely. The title reverted to the United States, the only country in which the event could have been held throughout the war years.

For sixteen years the U S A quartet won the international team race at Havana (it was not held in 1940) and each time by a safe margin But finally the worm turned and, in 1949, the Cuban team scored its first victory. This brings us up to date.

If you think that I am trying to sell you on the idea of going to Havana, either as a contestant or spectator, during the period of the Mid-Winters, you are perfectly right. Each fleet is entitled to two entries, but few of late have availed themselves of that privilege This means that if you own

MID-WINTER CHAMPIONSHIP RESULTS

Year	Yacht	Skipper	Crew	Fleet
1926	IREX III	E Ratsey	G Ratsey	Western L I Sound
	2 J Hayward (N O G)		3 Tie, Bedford-Inslee	
1927	SPARKLER	P E Edrington	G Gray	New Orleans Gulf
	2 E Ratsey (W L.I S)		3 J Miller (H R *)	
1928	BUDSAL II	F H Robinson	D Potter	Peconic Gardiners
	2 T Parkman (G B)		3 Tie, Ratsey-McHugh	
1929	COLLEEN	F T Bedford	W J McHugh	Central L I Sound
	2 G Elder (W L I S)		3 A Williams (G B)	
1930	JOY	C Ratsey	E Ratsey	Solent (England)
	2 A Iselin (W L I S)		3 F Teenes (W L I S)	
1931	JUBILEE	H B Atkin	J Atkin	Western L I Sound
	2 H Nash (C L I S)		3 G Patterson (H)	
1932	WINSOME	H Edwards	G Godwin	Peconic Gardiners
	2 D Atwater (N B)		3 M deSena (H)	
1933	WINSOME	H Edwards	G Godwin	Peconic Gardiners
	2 Arteaga (N)		3 M Rasco (H)	
1935	ACE	A Iselin	G Carricaburu	Western L I Sound
	2 M deSena (H)		3 E Jahncke (N O G)	
1936	ACE	A Iselin	E White	Western L I Sound
	2 C deCardenas (H)		3 R Symonette (N)	
1937	TWIN STAR	L M Pirie	J Pirie	Wilmette Harbor
	2 P Shields (P G B.)		3 A Iselin (W L I S)	
1938	CHUCKLE II	H C Halsted	L R Bowden	Moriches Bay
	2 S Smith (Ot L)		3 H. Nye (S L M)	
1939	CHUCKLE III	H C Halsted	C. Pflug	Moriches Bay
	2 H Nye (S L.M)		3 C deCardenas (H)	
1940	GALE	H C. Nye	W Etzbach	So Lake Michigan
	2 H Halsted (M B)		3 A Iselin (W L.I S)	
1941	GALE	H C. Nye	W Etzbach	So Lake Michigan
	2 vonHutschler (F H)		3 A Iselin (W L I S)	
1942	KURUSH	C deCardenas	G Aurioles	Habana
	2 J White (W L I S)		3 H Nye (S L.M)	
1948	TWIN STAR	L M Pirie	S Pirie	Wilmette Harbor
	2 R Cameron (St J)·		3 C deCardenas (H)	
1949	TWIN STAR	L M Pirie	F Dixon	Wilmette Harbor
	2 A Tounon (H)		3 C deCardenas (H)	
1950	SHILLALAH	W E Etchells	M Etchells	Western L I Sound
	2 L M Pirie (W H.)		3 C deCardenas (H)	
1951	GALE	H C Nye	L Gilbert	So Lake Michigan
	2 H Halsted (M B)		3 J Schoonmaker (Bis B)	
1952	MATE	R Lippincott	R Levin	West Jersey
	2 J W Price (Bis B)		3 L M Pirie (W H.)	
1953	DINGO	J Schoonmaker	D Pritchard	Nassau
	2 P Smart (C L I S)		3 A Debarge (FdeP)	
1954	FLOWER	R Lippincott	W Lane	South Jersey
	2 J Price (B B)		3 A de Cardenas (H)	

NOTE—* Fleet defunct Cancelled 1934, political conditions 1943 to 1946, cancelled because of war 1947, cancelled being too close to the World's Championship a Star and wish to go, there is nothing to prevent it, as the rules provide that a fleet must name any member willing and able to represent it, if those entitled to prior right, by reason of where they finished in the eliminations, do not exercise that right. This is one trip which every Star owner in the States owes it to himself to make. Do not be deterred by the fact that you feel you have no chance of winning or may make a poor showing Even if you should finish last, no one will care and you will never regret the experience or forget it. Where else within such an easy reach can Star owners in the United States step right into an old world atmosphere, with their own crowd, and enjoy a week of racing? It is completely different. Havana is a happy land of laughter, where you are royally entertained and where a Star membership button is open sesame.

CHAPTER VII

MERRILY WE ROLLED ALONG

THE BIG CUP BEGAN ITS ENDLESS JOURNEY in 1927, never again to be raced for on the same waters for two consecutive years except in 1950. The first stop, before making a complete circuit of these United States, was Naragansett Bay. Since then, in round figures, it has traveled about fifty-six thousand miles. By 1927 the Star class had spanned the Atlantic, having a small fleet on the Solent in England It also extended to the Far East. Stars were racing in the Philippines There were thirty-two fleets and we were really beginning to roll.

Headquarters were at the picturesque Warwick Country Club, with its vast expanse of lawn, overlooking Narragansett Bay. Prior to the series, torrential rains and winds, of gale force, lashed the New England coast. One entry, coming by water, was storm bound behind the Point Judith breakwater for two days and only just did reach its destination in time. The early arrivals did not find Warwick too cheerful a spot. The club had the bleak and desolate aspect of a summer hotel in winter The yachtsmen, unable to go out for so much as a tune-up spin, sat huddled around the open fires. Rhody, on her home waters, was the odds on favorite, with Ace second choice. Big Bogardus and his almost equally big crew Purvis, totaled over four hundred and fifty pounds. They had been sailing around there for some weeks and the locals had a high regard for their ability. The Hoku, from Hawaii, was, therefore, considered a likely dark horse, if Narragansett Bay lived up to its reputation for wind. On the morning of the first race, the sun broke through the clouds and Warwick Neck was revealed in all its glory.

This was the first time that our international race committee conducted a World's Championship. When the new blue and gold I.R.C. flag was broken out at the masthead of the C.G. seventy-five footer, which served as committee boat, another important step forward had been taken. Five clubs cooperated with the association, each sponsoring one race and presenting daily prizes for that race. Frankly we were a bit doubtful as to how the clubs might accept this new arrangement. Club officials, however, seemed happy over the fact that they did not have to assume the responsibility of running any of the races. By sponsoring a race the club received just as much recognition and did not risk any adverse post-mortem criticism or publicity if something went wrong. Much credit was due Sol Makepeace, in charge of advance arrangements. Today, as the result of many years of experience, the Star central office is able to send to the unfortunate individual assigned to this necessary but thankless task, many typewritten sheets of instructions covering all details. At that time Sol had to figure many things out himself To have what you want, where you want it, when you want it, makes officiating at such an event a pleasure. If, however, at the last moment you find that a hundred and one minor items have been overlooked, it's enough to permanently ruin the most amicable disposition in the world.

After the 1927 series we were completely sold on the idea of never using a private yacht as a committee boat, if it could possibly be avoided. Say what you like, on a private yacht the members of the race committee are placed in the position of being the guests of the owner. If the commodore's wife is late or the liquor has not been put aboard, and the owner says, "Let's wait another ten minutes," what can you do but wait and delay the start? You must ask permission for everything you do and the paid captain usually objects on general principles. If the owner and his guests invade the section of the boat restricted for the committee and begin to buzz about at the start or finish, you cannot tell them to shut up or to get the hell out of there. On a Coast Guard boat the committee is its own boss and is dealing with an efficient officer and capable crew. There is a wireless telephone at your disposal. Should a mark be out of place, or the like, you can speak with the nearest patrolling Coast Guard boat and have your instructions relayed immediately. You can contact the nearest station and get a weather report. If a spectator boat or some stranger, anchors too near the line, and is hailed, the voice of authority is recognized and obeyed. It better be, for otherwise the owner of that boat is subjected to a fine. From a private yacht you can yell yourself hoarse and no one pays the least attention.

I doubt if the Star class would have endured, had we not changed the system of conducting the World's Championship. What a contrast it was, at least to the three previous years. No friction among the contestants and no constant bickering with the club committees over petty questions of jurisdiction. Everything was harmonious.

The first visitation of the "mysterious white yacht," which Bill Taylor has referred to now and then, in Yachting, occurred, to the best of my knowledge during this series. Mark officials reported a foul. They had not seen it, because of intervening sails, but they heard the impact of several hulls. It was one of those crazy jambs, with all yachts trying to round a mark at once and everyone calling for room. It was generally agreed that a white Star, in the middle of the mess, did not bear away with those who were trying to give the inside boats room. Endless cross questioning failed to reveal which Star it was. Someone knew, but the boys were not talking Since at least half the seventeen entries had white hulls and all of them were in the mix up, we got nowhere fast. The I.R.C. was determined to strictly enforce the rules, in order to establish a precedent for the future, but was helpless. Its first official decision was a pretty weak sister. It read, that yacht "X" was at fault, but as its identity could not be established, there could be no disqualification—and that was true. To this day I have never received a hint as to which Star it was.

The very fact that Warwick was a rather isolated spot, with no conflicting outside interests, kept the crowd together and gave our members a chance to become better acquainted. There was no lack, however, of shore activities One evening we were taken to a Rhode Island clam bake For the benefit of those who have never attempted this pleasant method of suicide, let me explain the process. Red hot stones are placed in a pit and the food is put between layers of seaweed and allowed to steam for hours. You start with clams, followed by fish, lobster, corn, chicken, but that is not the half of it, and end up with indigestion. Another evening we were the guests of the Albee theatre in Providence. Bill Gidley drove me there. I was seated in the back of the car with his wife and others. It was dark and she evidently did not notice who we were. At one point in the conversation, which was about Stars, as usual, she said to her husband, "Bill, how much longer do we have to have this fellow Elder as president?" Bill momentarily lost control of the car and almost ran us into a ditch. On off evenings we entertained ourselves. Bogy and crew did the hula, with their coats tied about their waists, and Bill Henderson, the Chesapeake crew, sang "Whiskey Johnnie", which became the theme song of the series.

Oh whiskey is the life of man,
Whiskey Johnnie—
And I'll drink whiskey while I can,
Whiskey for my Johnnie

On the night of the final banquet, Jim Rockwell, Manila's first entry, was presented with a surprise package and told to take it back to the Philippines, where he could introduce a new fashion among the Igorots. Unwrapped, it turned out to be a starched high collar, such as those worn by Commodore

Corry, properly inscribed and signed by the contestants. Pop thought it a huge joke until he asked, "Where on earth did you find a collar like mine in Providence?" "We didn't," Johnnie Atwater informed him, "we took it out of your bureau drawer." It was Pop's last clean collar and there was another day to go, because the series had ended in a tie—but that is getting ahead of the story.

This was probably the most exciting and closest of all World's Championships. Fred Bedford, with Briggs Cunningham as crew, won the first race in Colleen. The next one went to Walton Hubbard, from Newport Harbor. He had only placed eighth the year before. On the wind, they showed us a new trick. Both sat completely outside of the Tempe III in rope slings, through which had been put a short length of rubber hose. Such devices and all forms of outriggers were barred thereafter. The next one went to Harold Smith, sailing Mackerel. That scrambled up the point score. Nor did Black Thursday pass us by. It was blacker than ever, rained and was blowing half a gale. This was the weather that Everardus Bogardus was waiting for. Hoku emerged from the curtain of rain, standing up like a church steeple, to win by two minutes. Mackerel was fourth, to lead in the point score, as Colleen fell back to twelfth. All the favorites were practically eliminated. Bedford, however, won the last race, ending up in a three cornered tie with Hubbard and Smith.

Never was there such a sail-off. The gallery had been small all week, as New Englanders do not leave their jobs on working days. Saturday, however, was another matter. Close to two hundred craft, of every description, turned out to witness the sail-off. Since the home entry was not involved, it was a good criterion of the interest created by the event, when held far enough away from the blase yachting element around New York City. Smithy could not get the Mackerel going and kept gradually falling back. He did not go home empty handed, however, having accumulated enough points in the last three races to take the Atlantic Coast Championship to the Chesapeake. Up to this point, being combined with the big event, the Pandora trophy was

looked upon much in the same light as the other special
prizes. The course was windward and leeward. Bedford
picked up about a minute lead on each beat, only to be over-
taken by Hubbard on the run downwind. As they approached
the finish, Colleen and Tempe III were neck and neck, see-
sawing on each sea. It was just a question of which one hit
it right at the line. Within ten feet of the finish, Colleen remained motionless at the top of a sea, while Tempe III flashed
across the line four seconds ahead. Then Colleen shot ahead
but the race was over. Two youngsters had accomplished
what all the veteran west coast skippers had failed to do in
five previous years and given California its first title. A fifty
piece brass band met them at the dock, the trophy was presented out on the lawn and then the association banner was
lowered.

Naturally no entertainment was scheduled for that added
evening. Senator and Mrs Gerry (formerly a Miss Vanderbilt), who owned a beautiful summer home within a stone's
throw of the club, decided to throw an impromptu farewell
midnight supper. Knowing that trunks and suitcases were
packed for an early departure on the morrow, they sent
word that the party was informal and to come as you were.
I fear that their idea of informal and that of a bunch of Star
sailors, tired out from a hard week of racing and having
worked until after dark to get their boats ready for ship-
ment, may not have been quite the same.

After tying on a good start, in "Bill's corner" of the
locker room, the boys invaded the Gerry domain in sweaters,
sneakers, etc., and various stages of unshaveness. The host,
hostess and Pop, were the only ones in evening clothes, except the butlers. There must have been ten of the latter. As
you entered, the majority of them were standing in a row
along the hall, noses pointed at the ceiling, registering dis-
approval, or perhaps they had never smelled sweatshirts
impregnated with stale salt water before. Number one took
your hat, if any. Number two was custodian of the ladies'
wraps and number three asked you for your name. He was
shocked when a few of the boys, who did not get the idea,

said, "Oh, just call me Butch" or something of the sort. Your name was relayed to the major-domo, who stood at the entrance of the drawing room and announced it in a very official manner. The befuddled Star member slunk in sheepishly to meet his host and hostess, then he was on his own. The big laugh came when Tim showed up escorting the twelve year old daughter of the senator's political rival and, due to a slight error, they were announced as Mr. and Mrs. Timothy D. Parkman. Never have I seen a more elaborate buffet supper. You were supposed to let one of the butlers serve you, but the boys were hungry, elbowed the said butlers aside and pitched in It was quite a night.

It may seem that an unproportionate amount of space has been allocated to this series, in comparison to those that follow, but in a sense it was an experimental year and an important one. This was the association's initial attempt to take complete charge of the event. While there were still to be a few minor changes, it proved conclusively that our rules and system of organization were fundamentally sound. It marked the beginning of a new epoch of better racing conditions, less friction and more harmonious relations with the yacht clubs.

By 1928 there were forty Star fleets, including two in France, which had been developed by the persistent efforts of Enrique Conill and his brother. To sell to European yachtsmen the idea of, what was looked upon as an American boat, was no easy task.

The scene of the World's Championship shifted to California. Prentice Edrington and Gilbert Gray gave the deep south its one and only world's title. Each race was won by a different skipper, namely: Adrian Iselin, Frank Robinson, Joe Watkins, Joe Jessop and Rey Schauer. That sort of thing has happened several times during the history of the event. Prentice annexed his gold star by consistent sailing, never bringing the Sparkler II in better than third in any race, to win by a single point. Again there was a sail-off for second place in the series, Watkins, of Central Long Island, defeating Jessop, of San Diego Bay. Further proof of how close the

competition was becoming, may be seen from the fact that
Walton Hubbard, the defender, only placed eleventh. True,
he suffered one disqualification, but he could not have placed
better than sixth anyway.

In that same race, Hubbard was protested for an alleged
subsequent foul, which protest was not heard. This is mentioned because for a long time it was ruled that a yacht,
from the moment it committed a foul, was automatically out
of the race and had no rights. Some years later the N.A Y.R.U.
ruled that regardless of fouls, a yacht retained its right-of-way.
That was a very sensible ruling, not only from the point of
view of safety, but because other skippers might assume that
a yacht was out of a race, fail to respect its rights and later
find out that the said yacht was exonerated.

At Newport Harbor there were the same number of
entries as the previous year. That, however, was remarkable,
since there were so few semi-local fleets to swell the list.
Cliff Smith, of San Francisco, was awarded the "Order of
the Golden Paddle," for four lasts and a D.N.F. It was an
ordinary canoe paddle, covered with gilt paint, but the
custom did not prove too popular and was abandoned

While the top flight skippers were fighting it out in
California, nine fleets along the eastern seaboard were represented in the Atlantic Coast Championship, on the Chesapeake, off Gibson Island. From that year on, it was held as a
separate event, sometimes as a three and sometimes as a
five race series. On alternate days, thirty entries competed
for the Chesapeake Lipton Trophy. That was over twenty
years ago and it would be a big entry today almost anywhere,
except on the Sound. Colleen again defeated Mackerel in the
title event and won the Lipton Trophy. Fred Bedford and
Briggs Cunningham were registered as joint owners and the
latter sailed Colleen to victory in the Atlantic Y.C. Race Week
and Atlantic Lipton Trophy series that same year. How Colleen
continued her winning way at Havana, in January, has already
been related. This, I believe, establishes a twelve month boat
record, but that is unofficial, since it was not done within a
calendar year and the same skipper did not sail the boat.

Only five yachts finished the final race for the Chesapeake Lipton Trophy. The air was so light on the second round that it was obvious that the course could not be sailed within the time limit The race committee established the finish line at the windward mark. While this is allowed under N.A.Y.R.U. rules, I have never seen a course shortened except at the end of the first round in any other locality, and it is contrary to Star rules to shorten a course at all, after the start, that is in a sanctioned event. We heard a gun and saw a lot of sails being lowered. We did not know that the boats which had tacked in shore, had been carried past the line and could not get back because of the tide. Those of us who tacked off shore, could have drifted over it, but a club launch came out and asked if we wanted to be towed in and we all said yes, assuming that the race had been called off The same thing has occurred several times since on the Chesapeake, which is very misleading. In that particular case I could not have helped but finish second or third in the series, although it might have taken another half hour to drift across the line.

The next year we headed for the southland. A special car was added to the train for those who went from around New York. This time the Southern Yacht Club, being the only club near New Orleans, bore the brunt of sponsoring the Whole series, and I must say they staged a gala World's Championship. Edrington, still being vice-president, was obliged to shoulder most of the work. Hence he made Gilbert Gray part owner of Sparkler II and they switched, Gray becoming the skipper. Many cots were placed on the screened-in sun porch of the Southern Yacht Club, for those who could not afford hotel rates. This was called the "convalescent ward" and looked it. It was a grand old club but in sad need of repair. Whenever any of the boys took a shower, the water dripped down on the tables in the dining room But what entertainment! And if you wanted a bootlegger, all you had to do was stick your head out of the window and whistle and one would pop up from nowhere.

One of the dinners was on the roof of the Jung hotel, the dome of which opens so that on a clear night you sit beneath the stars The wine and some of the food was imported from Europe for that meal. Vaudeville acts started at eight and continued through until midnight. On off days we went to such places as Antoines. Then there were the oysters Rockefeller. The boys did not do so well with them. Eight went to the hospital. Our hosts left nothing undone. Behind the club, in what I believe they called the pen, there was a concrete platform, with a whole system of tracks. Your boat was hauled out each night and the cradle, on wheels, was run along the track and switched into its place.

Some of the fellows took Pop on a sight-seeing tour of the red light district. A gal, with a highly decorated face, was leaning out of a window. As the commodore passed, she said, "Hello, Pop" The commodore stopped dead in his tracks His chest swelled out and he said to the boys, "It's funny, but no matter where I go people recognize me at once as the 'Father of the Stars'."

Frank Robinson brought with him spars, rigging and sails for the proposed tall Marconi rig. This was installed on a local boat and demonstrated. It made a very favorable impression. It took the annual meeting, however, eight hours to iron out all questions and adopt it. The chief bone of contention was the sail area Some wanted it reduced and others claimed that this would reduce the Star's speed and hurt its popularity. The latter won out. Prentice Edrington and Bill Gidley re-fought the Civil War, over the question of what would happen if a prospective fleet in Haiti (which never did materialize) should send an entry to New Orleans. It was the longest session I ever sat through, but much was accomplished before we adjourned. The new tall rig was made optional for the first year and word was sent immediately to Enrique Conill, whose insistance that the Star be modernized, if we hoped to develop the class in Europe, was the chief factor responsible for its adoption. Frank Robinson, Larry Bainbridge, Prescott Wilson and Ernest Ratsey were appointed as a committee to draw up the specifications

Lake Pontchartrain, in mid-October, proved that it could beat the Sound at its own game. The first race was won by Arthur Knapp, sailing Peggy Wee, in a brisk rail down breeze. The Western Long Island representative, negotiated the windward and leeward course in 1.40:21. This tied an unofficial record established by Bill Inslee in 1924, when the wind shifted and only one leg was a beat and stood until 1946 After that first race, Pontchartrain settled down to business and produced the lightest and most fluky winds that have ever disrupted a World's Championship. Sparkler II took the next race. Graham and Lowndes Johnson, undoubtedly the best combination that ever represented the Chesapeake, won the next three races with their new Star Eel. They seemed to like this light going, interrupted by endless called off races, which made it appear for a while as if we were destined to spend the rest of 1929 in New Orleans. Under the general racing rules, a yacht disqualified in the original race could not enter the re-sail. The I.R.C. would start a race in the morning, call it off when the yachts had little more than rounded the first mark and then attempt another in the afternoon, with no better success. Because of the light shifty winds there were several fouls, mostly at the start, and then another in the attempted re-sail. It became very confusing, as it was difficult to keep track of which re-sail applied to which original race and what entries could not start. That led to adopting a class rule that put a called off race in the same category as a cancelled one.

The final banquet was postponed so often that the food at the club went bad and the larder had to be replenished. At that, in entering the last race Gilbert Gray had a two point lead. He was actually talked out of winning. The boys began to tell him that he could never stand the strain and was bound to crack up, and he did. Instead of covering Eel at the start, he shot Sparkler II into what looked like a hole in the middle of the twenty-three starters. The gap closed and Sparkler II remained in a pocket throughout the windward leg, while Eel ghosted away to win the series. Talk about a war on nerves, that was a most successfully conducted one. At long last the series was over. Motorcycle police and fire engines, that had been waiting at the dock each day, escorted the victors through the streets of New Orleans to city hall, where the mayor made the formal presentation of the cup. It was quite a parade. I rode with the Johnson brothers and Pop was in the front seat. He was kept busy tipping his cap to the people that lined the sidewalks and cheered, not having the slightest idea of what it was all about.

One odd thing happened. The Barbados boat, by some error, was shipped to Halifax, so the I.R.C. was forced to allow the stranded crew the right to use a local Star At the final banquet, Bill McHugh made his famous impromptu speech, in which he referred to our commodore as, "The man whom we all love and revere, but do not respect."

That year of 1929 was an eventful one. There was a big increase in the number of entries for the World's Championship. There were one hundred and one new Stars built, another record, and the average boats per fleet were fifteen and three-tenths. The first official Star event in Europe was held by the Paris fleet, Enrique Conill winning the French Championship. The Great Lakes Championship, won by Max Hayford, became our third district title event. Frank Robinson won the initial series, on the Great South Bay, for the Corry Cup and yours truly took the Jersey Coast Challenge series, on Barnegat Bay, then called the Bamberger series.

As early as January of the next year, Enrique and his brother Fernan Conill began sending in applications for fleet charters. Just as the former had stated, the tall Marconi rig proved to be the turning point in Europe. There were now seven fleets in France and fleets in Spain, Portugal and Switzerland. In America, tall and short Marconis were racing against each other that year, nor did the new tall rig have things all its own way at first. Many of the old timers were unable to get the feel of the boat for some time and quite a number never did In a stiff breeze, short rigged Stars often came out on top, but that did not last long.

The next World's Championship was raced on the Chesapeake in 1930 not only with mixed rigs but mixed weather.

Gibson Island was a delightful place and in some respects reminiscent of Warwick, only more isolated There were no outside interests at all and no place for the boys to roam. Huge trays of mint juleps were passed around on the slightest provocation. They were much more potent than those in New Orleans. Except for the locals, two were apt to make you fall flat on your face. We all ate together at the club and the meals were excellent. Crabs were served in every form, except that we did not have crab ice cream. The bay was so full of crabs that one could not spit without hitting one. The dining room was bedecked with the flags of many nations, for the class was now truly world-wide—our first fleet, Lake Maracaibo, being established on the mainland of South America.

Gibson Island was one place where they really treated the I.R.C. with the dignity it was entitled to. We had our own room and a colored boy to look after our needs. No sooner was breakfast over than he was on your heels asking what you wanted to drink. Juleps or frozen rum on a warm day and rum toddies on a cold one. He followed us aboard the committee boat with huge baskets of food and carefully concealed liquor, since it was a Coast Guard boat. J. Rulon Miller, one of the best friends the Star class ever had and the leading spirit in that locality, was responsible for most of this —he was on the I.R.C. He started off by telling me that they were going to run the series in their own way, but actually was the most co-operative local official I have ever worked with When Bill McHugh walked into the bar and saw "J" he went over and slapped him on the back and said, "Damned if you and me ain't the homeliest two guys in the world." From then on they became great pals.

While there was one less entry than the year before, the series was the most international one to date. Rockwell was there again, from the Philippines, while Colin Ratsey represented the Solent and there were two French entries: Jean Peytel, of Paris and Jean Kelly, of Cannes, or what have you. The latter was the most international member we ever had. An American by birth, of Irish extraction, he was an English citizen, lived in the South of France and sailed a boat with a Chinese name. To be consistent, he later moved to Bermuda and was responsible for starting a fleet there. He was making a similar effort in Mexico, when he died. Jean, with his flowing blond mustachio, which wrapped itself around his ears in a breeze, was one of the unsung heroes of the class, who never lost interest and always kept working for it.

There was never a World's Championship in which Pop did not get himself all mixed up in something. On Sunday, Harry Reeves took Pop and Ma Corry to church. On the way back, Harry's mind was on one of those tall frosted glasses. He stepped on the gas and overturned the car. He then went about, shaking his finger in everyone's face, and saying, "I almost killed the commodore." Then he would laugh until tears came into his eyes. Pop did not think it very funny, he was darn sore. There were times that week when I almost wished Harry had been successful. Pop and Ma had the room next to mine, in one of the cottages. At six-thirty each morning, Pop woke me up by standing on his head, with his shoes on, and beating his heels against the reverse side of my bathroom door. Otherwise it was a most restful place, with a dip in the bay each morning and an occasional rail bird breakfast with Nat Kenney.

The annual meeting elected Enrique Conill to the office of vice-president. At the suggestion of the French delegates, it made, what I consider, a very serious error. It legalized the use of aluminum fittings, which had previously been barred. I have worked for years, but to no avail, to have this repealed. On salt water, they crumble without any advance warning. Many a mast has gone overboard as the result of using such fittings, in an attempt to save an ounce or two in weight.

It was the first time we met Sam Smith. He was sailing my Iscyra II, which I had sold him a few weeks before, and which he renamed Red Star II. After that Sam won three consecutive Twelfth District Championships. In 1930, however, he and his crew, Dot, were still novices. Herb Dowsett, who was serving on the I.R.C., spotted the boat as mine, since Sam had not yet removed the gold chevrons. As Sam crossed the line, usually a good last, Herb would bellow, in his bull-like voice, "Good boy, Elder."

Not to be outdone by New Orleans, the Gibson Island group built new docks, equipped with enough chain hoists to haul over half a dozen Stars at a time. These two fleets went to such great expense, in providing facilities for hauling boats out each night and launching them in the morning, that it was establishing a precedent, which most home fleets could not afford to live up to. After one more year, when haul outs were made optional, at a reasonable rate on a public dock, the association barred this practice during a series, except on rest day or by special permission for repair or hull inspection.

Arthur Knapp, of the veteran fleet, went out into an early lead, winning the first race and then finishing third to Slade Dale of Barnegat Bay, in the next. Walton Hubbard staged what appeared to be a comeback, by taking the next two races, to lead by two points. The last race was sailed on a cold day, with open fires burning in the club and a stiff twenty five mile wind. Arthur, thinking he had made a premature start, swung back. Actually he had not done so. He fell back to eleventh place and it looked like a California victory. At that point Arthur shook out a reef. Walton did the same, but was unable to carry his sail and kept falling back. Poor and deSena, from the Peconic and Habana respectively, both sailing old rigged Stars, finished in the order named. The boys had not as yet mastered the art of making the tall Marconi go in a breeze. Knapp and Weed gradually forged ahead, bringing Peggy Wee in fourth and winning the series, as Hubbard slipped back to ninth.

That same year, Joe Watkins and Briggs Cunningham, sailing on their own Central Long Island waters, tied for the Atlantic coast title, the former winning the sail-off. They were racing for a new Atlantic coast perpetual trophy, presented by F. T. Bedford. This was the first year in which the rules allowed two entries from each fleet, in major championships, other than the World's Championship.

Once again the world's title event returned to the western end of the Sound, but under different conditions. The association was now conducting the races and that fact was generally accepted. Headquarters were at the new Manhasset Bay Yacht Club, of Georgian architecture, overlooking the Bay and a swimming pool, which was illuminated at night. The flags of the six competing nations were flown along the sea wall and a huge red star, in electric lights, marked the entrance to the club.

Once again a different entry won each race, in a series so abundant with hectic incidents, that it is quite impossible to attempt to relate them race by race. Bill McHugh, a veteran of the gaff rig days and newly registered part owner of Colleen, with Joe Watkins as crew, was the eventual winner. Contrary to press reports, the series did not establish a new record for disqualifications, although there were plenty, to say nothing of withdrawals, where the skipper knew he had fouled, and protests that were not allowed. The I R.C. was busy every night and often on the following mornings, ironing out disputes. The real reason for this, was that in a field of twenty-six entries, there were at least a dozen skippers of almost equal ability. They took unnecessaray chances, knowing that to win would depend upon a very slim margin.

A sail-off was again necessary to decide second place, Colin Ratsey representing the Solent, with Joy, defeating Eddie Fink, of Long Beach, California, in Zoa. Eddie threw away second place and possibly the title in the first race. It was a three times around course, but he forgot and started home after the second round. He was awakened by a chorus of shouts, but before he could get his boat trimmed down, he had lost six places. Colin Ratsey came in for quite a lot of criticism by one of the papers, which referred to him as the English entry from City Island. That particular reporter was trying to create the impression that the Star Class was faking the international character of the event. He did not know that Colin owned two Joys, one in England and one which he kept at City Island, where for business reasons, he spent several months of each year. That same reporter took several other dirty cracks at the class and does not know to this day that I had considerable difficulty in preventing an irate bunch of members from tossing him off the end of the dock. When England named Colin to represent that nation in the Olympics the following year, he changed his tune. Like so many others, who criticised us at first, he became one of our strongest boosters thereafter.

No account of the 1931 World's Championship would be complete without mention of our old friend Doc Pflug, whose son Carl won the first race and was a contender right up to the end. The Doc, a great favorite with the Star bunch, held nightly court on the club porch. I was among those unfortunate ones who had rooms in the front, directly above said porch, and can still hear the Doc singing "The King of the Cannible Isles." Then he would tell endless stories about the Spanish American war. Every now and then he would say, "Am I right boys?" and they would shout "Yes" at the top of their lungs. It kept up until three a. m. One evening the Doc invited everyone over to his house for cocktails. He greeted us all dolled up in a tuxedo and no one recognized him—we had never seen him before with his shoes on or dressed in anything but overalls.

Another milestone was passed. Rhys-Price represented the Lake Maracaibo fleet, of Venezuela, bringing the mainland of South America into the picture. Later he moved to Trinidad and started a small fleet there, but made the same mistake that Colin Ratsey did with the Solent fleet. He paid all dues himself. When he left there, the other owners could not understand why they should have to pay for something, which they had been getting gratis before, and the fleet broke up. Later the Solent fleet folded up for the same reason, but was revived in 1948.

Although a year's grace was given to convert to the tall Marconi, no short rigged Stars sailed in the 1931 series. By this time the association had grown to sixty fleets, with Stars racing in sixteen nations.

It was only a short hop to the territory of Central Long Island Sound, where the event was held, off the Pequot Yacht

Club, the following year. In spite of the club being dry, we did very nicely. Most of the visitors were housed at a hotel in Bridgeport and the entertainments took place at widely separated points. This involved a considerable amount of travel, but cars were plentiful There were twenty-eight entries. In Europe, where the countries are as close together as the States in the Union, there had been regattas more international in character. This, however, was the second consecutive year in which three continents and the Far East sent yachts, to the same event. Even in those comparatively recent years, nothing of the sort had happened before. There was a strong representation from Europe, with entries from France, Sweden and Germany. Walter von Hutschler, who was destined to become famous, made his debut, but it was not a very impressive one, as he only placed fourteenth. Once again a different skipper won every race and the series was too much of a jumble to attempt a blow by blow description Remember that detailed results of each World's Championship can be found in the back of this book.

A most tragic accident marred the event. Bud Vanderveer, with his father, Steve as crew, won the third race. He won by a safe margin in a race against the time limit. Shortly after that, a little squall drove the tailenders up among the leaders and seventeen yachts crossed the line within less than a minute and a half This put Bud right back in the running, only seven points behind the leading Ralph Bradley. Then came rest day. That night there was a clam bake at some distance from the club Bud and three others drove over and, as the car passed through a little cloud of land fog, it struck a tree. Bud was taken to the hospital, where he died later that evening Flags were half masted. A futile effort was made to dispel the pall of gloom during the remaining two days. Steve Vanderveer presented the Vanderveer Trophy in memory of his son. It goes to the entry with the highest point score at the end of the third race and is perpetual.

Eddie Fink, sailing Mist, for Long Beach, obtained permission to use a substitute crew, his regular one having been one of those involved in the accident The other two, Glen

Waterhouse and Woodie Metcalf, who were allowed to leave the hospital that morning, insisted upon sailing, in spite of their injuries. Fink won the fourth race, but Ralph Bradley, of Illinois River, still had a four point lead. The last race was sailed in very light air. Bradley covered Fink throughout the first round. Then the wind shifted. Dave Atwater and Tubby Lawton, a quarter ton combination, who had won the first of their three consecutive Atlantic coast titles that year, took the final race. Fink, however, finished second, as a result of the shift, and Bradley ended up third in the point score. Mist was another of those so called million dollar Stars. It was said to have cost around twenty-five hundred dollars. Once again the rumor spread, as it has before and since, that the Star class was being ruined by allowing such expensive boats to be built. One might well ask at this point, how could a sports organization place a ceiling price on boats, sails or equipment, built in all parts of the world? The absurdity of such a suggestion was proven during world war two, when even government regulations could not prevent black market sales. This is not said as a reflection upon Eddie Fink's ability as a skipper. He was a most able one and would have placed in the money anyway. Ralph Bradley, however, sailing a Joe Parkman Star that cost around seven hundred dollars, had the series in the bag, except for a wind shift. That shows how some unjustifiable rumors are started.

The I R C. held its protest hearings in a two room suite at the hotel in Bridgeport. We had some little trouble with Dan Suden-Collberg, of the Stockholm fleet. He and Dave Atwater got into a rhubarb and Dan was convinced that an American committee was prejudiced. The fur flew and he had to be escorted out of the room. We were trying to keep this all secret from the press. The door was locked. No one could have entered the suite. In the middle of it someone opened the bathroom door and there was Anne Taylor, Bill's wife. She too was escorted to the door. She threw her slipper over the transom, however, and got in again. Once more she was put out and the door locked. We thought that at last we had complete privacy, but derned if she did not show up in the bathroom again. How she got in no one knows.

At the final banquet the national anthem of the skipper's country was played as he stepped up to receive his prize. We did not know just what to do in the case of Jean Kelly. So the band played "Has Anybody Here Seen Kelly?" and we hoisted a green flag with a golden harp. This brought to a close the first cycle of the World's Championship. The big cup, having made a complete circuit of the U.S.A. started back to California. The tall Marconi was in to stay and had brought about the desired results in Europe. Another phase of Star development was over.

CHAPTER VIII

THE OLYMPICS

STARS MADE THEIR OLYMPIC DEBUT IN 1932. Star sailors stole the show that year at Los Angeles, three out of the four yachting events being won by Star skippers. Aside from their own series, Jacques Le Brun, of France, won the little singlehanded one-design (Monotype) crown. Owen Churchill was at the helm of Babe, U S. winner among the Eight Metres. In contrast to other yachtsmen from different countries, Star members were old friends and spent much of their time ashore together It was the first time that the rest of the yachting world was able to witness the comradeship already developed by the I.S.C.Y.R.A.

Originally scheduled as an exhibition, a sort of unofficial test of popularity, Stars were eventually included as one of the regular classes on the Olympic program. It is doubtful if that could ever have been accomplished without the co-operation of the N.A.Y.R.U , which was recognized as the national authority of the U.S.A.

Getting back to Star competition, Gilbert Gray, of New Orleans, sailed Jupiter to a decisive victory. With Andrew Labino as crew, he won five firsts and was never seriously threatened. Gilbert rose to the occasion and sailed the best series of his career, giving the U.S. its first Olympic Star champion.

Colin Ratsey, representing England, was runner-up. He owned two Stars named Joy. He was not the only one who kept a second Star in the New York area, to save the cost of transportation. At that time Colin lived in England and was very definitely a Britisher, otherwise he could never have represented that country in the Olympics.

Gunnar Asther, sailing Swedish Star, won the bronze Olympic medal. As a matter of fact Harry Wylie, of Canada, tied for third. Due to a misunderstanding, Harry shipped his Star home immediately after the series was over, hence Sweden won the sail-off by default.

The one-man Monotypes, always furnished locally, were raced as a skipper's series in the mornings, each man sailing each boat once. Some Star skippers did double duty, racing these boats in the morning and Stars in the afternoon. As a result Cecil Goodricke, of South Africa, missed one Star race entirely. He was the dark horse, as we had no fleet in South Africa, and surprised the boys by winning one Star race. Fleets, of course, have nothing to do with Olympics. A national entry can build, or buy into, any specified Olympic class. Goodricke can best be remembered by the fact that he kept blowing a little tin whistle, when on the starboard tack, to warn others that he was coming. Such politeness! The average skipper keeps his mouth shut and his fingers crossed, hoping that someone will come close enough to be hailed about and commit a technical foul.

When the Maas brothers landed in New York, on their way back to Los Angeles, they dropped in at the office. They were only kids then, but full of enthusiasm. I remember that I took them out to lunch. The boys ordered rye bread and tomato ketchup, much to the dismay of the waitress, as both were "for free." I wish that other luncheon guests had a similar appetite, as that would help beat the high cost of living. Adrian Maas, however, has established a remarkable record. He has sailed a Star for Holland in the Olympics, ever since the Stars were included, and has won two Olympic medals.

I am not sure how all the 1932 Olympic yachting entries were selected, but most of them were the result of national trials. U.S. Star members have always handled their own method of selecting an Olympic entry. In 1932 and 1936 it consisted of fleet preliminaries, four regional semi-finals and finals. I am not apt to forget as I have two U.S.O.C. certificates framed and hanging on the wall as a reminder that I was also a contestant that first year and managed to tie for first at Narragansett Bay, but was beaten in the sail-off by Ed Thorn. The Great Lakes did not send an entry, so that there were only three in the finals. Gilbert Gray won, of course, and Eddie Fink was second, which made him the U.S. Star alternate.

The 1936 Olympic yachting events were sailed off Kiel, Germany. The courses were on the Aussenforde (Outer Bay) and radiated in all directions from the starting line. Every afternoon, when the race was over, crowds gathered on the Hindenburg Ufer, where the flags of the three nations that placed were hoisted. On the final day, when prizes were presented, Hitler was there in person. I was not there, but all who were, agree that everything possible was done for the comfort and convenience of the competing yachtsmen. To this I can add that the German yachting authority co-operated in every way with the I.S.C.Y.R.A. All our class rules were enforced, our measurement certificates were not questioned and even our total point score system applied to the Star series.

The Olympic Star title was won by Dr. Peter Bischoff, who sailed the German Star Wannsee, with Hans-Joachim Weise as crew. They won by a greater point margin than Gray did in 1932. Both were reported killed in the last world war. Laurin, of Sweden, placed second, but only one point ahead of Adrian Maas. The Holland skipper, however, won the first race in a howling gale, but was disqualified. He was really the only one that gave Bischoff a run for his money.

The best the U.S. entry was able to do was place fifth. Girogono, of England, is to be complimented upon finishing fourth, being a newcomer to the Star class. The French skipper Herbulot won the second race, but he also was disqualified. As a matter of fact the reader will get a much better overall picture of the series by reading the summaries.

Many have asked why Walter von Hutschler, who is credited with training Bischoff and Weise, did not himself represent Germany in the1936 Olympics. Walter was born in Brazil of Brazilian parents. He was not German and was not eligible to represent Germany in any form of Olympic competition. His name is of German origin, but so is the name of many Brazilians. Walter did, however, live in Germany for a number of years. Residence, not nationality, governs eligibility under Star rules. He had a perfect right, therefore to join the Star fleet in the locality where he then resided and to represent it in any Star event under the auspices of the I.S.C.Y.R.A.

The 1936 U.S. trials were held off Sayville, N.Y. Once again there were only three entries, the Great Lakes sending none. Glen Waterhouse, of San Francisco, won, but only after a sail-off with Eddie Ketchem, the eastern semi-finalist. The U.S. came very near to being represented that time by the old Draco, a relic of the days of Ike Smith. A couple of tall lanky Texans, who wore five gallon hats, represented the southland. Skipper Dan Ryan did beat Waterhouse once and was responsible for the sail-off, but finished the series in last place.

Only the fleet try outs and regional semi-finals in the New York area were reasonably well attended in 1936. Throughout the rest of the U.S., because of the additional time and expense involved, such preliminary events had very few entries. Yachting is one of the few U.S. Olympic sports in which contestants have to finance themselves. While that is bound to reduce the number and to some extent the quality of prospective Olympic entries, it's the only logical solution. The cost of the 1948 U.S. six meter entry, which was built especially for the Olympics, has been estimated at around ninety thousand dollars. If any such amount was taken from the Olympic fund, there would not be enough to take care of the other fields of sport. The I.S.C.Y R.A. cannot finance the U.S. Star Olympic entry, as it has no national subdivision of its funds. If it did that, it would also have to underwrite entries of twenty odd other countries.

The exploits of Glen Waterhouse and his crew Woodie Metcalf are worthy of mention. They were the "singingest" pair of Star members we ever had. They sang Abalone Moon, Hail To California, Eight Bells, etc. They even sang during a race. When they were not singing they were composing lyrics. Their first break came when the regional semi-finals at Santa Barbara were cancelled because their one rival there withdrew. That enabled them to ship Three Star Two east with the University of California rowing shells. Arriving at Poughkeepsie, they bought an old Buick for thirty dollars, with which to trail their Star to Sayville. The U.S.O.C. chartered the S.S. Manhattan that year, so the Star could be shipped on deck gratis, at the owner's risk. After loading it, they returned to the Commodore Hotel and parked. While discussing what to do with the Buick, a N.Y. cop came along and they thought they were pinched. All he wanted to know was what they were doing in Olympic uniforms. When they told him about the Buick, he gave them twenty dollars, got in it and drove away. Hence, except for loading costs and gas, it cost them only ten dollars to transport their Star to Germany.

I do not know how long they had been experimenting with them, but flexible spars were already being used on German Stars in 1936 and also on some Stars of neighboring countries. We all know today that flexible spars, properly handled, will always beat rigid ones. This is not said as an alibi, as German skippers were then highly efficient, but it may make Glen happy to know that he did not have a chance with the rig he was using.

Spar flexing is an operation. Star rules distinctly state that spar diameters and methods of rigging are optional. The Germans did not even violate the rules in principle, anymore so than if they had developed a new technique in seamanship. Every Star Olympic contestant in 1936 saw the rig in operation on German built Stars. Let me quote from an article by Woodie Metcalf, describing his Olympic experiences. "The specially cut German sails, with fullness along the foot, combined with a light flexible boom and method of trimming flat amidship, was a powerful and speedy combination." It will be noted that he even used the term flexible.

Waterhouse and Metcalf simply did not realize that they were seeing a revolutionary and almost automatic operation governing draft. That is no more surprising than that the hundreds, who read the above mentional article, also failed to grasp that fact. According to von Hutschler, the German skippers themselves did not yet fully appreciate the many advantages to be gained from what they had developed.

The 1940 Olympics, slated for Finland, were cancelled because of the war. The twelfth and thirteenth Olympiads (an Olympiad being a measure of time) were, therefore, skipped. The games were renewed and held in England in 1948, the yachting events being sailed on Tore Bay.

The Star was not one of the four classes originally designated for the Olympics. The unvarnished truth is that British top yachting brass, which practically controlled the permanent committee of the I.Y.R.U., did not like Stars. The chief bone of contention was the two man one-design Swallow. Like the jib and mainsail Firefly dinghy, it was a new creation by the English designer Uffa Fox. Being new, naturally there were only a few Swallows in existence, almost all of them being in England. The only measure of popularity in yachting is the international distribution and activity of a given class. Many countries thought it odd that the Star should have been replaced by an unknown quantity. Their overwhelming requests for the Star resulted in its being included as a fifth Olympic class, thereby establishing a new precedent.

Perhaps I better start by telling about the U.S. Olympic trials of 1948, because of a drastic change made in the system. Each fleet was entitled to send one entry direct to the finals. The skipper had to agree in writing to go if he won and, just to keep him honest, a fifty dollar entry fee was required The money went to help defray in part the cost of shipping the winner's Star.

The finals were sailed on the ocean side of Coney Island, with the anchorage and headquarters at the Sheepshead Bay Y C Because of the many fishing boats in that area, the co-operation of the Coast Guard was most helpful. Hilary Smart defeated Woodie Pirie by a single point in a close and exciting series. It was necessary to go down to a tie for sixth place between Cebern Lee and Ralph Craig, in order to find two alternates willing to make the trip. They were also named as alternates for several other United States classes.

Two girls were originally selected to represent the U.S. in the Swallow class, but the entry could not be accepted. That had nothing to do with yachting, but a general Olympic rule, which prohibits men and women from competing in the same event. On the night of the final Star banquet, Mr. Loomis, manager of the U.S. yachting team, came down to Sheepshead Bay and between us we persuaded Woodie to skipper the Swallow for the U.S. Owen Torrey, a good Star skipper in his own right, happened to be in London at the time and was willing to act as crew. I believe that the charter price of the Swallow was a suit of new sails, but anyway Woodie and Owen gave the U.S. a third place among the Swallows. There were other Star skippers sailing in that class, including Bellow, of Portugal, who owned his own boat. If I remember correctly, he placed second.

Durward Knowles, who was then international Star class champion, only learned at the last moment that the Bahamas were not entitled to a separate Olympic entry, but could compete only for Great Britain. He immediately shipped his Star from Nassau to Miami. He and his crew trailed it from there to New York, driving day and night. At that they would have missed the Queen Elizabeth, except for a bomb scare, which delayed her departure for several hours. Durward had no trouble in winning the finals in England, as he was sailing against a less experienced group of Star skippers. In the Olympics, however, he ran into tough luck. He was dismasted and disqualified in the last two races. At that he placed fourth

As the games originated in Greece, Greek athletes always lead the Olympic parade of nations. George Calambokidis headed that group as its standard bearer. Ralph Craig was elected to carry the Stars and Stripes. It was the second time he represented the U.S. In 1912 he had won both the one hundred and two hundred meter dashes. Hence two Star skippers had the honor of marching at Wimbly, in a temperature of one hundred and three degrees, carrying the flag of their respective countries.

Out of the scheduled seven races, an entry's best six counted in the point score. In other words a skipper could throw out any one race he desired. There are two schools of thought on the subject. If disabled through no fault of his own, perhaps the skipper should not have to suffer. Everyone will agree, however, that he should not be allowed to throw out a disqualification and nullify the penalty, as we must assume that officials know their business and that the disqualification was deserved. The point system was figured on a formula, which frankly I do not fully understand. It provides a big premium for winning, which conforms to Olympic principles. As you go down the list the difference in points between positions keeps diminishing, until very few points separate those at the bottom. My personal opinion is that the throw out system encourages reckless sailing, because the skipper knows that the race does not have to count. I also feel that the old fashioned total point system is a more accurate measure of ability, as yachting is about the only sport in which wind shifts, slants, puffs, etc., affect the order of finish and are unpredictable.

Whoever laid out the courses off Torquay must have thought that Stars were toy boats. The Star course combined a windward and leeward and a triangle, sailed three times around, for a total of about seven and one-half miles. One can judge from this how short the windward leg must have been. The seventeen Star entries could not get out of each other's hair and were constantly in danger of a foul. That accounts for the many disqualifications, to say nothing of the disallowed protests, in 1948. Most of the contestants had to wait around after each race to testify as principles or witnesses at the hearing of some protest. They would have been there yet, if the hearings had not been conducted with the dispatch of traffic violations.

The first four races were sailed in comparatively light air and, after a three day rest period, the last three races provided rather rugged going. Hilary Smart, with his father Paul as crew, made his best showing during the first part of the series, taking two firsts and a second. That gave the U.S. the 1948 Star Olympics by nearly one thousand points. Carlos de Cardenas, with his son as crew, finished in a blaze of glory Charlie, who has always liked plenty of wind, took a first and second to make Cuba runner-up. Adrian Maas was once again third. On the total point system, used in the two previous Olympics, the Holland skipper would have won. Italy's Straulino actually finished first four times, but was disqualified on two of those occasions and dismasted in the last race. Nevertheless, he placed fifth. His daily record and that of Maas, if the reader will look at the summaries, is a good example of the difference between the two systems.

Star contestants were plagued with unexpected difficulties and expenses from the start. Over here the right hand did not know what the left was doing. The U.S.O.C. was most helpful in arranging for the Star and Star contingent to go on the Manhattan with the rest of the Olympic team. I was given full authority to handle the Star entry, but someone else must have been given like authority. At the last moment the Star entry was switched to the Queen. Fortunately the boys could afford the additional expense.

Finalists and semi-finalists did not receive their U.S.O.C. certificates although I sent a certified list of those entitled to them to the secretary of the U S O. yachting committee. I learned two years later that he did not know that his own committee consisted of seven members. It is difficult to understand why, as my name appeared on U.S.O.C notices He only recognized the five N.A.Y R U. delegates and did not know that I had been appointed a Star delegate over a year before they were eligible. How could things be expected to run smoothly? The man responsible for allocating the work, and there was plenty of it, openly admitted that he disapproved of the Olympics and even told members of the committee that their jobs were really only nominal.

What happened in England is only heresay and I cannot vouch for its authenticity. No provision had been made for getting Stars from where they were unloaded at London to Torquay. Commercial transportation had to be arranged for and cost plenty. It is said to have cost fifteen dollars to either launch or haul a Star at Torquay. One alternate told me that the only way he could see the races was to buy a ticket on the public observation boat. After the Olympics, over half the Stars had to be shipped to Portugal for the World's Championship. Finally a tramp was diverted to Torquay. I understand that it could have come alongside the dock and loaded the Stars, except possibly at dead low water, but the port authorities would not allow it. So the boats had to be taken by a lighter to where the tramp was anchored, a short distance away. The consensus of opinion was that the tradespeople heaped every expense they could think of upon the rich yachtsmen.

Do not think that I am criticising the local yachting organizations. Remember that there was a lot of discussion as to whether England was in a position to hold the games that year. I believe that the local yachtsmen did all they were able to do under existing conditions. Even in our own World's Championships some localities are able to provide better and cheaper facilities than others.

The 1952 Olympics, after a wait of twelve years, were held at Helsinki, Finland. The yachting was on more or less protected waters. The start was about four miles from the harbor, where excellent facilities were provided The yachtsmen were housed in clubs on small islands near the mainland. They were divided according to nationality, not classes, hence the Star members did not see too much of each other. The point and throw out system was the same as in 1948. Everyone agreed that the races were most efficiently conducted.

The Star course would have been over the same triangle as the one for the one man monotypes, had it not been for Jean Peytel's strenuous objection. As instructions had already been printed, the only thing that could be done was to send the Stars over the next larger triangle, a total of about thirteen and one-quarter miles. It was longer than the regular Star championship course, but a great improvement over the wild scramble of 1948. As a result of the longer course there were no disqualifications. There were no dismastings and only five did not finish, although there were twenty-one entries —a new Olympic record for a class bringing its own boats.

The U.S. finals were sailed on the Great South Bay, with the Bay Shore Y.C. sponsoring the event and the Bayberry Point Y.C. providing the anchorage. Owing to the early shipping date, comparatively few clubs were as yet in commission and we only had just enough powerboats to handle the marks Shoal water eliminated the help of the Coast Guard and its telephones. Establishing reasonably accurate courses and starting on time was not easy. I know, as I was chairman of the special R.C., but weather conditions were good.

The series quickly developed into a duel between the two Florida entries. Jack Price and Jack Reid, of the Biscayne Bay fleet, won by four points. Jim Schoonmaker was runner-up and became alternate skipper. To avoid misunderstanding, he also lives in Miami, but belongs to the Nassau Star fleet. Nye, Ulmer and Smart followed in the order named. Paul Smart, however, finished ahead of anyone else seeking a substitute berth and became alternate crew. Thus the U.S. was fortified with a second string Star combination at Helsinki that was almost as good as its first.

Commanders Straulino and Rode, of the Italian navy, won an impressive Olympic victory. They would have won under any point system the writer has ever heard of, never bringing Merope in worse than second in any of their seven starts. Agostino Straulino deserved to win. He was finally able to shake off the ill luck that pursued him for years and his tendency to take rash chances. As a result, he won the three major Star championships held in Europe in 1952.

Price and Reid came nearer winning than most people realize. Had Jack been able to place on the final day, regardless of Straulino winning, he could have thrown out Comanche's seventh and won the series. That sort of thing can happen under the premium point and throw out system. At that the Italian and U.S. entries finished with over two thousand points more than anyone else.

It is interesting to note that of the first five entries to place, Price was the only newcomer to the Olympics. Fiuza and de Cardenas, a Star veteran of twenty-seven years, placed third and fourth respectively. Knowles was fifth and gave the Bahamas their first Olympic points, as the Bahamas only recently had been granted recognition as a separate nation.

An eyewitness reported a twenty mile wind in the first and third race, with fair seas and whitecaps. The other races were sailed in from medium to light weather. It is also reported that the final race was started in no more than a five mile zephyr. The light going may have somewhat cramped Price's style, as he was never an outstanding drifter. My own feeling, however, is that Straulino was finally hitting on all fours in 1952 and that no one could have beaten him. In the second race, Straulino sailed through all seventeen Dragons and all except five of the 5.5's, which classes started ten and twenty minutes, respectively, ahead of the Stars.

I have only spoken with three Star members who were at Helsinki and cannot add much in the way of sideline gossip. Charlie de Cardenas seemed to be more impressed with the fact that women masseurs were in attendance at the steam baths, which he took, than anything else. Perhaps this will add a splash of color to an otherwise rather drab routine account.

1932 OLYMPICS, Los Angeles, U S A

Nation	Skipper	Yacht	1sts	2nds	3rds	Pts
United States	Gilbert Gray	Jupiter	5	1	1	46
United Kingdom	Colin Ratsey	Joy	1	1	2	35
Sweden	Gunnar Asther	Swedish Star	—	1	2	27*
Canada	Harry Wylie	Windor	—	2	—	27
France	Jean Herbulot	Tramontane	—	2	2	26
Holland	Adrian Maas	Bem	—	—	—	16
South Africa	Cecil Goodricke	Springbok	1	—	—	7

Winning yacht built by Joseph Parkman, Brooklyn, U S A   *Tie for third won by default
Total point system
NOTE—All daily positions not obtainable Hereafter official results were copied from bulletin board by a Star member.

1936 OLYMPICS, Kiel, Germany

Nation	Skipper	Yacht	Daily Points							Total
Germany	Bischoff	Wannsee	12	9	12	12	11	12	12	80
Sweden	Laurin	Sunshine	11	12	10	11	1	10	9	64
Holland	Maas	Bem II	0	11	9	10	12	11	10	63
United Kingdom	Girogono	Poka	9	10	11	6	5	8	7	56
United States	Waterhouse	Three Star Too	10	8	5	4	10	9	5	51
Norway	No Record	K N S	8	3	6	7	9	7	4	44
France	Herbulot	Fada	3	0	4	9	8	6	11	41
Turkey	Ulmann	Marmara	6	7	7	1	7	2	8	38
Italy	de Sangro	Pegasos	5	6	8	2	4	3	6	34
Portugal	Fiuza	Vicking	7	0	0	8	6	5	2	28
Japan	Takarbe	Mayojo	4	5	0	3	2	4	1	19
Belgium	Godts	Freddy	2	4	0	5	3	1	3	18

Winning yacht No 1287, built by Caesar Fuhlendorf, Hamburg, Germany, 1936 Total point system

1948 OLYMPICS, Torquay, England

Nation	Skipper	Yacht	Placed in each race							Points
United States	H Smart	Hilarius	4	1	2	1	3	dq	6	5828
Cuba	de Cardenas	Kurush	7	dq	7	2	7	1	2	4849
Holland	Maas	Starita	3	5	5	3	4	2	7	4731
United Kingdom	Knowles	Gem II	2	2	6	4	2	dq	dm	4372
Italy	Straulino	Legioario	1	3	3	dq	1	dq	dm	4370
Portugal	Fiuza	Espadarte	11	6	1	5	12	5	3	4292
Australia	Sturrock	Moorina	0	4	15	6	10	4	1	3828
Canada	Gooderham	Ariel	9	14	4	14	8	6	10	2635
Spain	Allende	Galerna	15	7	16	10	5	7	8	2564
Greece	Calambokidis	Nephos I	8	12	9	12	11	9	4	2532
France	Lorion	Aloha II	12	5	8	8	6	3	dm	2515
Finland	Nyman	Lucky Star	13	11	13	13	9	11	5	2058
Austria	Obermuller	Donar III	10	15	14	15	15	8	9	1661
Brazil	Bracony	Buscape II	16	13	11	11	1	10	11	1644
Switzerland	Bryner	Ali Baba II	6	9	12	9	dq	dm	dm	1610
Argentina	Piacentini	Acturua	14	10	10	7	13	dm	ds	1551
Sweden	Melin	Lotta IV	5	da	17	16	dq	0	ds	888

Winning yacht No 2570, built by Old Greenwich Boat Co, Old Greenwich, U S.A, 1947 NOTE—Premium point and throw out system

1952 OLYMPICS, Helsinki, Finland

Nation	Skipper	Yacht	Placed in each race							Points
Italy	Straulino	Merope	2	1	2	2	1	2	1	7635
United States	Price	Comanche	1	7	1	1	3	1	8	7216
Portugal	Fiuza	Espadarte	4	8	3	3	5	6	3	4902
Cuba	de Cardenas	Kurush IV	5	12	4	4	6	3	7	4535
Bahamas	Knowles	Gem III	3	6	6	10	2	8	9	4405
France	Chabert	Eissero	6	11	7	7	4	4	10	3866
Sweden	Melin	Lotta IV	7	9	5	5	9	10	4	3785
Holland	Maas	Bem II	9	3	9	11	8	5	11	3510
Switzerland	Bryner	Ali Baba IV	13	2	14	9	7	7	18	3400
Canada	Woodward	Whirlaway	12	13	11	16	10	14	2	2889
West Germany	Fischer	Paka	8	10	nf	14	21	11	5	2367
Brazil	de Paula	Bu III	11	4	13	19	12	16	15	2350
United Kingdom	Banks	Fortuna	15	5	nf	20	15	18	6	2178
Austria	Musil	30 Februar	16	15	18	8	13	9	14	2092
Greece	Timoleon	Marie-Tim	19	16	10	6	18	17	13	1983
Argentina	Vellebona	Arcturus	10	19	nf	13	11	12	17	1833
U S S R	Chumakov	Uragan	18	14	16	12	16	15	12	1660
Australia	Harvey	Hornet	14	20	8	18	20	13	20	1575
Finland	Nyman	Lucky Star	17	17	15	17	14	19	16	1522
Yugoslavia	Fafanceli	Primorka	20	18	12	15	17	20	21	1218
Monaco	de Sigaldi	Hirondelle	nf	nf	17	21	19	21	19	560

Winning yacht No 2958, built by Old Greenwich Boat Co, Old Greenwich, U S A, 1949 NOTE—Premium point and throw out system

CHAPTER IX

REASONS UNDERLYING STAR RULES

R̲ULES ARE THE STRUCTURE of competitive sport. Rule books do not have space for lengthy explanations, nor can all reasons for a rule always be made evident by its wording. A superficial knowledge of rules, therefore, is not enough. Officials that understand the intent and purpose of rules can better enforce and interpret them. Contestants with that knowledge are less apt to unwittingly violate a rule in principle.

The writer will try to explain the less obvious reasons behind certain Star rules, which even many Star members do not fully grasp. Being an exhaustive subject, only the more important rules can be touched upon. The casual reader, not interested in a rule discussion, is advised, therefore, to skip rather lightly through the contents of this chapter.

To begin with, a one-design class serves two masters. Rules of the parent unions (I.Y.R.U. and N.A.Y.R.U.) govern right-of-way, most race procedure, rating formulae and time allowance based thereon. Union rules are essential to preserve a reasonable degree of uniformity in yacht racing and the conduct of large regattas These rules, however, are primarily written around and intended for the rating (open design) classes. Each one-design and special class is responsible for its own class rules and must file a copy with the R.C. conducting the event That, in a nutshell, is the setup.

The basic principle of open design and one-design racing is the exact opposite. Races in the rating classes are contests of design, intended to prove which is the fastest boat. The purpose of a one-design class, however, is to provide theoretically identical boats in order to prove who is the best skipper. It stands to reason, therefore, that neither can race under all the rules of the other without causing many inconsistencies Nevertheless, one-designs were forced to race under open design rules in the past and still are in many large club regattas. Worse still, some of the strictly local one-design classes seem perfectly satisfied with that arrangement, thereby nullifying the very purpose for which they were organized.

The most striking example of this is the usual practice of awarding series points to the boat, regardless of the type or class. While it is quite correct to continue that practice with the rating classes, it is all wrong in the case of the one-designs. If two or more skippers sail the same one-design boat in different races, their combined point score does not prove who is the best skipper. Probably more than eighty-five per cent of the starters are one-designs in the average large club regatta today. Does it make sense to impose a practice, which now only applies to a small minority, upon the great majority?

The problems of an R C. conducting a regatta for many classes have not been lost sight of. It is just as easy to award points to the boat and its skipper as it is to the boat and its owner. Entries have to be filed with someone, either the club or its local Y.R.A. It is a simple matter, therefore, to obtain the name of the skipper of record by asking for it on the entry blank. No one expects the R.C. to know who is at the helm of each boat in a big regatta. If one of the small boat skippers is a professional, that would be a violation of Union rules What would the R.C. do? It would wait for a protest and then disqualify. Is there any reason why it cannot follow the same procedure if the eligibility of the skipper is protested on other grounds? Those racing in a class know whom they are sailing against. It is definitely their responsibility to protest an ineligible skipper, just as it is an ineligible boat. No additional work is asked of the R.C.

A great many persons do not seem to realize that class rules do not refer to measurements only, but include all regulations and restrictions necessary to properly carry out the principles for which the class was created. They also do not seem to understand that individual ability is just as great a factor in yacht racing as in any other sport and that ability is not just confined to helmsmanship. A skipper can definitely increase the speed of a boat by condition and tune. Some can do it quicker than others, but all must have the boat in their care for an appreciable time to accomplish this. That is why nothing conclusive can be proved except by the performance of a given skipper in a given boat.

If too great a curb is placed upon a skipper's ability, it defeats the purpose of one-design racing. The extreme of this has been tried in club owned classes, where the skipper draws for the boat he is to sail just before the race. Such boats are never in anything like the condition of privately owned ones. Since the skipper is not allowed to adjust anything, they are never in tune and do not even provide an accurate test of helmsmanship between skippers of more or less equal caliber.

Under Star rules a skipper can take full advantage of his general boating knowledge. If he does not attempt to change the basic design of hull, spars or sail, he can do or use almost anything he wants. He can even shift the position of mast and keel within limits. He can tune the boat to his own style, the weight of its human cargo, weather conditions, etc. Then if he does not win, it's because others possess greater ability. On the other hand, he cannot spring a surprise attack by using something new. If he wishes to try anything not mentioned in the rules, he must first obtain a ruling in order to be sure it does not violate them in principle. If allowable, others can see, or at least, hear about it. If it has merit, they can copy it. That policy is chiefly responsible for the continued improvement in a Star's speed and appearance throughout the years.

The foregoing describes the fundamental principles behind almost every Star rule. From this point on I will deal with the less obvious reasons for certain specific Star rules, which is the real object of this chapter.

Sanctions and Classifications — All strictly Star events of inter-fleet character must be sanctioned. That is necessary to prevent conflicting dates. All championships are inter-fleet championships. Entries are restricted to those that win their fleet trials. Such events range from the AA World's Championship down to the 2-B novice district championships. A skipper does not have to qualify for a C or D event. Any number of skippers from the same fleet can enter, as well as isolated ones that are not within the territory of any fleet. Class rules for these events are not as strict, especially with regard to the crew. Some D events have even become part of open regattas. This brief explanation should clarify the rules governing substitutions.

Substitutions — A skipper cannot substitute for himself in his fleet trials, the purpose of which is to select the best skipper for some championship. The same is true of other non-title events, which are also contests between skippers. It would be just as absurd to allow a tennis player to substitute for himself in the preliminary rounds of a tournament. Fleet trials, however, are usually held on consecutive weekends. If a fleet fears that its favorite is apt to be eliminated because of illness or disqualification, there is a simple solution. It can schedule, say seven races and require five to qualify on a percentage system, or five to count on a throw out system. The I.S.C.Y.R.A. does not care, provided that no form of arbitrary selection is used.

Championships are a different story. An entry represents a fleet and they are contests between fleets. The skipper, crew and yacht are supposed to be the fleet's best combination. A duly appointed alternate, therefore, can be substituted in an emergency. The Star officials in charge, however, must approve of any substitution after the series has started. Otherwise a fleet might fake an emergency in an effort to gain an advantage by using a substitute under certain weather conditions. Actually there have been only a few rare cases of an alternate being substituted for the starting combination, and to the best of my knowledge, it has never affected the point score of the leaders. My personal feeling is that any substitutions after the start should be barred, since they serve no good purpose and only force the R.C. to occasionally render a difficult decision, without sufficient time to investigate the circumstances.

Outlawed Events — A rule exists authorizing the I.S.C.Y.R.A to outlaw any established event in which Star class rules are wilfully ignored. While this is a necessary protection, the rule has only been invoked twice. Both cases were in sanctioned Star events for the flagrant disregard of agreed conditions and inexcusable failure to enforce obvious violations of rules.

Protests and Protest Flag — Star rules seek to minimize protests in sanctioned events, as protests cause bad blood. In championships, officials are stationed at each turning mark and follow the race. If a probable violation is reported, the R.C. must investigate. In a large regatta for many classes, of course, it is impossible to provide officials to watch every course. Yacht racing is the sort of sport in which a foul may not be seen by an official, even in a championship. A skipper, therefore, must be given the right to protest. Rules are made to be observed and not to give the R.C. excuses to avoid its duty. The points of every entry in a series are affected by a disqualification. A foul is not a private matter between the two skippers involved. What most R.C.'s do not seem to understand is that it is often to a skippers advantage not to protest. If the fouled skipper beats the one that fouled him and puts a point between himself and his closest rival, why should he protest? By the same token, as that point could mean the series, why should the said rival be prevented from protesting, whether involved in the foul or not? Certainly the outcome of a series should not depend upon whether or not a contestant protests.

Protest flags are not required. Like displaying the owner's private signal, it is a regulation handed down from the days of large yachts. A Star is very sensitive to any movement aboard. Its one man crew hangs over the rail in a breeze and must remain motionless in light air. If he shifts about hoisting a flag, seconds will be lost and Star competition is usually so close that a couple of places could easily be lost. If a boat is disabled, or the skipper does not see a foul, a protest flag cannot be displayed anyway. About the only purpose it serves is to provide the R.C. with another technical excuse to refuse to hear a protest.

Hearings — At a collective hearing a skipper's crew and witnesses will substantiate his testimony. A Star R.C. hears every witness separately. While the testimony will vary to some extent, just as no two people see a street accident exactly alike, the R.C. gets a better picture of the true facts and can tell who is trying to distort them, if anyone.

Appeals — Only I.R.C. decisions cannot be appealed. That is because our best rule talent is usually available at a World's Championship and, since entries come from all parts of the world, an immediate decision is necessary. Even right-of-way rules can be appealed to the I.S.C.Y.R.A. in other championships. While we would prefer that the Unions decide right-of-way violations, the channels provided by them move too slowly If the winner of a fleet's trials rested upon such a decision, not only would the championship be over, but the season would be ended before a final opinion was rendered. Union procedure is intended for local conditions, where prizes are not usually presented until months after the active season is over.

Registered Skipper — It is impossible to prove ownership, nor has it any bearing upon who is the best skipper. That owners and part owners are mentioned in the rules is a figure of speech, as the owner and skipper of a Star is almost always the same person. What the I.S.C.Y.R.A. is interested in is the registered skipper, the skipper that is identified with the number of a given Star. I say "number" advisedly, since a boat's name can be changed, but its number cannot.

Membership — Only members of the I.S.C.Y.R.A. are eligible to race Stars. The reasons for this should be obvious. One-design skippers are entitled to race under their own class rules. Every Star skipper must sign a pledge agreeing to abide by Star rules, when applying for membership. There is no other way of putting teeth into the enforcement of rules. Only those on the membership list can be sure of automatically receiving the rule book and being advised of any changes. Skippers that do not know class rules are a menace to the rest. Aside from this, a world-wide organization cannot be properly run without funds. An international class like the Stars cannot be supported year after year by large contributions from enthusiastic individuals. Necessary funds can only be obtained from small dues paid by all members. Only in that way can the organization's revenue keep pace with its growth and the increased cost of running it. A Star active member must also belong to a recognized club. The only purpose of that requirement was to play ball with the clubs. Star dues are little more than nominal, whereas club dues are much more and in many cases amount to several hundred dollars per year. I mention this to show how narrow minded and ignorant some club officials were in the past, when they claimed that the I.S.C.Y.R.A. was trying to make them its collecting agents, although the reverse was really the case.

Verbal Instructions — There is no reason why understandable printed instructions cannot be available to contestants. Even supplementary verbal instructions are barred and cannot constitute grounds for a protest. Seldom can a skipper be sure that his hail for information is answered by an authorized official. He can easily misunderstand and, on the spur of the moment, the official is apt to give misleading answers. If the printed instructions are open to an honest misunderstanding, the race can be protested and declared no contest.

Star Rules Unbeatable — The by-laws instruct Star officials how they must interpret the rules. This article reads in part, "In deciding any question the intended meaning of the rules shall be considered rather than any technical misconstruction that might be derived from the wording . . . Precedent and the established policy of the association shall be taken into consideration in interpreting any rule or regulation of obscure meaning or not covered at all." Builders are also warned not to copy the dimensions of any Star known to have a measurement certificate, as some of the limitations may have been narrowed since the boat was built. If a bright lad thinks he has found a loophole in the rules, because what he had in mind is not mentioned, he should remember that the responsibility of obtaining a ruling rests with him. Disqualification is the penalty of violating a rule in principle just as much so as violating the letter of the rule. That is why I say that Star rules cannot be circumvented.

Team Racing — Sanctioned Star championships are contests of individual ability and team racing tactics are prohibited, even when a fleet is entitled to more than one entry. I know of no other racing class where such a rule exists. It's -simple enough. A skipper may cover or luff as much as he pleases, where allowed by right-of-way rules, provided he does so in a manner consistent with maintaining or improving his position. If he sacrifices his position in the race and thereby improves the series standing of another, that is team racing. It is easily detected. If he helps a teammate, or one from his own general locality, the reason becomes obvious The reason, however, cannot be considered by the R.C., as it is sometimes obscure. It could be due to a personal like or dislike. A skipper could even favor another, so the event would be held the. following year at a place he would like to visit. Disqualification, in a flagrant case, would not help the injured party. Hence the penalty can include suspension and the R.C. has the power of ordering the race resailed, if the incident materially affected the series score.

Shortening Course — The total distance of a standard Star course is only approximate, otherwise any race could be protested Star rules prohibit shortening the described and signaled course by stopping the race at the end of the first round or at any point short of the regular finish line. Such practice is allowed by Union rules and is probably all right in a large regatta for many classes In an important event for a single class, however, it gives the R.C. too much power to affect the results. If the race is stopped at the end of the first round, the R.C. is accused of wanting to see the entry, then leading, win. If it is allowed to continue, then it is accused of not liking the positions and hoping that the time limit will cancel the race. In other words it's damned if it does and damned if it doesn't. The R.C should not be placed in that position. Aside from this, it has hurt the chances of entries in many C events. Knowing the rules, hearing two guns, and seeing the leader apparently withdraw, other entries have assumed that the race was called off and sailed for home. Then they have learned that had they continued for another hour or so they could have drifted across the line and probably won or placed in the series. This is a good example of why it is dangerous to have sanctioned events run by club R.C.'s, no matter how cooperative they may be. They do not usually know Star rules and act without checking up on them. They do not realize how unfair that sort of thing is to a visiting skipper, who has spent a lot of time and money to enter the event.

Resails — The status of an unfinished race is the same as a cancelled one. The Star class adopted such a rule over twenty years ago. I am happy to say that at least one Union has recently followed suit. The old procedure allowed an entry to be disqualified in the attempted race and barred from the resail, as well as any new entries. In an unfinished race practically every entry picks up a tow before the time limit has officially expired, thereby disqualifying themselves While confusing in a championship, it is worse in a regatta held for many classes The entries are too far away for the R.C. to identify them and too numerous to keep track of An unfinished race is no contest anyway and the only fair way to handle such a situation is to make a resail a new deal in every respect

Special Rules — If a race is declared "no contest" on appeal and the entries cannot be reassembled, the results of the series are determined upon the races that were completed. This must not be misunderstood as giving the R.C. the power of shortening a scheduled series. It is not a very desirable rule, but the only way of handling an otherwise impossible condition.

If an entry fails to start within thirty minutes after the starting signal its time shall not be taken, or if it fails to return within that time after being recalled, it shall be disqualified. The purpose is to prevent a skipper from remaining at anchor in bad weather and only deciding to start after he has found out how many of the entries were disabled, which might be hours later. It also prevents a skipper from starting perhaps hours after his recall, if he figures it would be to his advantage. Union procedure places no time limit on this sort of thing, which could easily keep the R.C. up all night.

An entry maneuvering in close proximity to the starting line is considered a starter, even if it does not cross said line. This and the above paragraph are primarily intended for a series in which only a given number of starts are required to qualify. It prevents an entry from bothering others before the start and then withdrawing.

Whisker Pole — A Star has no light sails and must, therefore, use a whisker pole to hold out its jib while running down wind. The writer has heard several times (not in the too far distant past either) Star skippers hailed from the committee boat and told to take down their whisker poles, as they were illegal. Those hails probably came from a talkative guest or greenhorn R C. member. I mention this only to show that hails cannot be considered official and that even the best club R C. is not always familiar with the obviously necessary class rules of every class

Sculling With Rudder — The Star class was the first to recognize the fact that some types of boats can be given increased speed by sculling with the rudder and passing a rule against that practice. A Star's bow can be swung in one given direction to go about or round a mark. Additional forward speed, however, cannot be imparted to the boat by short quick motions of the helm. Of course this is technically barred by the rule which provides that a yacht can only be propelled by sail. Large yachts cannot be sculled by the rudder and it was practically impossible to make the average club R.C. believe that a Star could until this rule was passed.

Amendments — While this has to do with organization rather than racing, a brief explanation seems in order. A proposed amendment must be published in Starlights four months before the annual meeting. That gives fleets a chance to discuss it and instruct their delegates. The annual meeting must then approve of the proposed amendment by a majority vote, to prevent crackbrained schemes from being submitted. Finally the resolution is voted upon by the membership with the annual ballot and a two thirds vote is required to pass it. Hence no change can be made in the rules unless desired by a substantial majority.

Team Racing Tactics — Such tactics are prohibited in any Star championship. I doubt if this rule exists in any other class. A skipper has a perfect right to sail a normal race and cover any rival he likes, provided he observes the right-of-way rules. He cannot, however, sail an abnormal course, which hurts his own position, and prevent another skipper from sailing a normal one. Team racing is easy to detect and there is nothing complicated about the rule. Since its adoption, there have been no marked cases of that practice. It's a necessary rule, as it's impossible to know the causes for team racing. It by no means always applies to skippers from the same district or nation and is often due to some private grudge, which no one knows about.

Race Circulars — Many of the requirements on a race circular are simply established practice and not rules to be found in the rule book. Probably the least obvious of these is the requirement that the red starting signal remain up until the race is over That red visible signal can be seen from a distance, whereas a gun often cannot be heard against a strong wind, nor can code flag J be seen.

Economy In Words — Star rules have often been criticized for being too lengthy and including too many repetitions. It should be known that this is mostly intentional. Unless the purpose of a rule is impressed upon the mind of a contestant, when excited he is apt to do the very thing the rule was intended to prevent. Those who write sports rules try to make them as brief and to the point as possible, which is highly commendable. They are inclined to think, however, that the average contestant understands the purpose of rules as well as they do, and that is not so. Hence, in their effort to be concise, they are apt to word a rule much as they would a telegram. If the intent of a rule is not clear, officials in various localities will interpret it a little differently, in fact. Except for that, appeals would never be necessary.

It has already been stated that there is not enough space in any rule book to publish a thorough explanation of every reason for every rule. It has always been the policy of the Star class, however, not to economize in words and to make the intent of a rule reasonably understandable. Repetitions sometimes cannot be avoided, since the same underlying purpose applies to more than one situation and may have to be emphasized again under another heading. Of the two evils, too many words can do no harm.

Right-Of-Way — There can be only one code of right-of-way rules for an international class. All Star championships and sanctioned events of international character are sailed under the right-of-way rules of the I.Y.R.U. When I.Y.R.U. and N.A.Y.R.U. rules were identical, Star races were sailed under both. Then the N.A.Y.R.U. adopted new right-of-way rules, that were considerably different. Uniform rules are far more important to any international sport than improved ones, hence the I.S.C.Y.R.A. was forced to recognize the rules that applied to yacht racing all over the world and not those that applied only to races on one continent.

The North American Yacht Racing Union — The N.A.Y.R.U. was the late Clifford D Mallory's brain child. For over a year a small group of yachtsmen, including the writer, lunched with him at India House monthly and discussed preliminary arrangements. Having been on the ground floor, I know what happened and this seems like the logical place to tell of the modest part played by the Star class in helping to launch Cliff's pet project.

Right-of-way rules were then pretty much the same the world over, but not identical. Europe had had its I.Y.R.U. since 1908, although few over here had ever heard of it. Racing on this continent was handled by various Y.R.A.'s. Each printed the rules in its yearbook, as did many clubs. Those rules must have been originally copied from the New York Y.C., as the more important ones were the same in principle, if not in wording. Many revisions, made in an effort to clarify them according to local understanding, probably accounted for this. Less common situations, however, were open to somewhat different interpretation and, of course, procedure varied widely. The object of the proposed N.A.Y.R.U. was to give North America uniform rules and provide a parent *advisory* body. Even appeals could not be carried on up to the Union without permission of the Y.R.A. having jurisdiction over the event.

The first difficulty encountered was to interest these Y.R.A.'s Letters remained unanswered That was where the Star class was able to help. The I.S.C.Y.R.A. was already in existence. Its members appreciated the advantages of a parent body. Star members were also officers of quite a few Y.R.A.'s. When I advised them what was afoot, they began to use their local influence. As a result, the Star class was instrumental in bringing in five of the ten Y.R A.'s that formed the N.A.Y.R.U

Its first session was held in New York City in 1925. Close to one hundred yachting organizations (Y.R.A.'s and clubs) were represented by delegates or proxies, mostly the latter. Each was entitled to one vote and about sixty-five per cent of those votes were cast by Star members. I know that I held five proxies myself. There was nothing unusual about that. Distant groups naturally appointed a proxy, living near New York, whom they knew well and the only ones they had met were Star members. The Star class is not trying to claim any credit whatever. These matters are simply explained to show that it did its best to help the N.A.Y.R.U. get started.

After deciding a few basic principles, the meeting appointed a committee to draw up a constitution and adjourned. That committee consisted of W. A. W. Stewart, chairman, the late Samuel Douchy and myself. The only two rule books referred to were the Log of the Star class and the yearbook of the Lake Michigan Y.R.A. That constitution was ratified the next morning and the N.A.Y.R.U. came into being. Of the seven officers elected, four were Star members. Later the N.A.Y.R.U. officially recognized the Star class and its class rules. It was the only one-design class mentioned by name and to which a paragraph was devoted.

When suggestions were asked for that might improve right-of-way rules, I know that I wrote Harry Maxwell, chairman, about fixing the burden of proof. Others may have also, anyway it was done. Before that an R.C. might just as well have tossed a coin to know who was telling the truth, if there was no impartial corroborative evidence. Naturally one hesitates to disqualify a skipper when there is a fifty per cent chance that he is innocent. That probably accounted for more disallowed protests in the past than anything else. The element of guess work has now been practically eliminated. Furthermore, if a skipper knows that the burden of proof rests with him, he is apt to be much more careful.

Primarily through the efforts of Cliff Mallory, the rules of the I.Y.R.U., N.A.Y.R.U. and N.Y.Y.C. were brought into conformity in 1929. That was the most constructive action ever taken for the benefit of yacht racing as a whole. It was all undone, however, about twenty years later. During the second world war clubs were requested to unofficially test the Vanderbilt rules. After the war, they were somewhat revised and the N.A.Y.R.U. officially adopted the new right-of-way rules. The Star class and the Snipe class wrote lengthy letters to the Union objecting to the idea. One-design classes, of course, had no vote. They stated that an international class could not hold important races under right-of-way rules that conflicted with those used by the rest of the world. They also pointed out that, especially in small classes, because of the number of entries and close proximity of the yachts, that fouls were constantly averted by instinctive action and that U.S. skippers would soon be at a great disadvantage by having to memorize two conflicting codes of rules. Nevertheless the new rules had gained popular favor and were adopted.

In 1950, however, the pendulum began to swing back the other way. At that years meeting of the N.A.Y.R.U., once again there was a strong sentiment in favor of bringing the rules into accord and even of having the N.A.Y.R.U. join the I.Y.R.U.

CHAPTER X

CALIFORNIA'S HEYDAY

CALIFORNIA CAME INTO ITS OWN in 1933, when Eddie Fink brought the world's title back to its shores for the second time. During the lapse of five years, yachtsmen of the fifth Star district had not been idle. They took their Star racing seriously, trained teen age youngsters and, with twelve months of the year to sail in, talent developed very rapidly. It is safe to say that in 1933 the Pacific coast of North America had, and still has, more good Star skippers per capita than any other distinctive locality. Almost every California fleet is so strong in reserves, that if the winner of its eliminations cannot attend a title event, it can send the third or fourth best skipper, who will perform just about as well. Furthermore, the majority are young men, with many years of Star racing ahead of them.

To substantiate the above statement, let me point out that California skippers have won eleven of the thirty-one World's Championships. That is a remarkable record in world-wide competition. Long Island Sound skippers, who rank next have won only seven out of thirty-one world's titles. It must also be remembered that in the early days of this event,

Sound skippers had a decided advantage having sailed Stars
for more than ten years before any other fleet. California's
record is still more impressive, because of the few entries
which they have sent to this event. Even when it was held
on their own coast, they had no preponderance of entries,
due to the fact that there are only a few scattered harbors
along California's lengthy coastline and hence only a small
number of fleets. Since it is almost the most remote point
from all thickly populated Star centers, for three years, beginning in 1933, World's Championship entries fell off to the
numerical standard of a decade before.

Glen Waterhouse and Woodie Metcalf brought Three
Star Too down from the north, to give San Francisco its
first gold Star. The event was sailed off Long Beach. The
Thorne brothers, in Mist (the same boat with which Eddie
Fink, as part owner, had won the event the year before)
were runners-up. Herb Dowsett, Jr. brought Hawaii into
the picture by placing third. The writer was not present in
1933, or the two following years. In covering these three
series, which were held in California, I must confine myself
to what appears in the records, as I have learned that hearsay
information is not always too accurate.

Eddie Fink won three of the five World's Championship
races of 1933, but was disqualified in the other two. In the
second race he became involved in a foul with Paul Shields,
right under the nose of the committee. At that Eddie could
have finished in the money, except that his boom swept
across a stakeboat on the last day. A group of Eddie's teen-
aged cohorts became very angry and expressed their dissatisfaction in no uncertain terms and caused a lot of trouble.

The I.R.C. that year, as I recall it, consisted of a Hawaiian
chairman, three Californians and one easterner. Perhaps those
youngsters felt that such a predominantly west coast committee should have closed its eyes to any rule infringement on
the part of a native son. I can think of no other explanation.
If anyone ever questioned the legality of those two disqualifications, it never reached my ears. Those boys became
imbued with that "kill the umpire" spirit, which is sometimes

found among a group of disgruntled local fans at a baseball game. The allegations made were so serious that the governing committee was forced to hold an investigation. Those unruly kids were never identified as Star members or by name. One member, however, was recognized as being among them. The association had jurisdiction over him and he had to take the blame. Perhaps he was guilty of nothing more than being in bad company, I was not there and do not know. All I know is what was testified to at the G.C. investigation. The details can be found in the minutes thereof.

The above-mentioned incident is past history and forgotten. I speak of it only because it bred an unjustifiable feeling of antagonism on the part of Pacific coast skippers against the administration and Atlantic seaboard Star members in particular, which has flared up several times since. Why, I have no idea. Neither the administration or eastern skippers were involved or benefited by those two disqualifications in any way. All this has been confined primarily to the younger element. The I.S.C Y.R.A. has had many older members from the west coast in responsible jobs and they have always proved to be most efficient and fair minded officials. Keen rivalry is to be encouraged, but let us hope that the new generation of Star skippers from the east and west coasts of North America will bury the hatchet. What is the sense of carrying on a feud that was started by a group of offensive youngsters, who did not even belong to this organization?

The Star class was spreading like wild fire. Our first fleet was formed in Africa, at Bonne. Central Europe and Scandinavia were becoming Star minded. The roster showed seventy fleets. Many national and district championships were in full swing. They were becoming so numerous that henceforth I shall only deal with the outstanding features that cropped up every now and then and played an important part in Star history.

The 1934 I.R C. had little to worry about in the way of protests. It did have its troubles, however, with the gentlemen of the press. They could not understand why the races were not sailed on the San Francisco side of the Bay, where local regattas were held and where the public could stand on the shore and see the start and finish. The fact that there were very tricky tides in that part of the Bay, which would have given the defender a decided advantage, did not seem to register. Sam Smith had to bear the brunt of the criticism. He was spoken of as the chap from Boston, who was trying to run their races for them. Why Sam was identified with Boston, I am sure I do not know. To the best of my knowledge he never went to that city but once in his life and he is not even a New Englander.

The story of that World's Championship can be told in a few words. It was all Hook Beardslee and Barney Lehman. By-C won four races and took the series by a safe margin of ten points over Johnnie Arms, with Adrian Iselin doing remarkably well in heavy weather, placing third. The only dent made in Beardslee's otherwise perfect record was made by Harry Meislahn and Reeve Bowden, from Moriches Bay. They won the second race. One surprising thing was the poor showing of Thorne and Dowsett, Jr., who finished way down the list. Even Gilbert Gray, Olympic champion, could do no better than seventh. Villefranche, the only European entry, was represented by Mme. Judith Balkan. She picked the wrong event to enter in California. Had she selected one of its famous beauty contests, she would have won hands down instead of finishing last. Over seven hundred persons attended the final banquet, held in the Palm Court of the Palace Hotel. Three Star Too, under full sail, was at one end of the room. When the World's Championship trophy was presented, Waterhouse's sail was lowered and that of By-C was hoisted.

Just in case the reader may think that Pop Corry has been lost in the shuffle, I had better state that he was there and tell of an experience he had on the way home. He drove out and back, from Chicago, with the Pirie brothers, who were trailing their boat. They were driving along a mountain trail, with a precipice on one side and solid rock on the other. Coming toward them at full speed was a model T Ford, swaying all over the road. Just before it reached them it swerved and went over the precipice, a sheer drop of several hundred feet. They looked over the edge and saw it rolling down the mountain, until it went out of sight. They were still debating upon what to do, when up over the edge crawled a drunk. He sat by the roadside and began to cry. No, it was not because of the lost car but his poor little dog. They had just persuaded the drunk to get into their car, so they could take him to the nearest town, when there was a scratching sound and up came the dog. Both had been thrown out of the car, as it rolled over, and did not have so much as a scratch on them.

That was the first year the Spring Championship was held at Bermuda and won by Adrian Iselin. It was also the first year of the championship of North Africa, won by Grima, against sixteen entries. Harold Halsted was listed among the winners of important events for the first time in 1934, when he won the Atlantic Coast Championship and Corry Week on the Great South Bay.

The scene now shifts back to southern California, where the 1935 gold Star event was sailed off Newport harbor. This was indeed a turbulent series, a cat and dog fight between Beardslee, the defender, and Iselin. Waterhouse would also have been in the thick of it except for a tenth place on the first day. Johnnie Arms, runner-up the previous year, was only able to beat five boats. And so it went—in the money one year and down in the ruck the next. The closeness of the competition becomes much more evident by consulting the results over a number of years, rather than the point score of any given series. A study of the World's Championship results, especially around this period, is very interesting. In most cases skippers worked their way up, attained fame for a year or two and then gradually slipped down the list. A few, not many, have staged brief comebacks. It is not unusual for a decisive winner one year to fail to qualify in his local eliminations the next The most consistent performance, I would say, has been that of Adrian Iselin. Next to Charlie de Cardenas, of Habana, he sailed in more worlds title events than anyone else. Adrian also had his off seasons, but unlike the majority, he had the faculty of bouncing back. During his long career, he has two firsts, a second and a third to his credit. His worst performance, was an eighth against thirty-six entries. He won his second gold star eleven years after the first one and his second Atlantic coast title twenty years after the first one, and always with the same boat. He is still going strong—all power to him.

Except for a thunder squall on the third day, which the Californians said was "most unusual weather," the 1935 series ran smoothly enough until the last race. Then the fireworks started. By-C entered that final race with a three point lead over Ace, but then Beardslee cracked. On the last round, he was far down and Iselin, while not the leader, had several boats between his and By-C. Under ordinary circumstances, Iselin would have won his second gold Star that year.

At this point a young skipper, representing another west coast fleet, decided to take a hand in the game. He claimed afterwards that he was inspired to do so, because he saw a Star sailing on By-C's wind. That was found to have been the case for a while, but the skipper of that Star was minding his own business and violating no rule. He was completely exonerated and the incident had no bearing upon what followed, except perhaps in the mind of the young skipper who caused all the trouble.

I did not attend the World's Championship that year and want it distinctly understood that I am not repeating idle gossip. What happened was established by the evidence given at an investigation conducted by the governing committee that fall. It is described in the minutes of that investigation and, in brief, follows:

On the last round, the young skipper first mentioned, was ahead of Iselin and about two hundred yards from the weather mark. Instead of tacking, when he could have made it, he luffed, waited for Ace and then bore down on it. Iselin let his jib go, to slow the boat and try to get about. The Californian did the same, to prevent Iselin from doing so. Then he sailed the Ace past the mark Finally Adrian was able to shake off his tormentor. In the meantime, however, the

Stars that had been between Ace and By-C had rounded the said mark, as well as Beardslee. Ace caught and passed By-C on the final leg home, but not the other Stars that it had been ahead of. That gave the series to Beardslee by two points. The G.C. minutes state that Iselin was "willfully and deliberately" fouled to prevent him from winning the series.

Had Iselin protested, the I.R.C. would have been forced to disqualify, but he did not and there was no disqualification. For that matter the I.R.C. had the power to investigate and act on any known infringement, without a protest. That is mandatory under Star regulations, which these officials are pledged to uphold before being ratified. A disqualification, however, would not have affected the point score with respect to Beardslee or Iselin.

Let me make it very clear that Hooks Beardslee was in no way implicated. It was not his fault, if some other skipper, from the same general locality, messed up the point score Likewise, there was no appeal. An appeal cannot be taken from a decision, or lack of one, by the I.R.C. Charges of unsportsmanlike conduct were brought against the offender. After the evidence was heard he was indefinitely suspended. He was reinstated, however, at the annual meeting the following year.

There was another minor incident at the finish, which was investigated at the same time. Two entries luffed along the line. It was evidently the intention of one of them to try to slip across between Ace and By-C. The other's motive is not too clear. Perhaps that skipper also wanted to help Iselin, as it would have taken two points to bring about a tie. The governing committee found that neither skipper had violated any existing rule of right-of-way, but that their actions were most unethical. In any event, whatever they intended to accomplish failed. Both these skippers, however, were given a short suspension.

I hate to wash our dirty linen in public, but in an authentic story of the Star class the bad must be told along with the good All this may have been a blessing in disguise.

It brought about the adoption of a team racing rule, explained elsewhere, and the aggregate point score rule, which causes the World's Championship to change locality annually. Obviously the series could not be awarded to Long Island Sound. By the same token it was felt that it should not remain on the Pacific coast. A special meeting of the association was held in New York City during the winter. It decided to award the series to one of the neutral lake fleets, a region rich in old Star traditions, but one that had never held a world's title event. Chicago and Rochester bid for it, but it was awarded to the latter by a very close vote.

Two new national championships and two perpetual trophies for race weeks were inaugurated in 1935. The Swedish Championship, won by Dan Sudden-Cullberg and the Italian Championship, won by Enrique Ducrot. At Marblehead week, the Charles Francis Adams trophy was raced for and won by Homer Clark, while Walter von Hutschler took Kiel week.

Awarding the title event to fresh water was no mistake. It brought it within reach of many Great Lake and inland lake fleets, which had never had an opportunity to participate before. With thirty-five entries, all previous records were shattered. A different skipper won each of the five races. While the writer was present, to attempt to describe these races is next to impossible. It was like watching a three ring circus.

By-C won the opener and it began to look as if it was going to be the same old story all over again. Following this came two days of flat calm. Races were attempted, but did not come anywhere near finishing within the time limit, which was fortunate for Ace and By-C, who were way down in the ruck. The next official race might have ended in the same manner, if the race committee had not postponed it within a few seconds of the start. While there is no tide on Lake Ontario, it had been blowing hard for several days before the series started and there was a strong set. Between the preparatory and the start the wind died out completely and several yachts, which had been playing it close drifted across the line and could never have returned. A number of them did not make an attempt to do so, questioning the right of the I.R.C. to order a postponement at the last instant. It was necessary to send launches after them, as a light breeze sprang up a few minutes later. There was quite a commotion about it, until they were shown an N.A.Y.R.U. rule book that evening. It was a wise move, for after a short wait we were able to give them a real race and, at last, the series got underway, with Harold Halsted winning that race.

From then on it became another battle between Iselin and Beardslee. No one else really had much of a chance. Sam Smith suffered most in the third race. He made a premature start and did not see or hear the recall through the forest of sails between him and the committee boat. Sam finished fourth, but naturally was disqualified. That cost him third place in the series. Horace Havemeyer, Jr., took that race and Jack Keith the next, while Iselin picked up a few points on Beardslee. In entering the final race, however, Beardslee still had a one point lead. Would history repeat itself? That final race was just about as fluky as one could ask for. The wind shifted many times, as little rain squalls made up and vanished just as quickly. For some reason best known to himself, Beardslee made no attempt to cover Iselin, but went off wind hunting on his own. That was courting disaster, as Adrian has always been a past master at keeping his boat going in that sort of weather. He finished second to Doc Martin, of Santa Barbara, and won his second gold Star. Harold Halsted, who had been improving year by year, also crashed into the golden circle by placing third in the series.

The Rochester yacht club had really an ideal setup for a World's Championship. Most of the yachts were moored in little slips along the club dock and it was only a short sail out to the starting line. All festivities were under the same roof, so there was no running about in cars or taxis, except for those who were quartered at some hotel in the city. Personally, I had only one complaint. For nearly two years I had been on a strict vegetable diet. The first thing I was allowed to eat, in the way of fish, flesh or fowl, was frogs legs. The program called for a frogs legs feast. I was told that the frogs up there had legs as big as chicken legs and that two were a meal in themselves. I had been looking forward to this feast for some time. When Tim Parkman and I arrived at the club that evening, we were told that there was no more room. We explained that we were president and secretary of the association, but the attendant at the door was not impressed. He pointed out a big tent which was to take care of the overflow. What they had in the club, I do not know, but the frogs legs served in the tent would have made a canary bird blush, if it had such scrawny little limbs. It was a great disappointment.

The annual meeting was a somewhat stormy session. There seemed to have been a whole flock of kids that year, who were delegates. When any serious subject was brought up for discussion, they acted like a lot of unruly little school children. They clapped and hissed and raised hell in general. I never presided at such a meeting before or since. It was certainly a far cry from the competent and sober minded group of delegates who have the interest of the association at heart and with whom one usually has to deal. Adrian Iselin introduced his pet mast band idea again. It had been adopted and rejected several times throughout the years, without affecting conditions one way or the other. This time, however, his motion was shouted down. He was given no chance to explain and walked out of the meeting, nor do I blame him. I thought at the time that it might be a good idea to place an age limit on delegates, but we have never had any such juvenile assemblage since and I never pressed the matter.

In relating the history of the Star class, I feel that facts, even unpleasant ones, should be recorded. Another very unfortunate thing happened at that meeting, which was largely my fault for not having discussed it in advance. Tim Parkman had been our secretary for a long time and a most efficient one The association was spreading rapidly, especially throughout Europe. We had fourteen districts and one hundred and nine fleets. Tim had a new job as a vice-president of a bank. He had the files and in order for me to answer the deluge of letters we were receiving, I was obliged to phone him several times each day. If he was busy or out it meant a delay. Sam Smith, on the other hand, was treasurer and had an office next to mine. It was my bright idea that they switch jobs. Tim, who was in the bank where we kept our account, seemed an ideal treasurer, while with Sam next door, I could get any information I needed at a moment's notice. Tim agreed on the spur of the moment and the elections went accordingly. At that time association officers were still being elected at the annual meeting. On thinking it over, I fear that Tim felt that he had been demoted and that it was a put-up job. Such was not at all the case, but I believe that he still thinks so and never really forgave me. Combining the work of the president and secretary, so it could be handled in the same office, was something which could not have been delayed another year.

And so the big show was headed back for another old home week on the Sound, the cradle of the Star class. Charlie Lucke, who was editor of the Log, made a very accurate prediction, when writing the account of the 1936 series. He stated that if the record entry of 1936 was ever exceeded, it would be the following year on the Sound. That proved to be the case, at least up to then.

Speaking of record breaking entries, that same year seventy-five Stars, sailing in two divisions, competed in Larchmont race week. The ten (or it may have been fifteen, that year) leading yachts were re-grouped into a championship division for the last three days. Frank Campbell, sailing Rascal, won by a single point over Johnnie Arms, in Andiamo. Frank, therefore, still has the distinction of beating the greatest number of Stars that ever sailed in any series, but not the greatest number to start on the same gun. The latter honor goes to Herc Atkin, in a race for the rear commodore Rafael Posso cup, held by the Manhasset Bay yacht club. There were fifty-one starters in that race. Due to some mix-up between written and verbal instructions, about half the Stars rounded the windward mark one way and the other half the other way It took most of the winter to decide whether Harry Nye or Herc won, but the latter finally got the nod.

CHAPTER XI

FLEXIBLE SPARS AND
GERMANY'S BRIEF SUPREMACY

SPAR FLEXING WAS FIRST WITNESSED in America during the World's Championship of 1937, when Walter von Hutschler brought his Pimm to Long Island Sound. The exhibition put on by him and his crew Joachim Weise, in the art of manipulating spars to control draft, was a revelation. As in the case of Waterhouse, at the Olympics the previous year, few, if any, realized what they were seeing. They attributed Pimm's showing to the marvelous coordination between skipper and crew in handling the boat. That too deserves mention, for I have never seen more perfect teamwork. It was not until the series was over that some inkling of the theory involved began to dawn upon those, who had an opportunity to study Pimm and its equipment at close range. It was 1938, therefore, before Star skippers in the western hemisphere, and such other parts of the world that knew little about it, began experimenting with flexible spars.

The Manhasset Bay yacht club was again headquarters. The entry list reached a new high, thirty-six, which was one more than the year before. While the event could not have had a more gorgeous setting, getting thirty-six Stars out to

a starting line, a good six miles distant, was quite a problem. The local clubs and the home fleet are to be complimented upon the efficient manner in which this was handled.

As to the series itself, Milton Wegeforth, of San Diego
Bay, was the eventual winner. Duplicating Iselin's performance of the year before, he took the series without finishing
first in any race. Without intending to detract in any way
from Milton's well earned victory, for after all we pay off
on the point score, it was von Hutschler who stole the show.
Except for a freak accident in the first race, which was won
by Harold Halsted, he would have made a clean sweep of
the series. It was blowing hard that first day, in fact for the
Sound it was pretty rugged going in the majority of the races.
There was nothing new about grooved or slotted masts, hence
what happened had no bearing upon flexible spars. The slot
in Pimm's mast must have been cut slightly off center, so that
there was not quite enough wood left in the lip, which forms
one side of the slot, as it neared the top of the mast. The
lip split and broke off, allowing about three feet of bolt rope
to come out of the groove. That distorted the shape of the
mainsail. Pimm gradually fell back and finished in twenty-
second place. That did not even cause a ripple of interest, as
no one yet realized that Pimm's spars differed from the
rest. It was blowing hard and a number of the entries had
sail trouble of one sort or another. Barney Lehman, in fact,
carried the stick out of the Pasha, a regular rigid mast I
mention this because people are prone to blame dismastings
upon flexible spars, having forgotten that in heavy weather,
some masts went over the side in the Star class, long before
there were flexible spars, and in all other classes as well.

After that first race, it was all Pimm. The German boat
took the next four races and its performance was equally
impressive in all kinds of weather. Two of the races were
sailed in heavy winds and seas, one in a medium breeze
with a cold driving rain and another, after many postpone-
ments, was started as the sun was sinking in the west and
was a light air race throughout. It was not unlike the old, but
apparently erroneous saying, "There is no second," which

was handed down from the first race for the America's cup in 1851. According to the book, "The Yacht America", written by Messrs. Thompson, Stephens and Swan, the authentic hail was, "what's second," and the reply was "nothing." It was not quite as bad as that, but almost, considering the length of the course. Certainly no Star has ever defeated the field in four World's Championship races by any such decisive margin, before or since In spite of that first race, Pimm was runner-up and only five points behind the winning Wegeforth. There is always some aftermath to every world's title event, based upon IFS. In this case, however, there was no doubt in anyone's mind as to what the result would have been except for that freak accident in the first race. In the light of what we know today, there was really nothing astonishing about it. Flexible spars, properly handled, will always run away from rigid ones.

On the opening day the boys were gun shy, as usual, and the start was ragged. Sam Smith and Ed Doyle passed close to the committee, before the half hour gun, and were checked in as "accounted for" They were in tow of a Coast Guard boat, which took them a little too far to leeward, but they must have heard the bark of the one pounder, calling attention to the signals. For some reason, they did not board their Stars and bend on sails in time, and started five minutes after the rest. In spite of that, Sam had his boat going and picked up sixteen of the entries before he finished. For the second year in a row, by not paying sufficient heed to the signals, he muffed a good chance of placing in the money.

Ed, who did not finish that first race, I fear was greatly disappointed in his showing. He had allowed himself to be talked into the idea that he had a good chance of winning against the galaxy of talent Many a neophite has gone home happy for having beaten half a dozen boats. With no big league experience and his younger daughter as crew, Ed should have realized that he was in that category. Then too, the year before he was the host commodore, around whom all interest centered, in a one club show. At Manhasset Bay, with all the neighboring clubs, brass was scattered about as thickly as fleas on a dog's back. The limelight could not be kept focused upon any one club dignitary, besides which his status was different—he was a contestant. I believe he felt slighted and that added to the letdown. From then on he lost interest in Stars. It was a shame, as he was a promising skipper, if he had only given himself half a chance.

Another, who practically eliminated himself from the series before it even began, was the Italian skipper Mario Perretti. He risked a port tack start, only to find a whole flock of starboard tack boats headed at him. He went about, but had no place to go except into the committee boat. I was watching the line, with the microphone near my mouth, ready for a possible recall. Turning my head, I told the spotter behind me to make a note that 1456 was disqualified. Of course, you have no right to tell a contestant that, for no matter how obvious the foul, he is entitled to sail his race and be heard. It was not intended for his ears and he was not supposed to be able to understand English, but he got that. Mario let fly a volley of Italian cussing that would have even put Earl Blouin to shame. It was probably a good thing for him that we did not understand what he called us. I mean a good thing for him.

That was the first time we ever used a loud speaker. They are certainly a great advantage, not only for recalls, but in keeping spectator boats away from the line and for instructing mark and course officials, without having them come alongside. I had not yet learned, however, that it was a good idea to shut the dern thing off, when not in use. Bob Atwater, who had his own ideas as to what the angle of the line should be, decided to change it just before the preparatory. He told a couple of the Coast Guard boys to let out more chain. The rest of the I.R.C had not been consulted about this. I heard the chain running through the hawser pipe and asked Bob, in no uncertain terms, who was chairman of the committee. I learned later that my voice was heard within a radius of half a mile. So the spectators that year were treated to plenty of choice language, in both English and Italian

A peculiar incident happened in the fourth race. Woodie Pirie had brought a Star from the Lakes, which had nothing but aluminum hardware. It was blowing hard. His rudder post broke just before we made the warning signal. He hailed us and wanted to know if he could use a substitute boat. We asked if he could get one on such short notice, and he said that he could. There is a rule allowing emergency substitutions, so after a brief consultation, permission was granted and it was anounced over the loud speaker. We had no idea that he intended changing boats with Phil Upton, another contestant, nor would it have made any difference if we had. There was so little time to make the exchange of boats, that Phil had to jump overboard and swim to the Gemini, in order to be off the Ibis before the preparatory. Pirie finished fourth, and if it had stood, he would have placed third in the series. He was protested, however, and the I.R.C. was forced to reverse its own original ruling. The protest was based on the fact that the rule further states that no emergency substitution can be allowed, if the entry gains any advantage thereby. What we did not know was that Ibis, in the lake region, had the reputation of being a good heavy weather boat, while Gemini, with her aluminum fittings, was considered a light air craft. I still do not see what else the I.R.C. could have done on the spur of the moment. There was nothing in Ibis' performance to justify its local reputation and no time to hold a debate. Had this condition (of which we knew nothing) not existed and had we refused Pirie's request, we might have been acting contrary to rules.

There was a lot of international Star racing in Europe in 1937. The class continued to grow. Each year we were showing a profit and our surplus kept growing. It was at the annual meeting that year that we decided to impose a twenty-five cent World's Championship tax upon each active and associate member. This, plus interest on our savings accounts and securities, computed as of July 1, was to constitute the World's Championship fund. That money was to be sent to the fleet holding the event. We knew it would only partly defray expenses, but we expected it to grow, until the point was reached where a small fleet, without any other local backing, could at least hold the series and give prizes. Except for the war, the fund would have been sufficient for that purpose today. Of course, it would not have covered any extravagant entertainment. There are two schools of thought on that subject. Some feel that fleets with almost unlimited financial support, should not be allowed to establish a precedent that others cannot afford to live up to. On the other hand, you cannot very well tell your host how much money he should spend on your entertainment. A poor man cannot be expected to entertain as lavishly as a rich one. Everyone understands that and does not expect it.

There being nothing else of outstanding note to report for 1937, this seems like the logical place to take up the matter of spar flexing. Let me impress it upon the reader that the following is only a very crude description and simply intended to give the layman a general idea of the theory, so that he can visualize the process.

In making a mainsail, the luff and foot are cut, generally speaking, with a convex (outward) curve. When the sail is roped and the luff and foot are drawn taut in a straight line (as is the case when pulled out on straight spars) the material in the cured segment flows into the body of the sail, giving the sail its draft. Remember that on rigid spars, that draft remains in the sail and nothing much can be done about it. Only time and use will gradually flatten the sail, until it has to be put aside for heavy weather days.

Now then, with flexible spars, if the mast is given a forward bow and the boom a downward bow, approximating the curve that was cut in the luff and foot of the mainsail, the sail will be pulled back into its original unroped shape. That is to say flat, approximately as it first lay on the sailmaker's floor. Another very crude example would be to flatten one side of a drum. The drumhead would naturally become baggy. Spring the rim back into shape and the drumhead again becomes flat and taut. Of course no one wants an absolutely flat sail, nor could it be obtained, since the curve in the luff and foot is not a true arc The amount of draft, however, retaining what there is of it in the proper part of the sail, can be regulated by the amount of curve given the spars. This should enable anyone to understand the theory. Not only was it a new theory, but a fundamentally sound one. It is the only effective method of controlling mainsail draft ever devised.

I do not profess to be an expert on flexing spars. My authority for most of the statements I make on this subject, comes from a pamphlet called "Flexible Spars", written by Walter von Hutschler, who developed the theory and probably knows more about it than anyone else. He was also employed for a few months by a firm with which I was connected and I had quite a number of long talks with him on the subject. Some years before that, the same firm took care of the Stars from abroad that were entered in the 1937 World's Championship, Pimm among them. By this I mean that it delivered them from the steamer to Port Washington and back. Little attention was paid to Pimm on arrival. It did not have an exceptionally fine finish and its fittings were more or less of a homemade variety. On the return trip, however, it remained in the shop for two nights, and Tom Parkman went over it with a fine tooth comb. The mast was weighed and every inch of it was calipered Tom built many masts similar to that one; more, I believe, than any other builder has ever turned out. They weighed about forty pounds and very very few of them have ever broken. That fact will be confirmed by Donald M. Walker, Star insurance officer.

When flexible spars were first introduced in North America, we made several glaring errors. We had a pretty good idea of the theory but did not understand how to properly handle them. We thought that the curve in the mast was produced by force. We believed, when close hauled, that this was done by keeping the step aft, the backstays taut and then forcing the mast forward at deck by means of the partner. A mast can be curved that way, but it means making constant and none too accurate adjustments. The position of the mast at step and deck is something which should be taken care of during the tuning up process. After that, the whole thing should be practically automatic, as I will try to explain.

Contrary to the usual method of rigging rigid spars, the middle shrouds (which fasten to the mast about twenty-two feet and three and one-half inches above deck) are kept taut and are aft of the lower shrouds (which are slack) on the chainplate. The jib stay is kept taut and the headstay slack. While the mainsheet trims to the center of the cockpit, its dead-end fastens to the end of the boom. Hence when the sheet is trimmed (which is the only force used) not only is it bowed downward in the middle, but the end of the boom is also pulled down. That takes care of the curve between the middle shroud and the top of the mast. The aft pressure of the middle shroud and forward pressure of the jib stay, produces the forward curve between the middle shroud and the deck. On a puffy day, as the pressure of the wind on the sail increases, so does the tension of the middle shroud. That causes the bow to increase and the sail to become flatter. Thus it will be seen that the draft automatically regulates itself. When the sheet is eased, for reaching or running, the spars straighten and the draft is restored. When properly set up, the skipper seldom has to touch anything during a race.

Two other grievous mistakes were made in the beginning and, in some instances are still being made. The one led to the other. Skippers had an idea that they could have a sail cut with as much draft as a tent and, by flexing their spars, could make it as flat as a board. They thought that one sail would answer all purposes from a drift to a gale. That is not the case, because wood is not rubber and there is a limit as to how far you can bend it before it snaps. Flexible spars, however, do make it possible for one sail to serve the purpose of two, namely a flat and medium sail or a medium and full sail. Spar flexing will not cover the entire gamut, but in an effort to do this, thinner and thinner masts were built. Those have been the masts that have broken and have given flexible spars, and quite unnecessarily so, a bad name. Of course all dismastings, and the number has been greatly exaggerated, cannot all be attributed to these buggy whip masts. Collapsed spreaders, due to fragile fittings, and inexperienced handling account for probably better than half the dismastings. In like manner, winning in light air has had little to do with spar flexing. It is always an advantage to reduce the weight aloft, if you can keep the mast in the boat.

Unfortunately the very word "flexible" creates the impression of something very willowy and light. Actually extreme elasticity does not make for more efficient spar flexing. On the contrary, these willow wands are very difficult to control and, upon the least provocation, will take all sorts of fantastic curves and twists. Ultra slender masts were tried out on Stars long before flexible ones were ever thought of. Tim Parkman's famous "rubber mast" that weighed about twenty-six pounds, is a good example. It cost Tim more than one series before he realized that he would have to discard it. There are quite a few Star skippers today that are suffering from the same trouble he did.

The most efficient flexing is obtained with a fair curve, but not an extreme one. By fair curve, I mean a curve such as you see in an archer's bow, when the string is drawn back before the arrow is released. If the bow was just a slender willow wand, what would happen? When the string was pulled back, it would almost bend at a right angle and not be an arc at all. To a lesser degree that is what often happens to an ultra-slender mast, usually where the jib-stay intersects it. In some cases the top of the mast takes a hook, not unlike the steam bent masts we once saw on the old "R" boats. Then too, there is the corkscrewing. Any of these gyrations throw a hard spot into the sail. The more experienced skippers can control this to some extent, but the less experienced ones have great difficulty in doing so.

In von Hutschler's pamphlet, he calls attention to one very important thing He points out that the most vulnerable part of the mast is between the deck and the lower spreaders, which is about the same position as the one pair, used in the single spreader rig. If there is not enough wood in that portion of the mast, it is apt to buckle fore or aft and, when the boat pounds in a heavy sea, it is apt to break from compression about eight feet above deck. This is something which there is no way of staying against.

Frankly, for the foregoing reasons, I would like to see some restriction placed on masts, which would eliminate the buggy whip and produce masts of the Pimm type. We know that the latter are substantial and flex more efficiently. Too much thought is being given to keeping light sticks in the boat and not enough to developing the art of spar flexing, which is still, to some extent, in the experimental stage. A weight restriction would not do. Aside from the fact that the same woods are not obtainable in all parts of the world, moisture in the woods is too great a factor. A mast that weighed in, when new, after a winter in a dry shed, might easily be a couple of pounds lighter by spring and be thrown out. Circumference measurements at three or four stations should be able to control the situation. Aluminum fittings should be barred. They disintegrate without warning, especially on salt water, and are a menace.

It might interest the reader to know that a resolution to empower a special committee to formulate rules to strengthen masts, was submitted to the membership, by ballot, and overwhelmingly voted down. Except for the length, most everything connected with spars and rigging has always been optional. Star members resent anything that appears to be an attempt to infringe upon their liberty. They feel that the leeways allowed in the past were responsible for the continued development of the Star class. For years Star members have borne the brunt of expense and criticism, connected with experimenting with various ideas to improve one-design racing. Once the idea was perfected, other classes have copied it It is nothing new to them and they do not give a hoot in hell about outside criticism. The Star owner feels that if he wishes to take the risk of losing his stick, that that is his business and his only. This and the fact that Star members make their own rules, and do not have them made by a small group of officers, is something that the outsider does not, and probably never will, understand.

Time cures all evils. It will not be long, I believe, before the buggy whip mast and aluminum fittings die a natural death. In the average series there is at least one good hard blow or squall. Those who gamble on light air and light rigs, will soon get sick of seeing the point score, which they built up in four races, thrown into the ash can on Black Thursday. I do not mean by dismastings, which are really infrequent, but by other troubles resulting from too light and fragile equipment. Remember that the great majority of Star owners have never lost a flexible mast, the writer among them.

Again let me impress it upon the reader that flexible spars are not a crackbrain contrivance. The art of draft control, by means of spars, may still be in its infancy, but flexible spars, after sixteen years of use, have proven sound in both theory and practice. For yachtsmen in general to close their eyes to anything so basic, is sheer ignorance. I dislike making predictions, but flexible spars are here to stay and will eventually be used by all racing yachts in some form. The word flexible, in some minds, may be synonymous with fragile and that is probably why other classes fear that adopting such spars would involve danger and expense. They should realize that you cannot condemn an idea because a few people have overdone it, to their own detriment. There has never been an injury caused by flexible spars and, properly used, they are an economy. Right now, benefiting from our experience, other classes could adopt flexible spars, under common sense restrictions, which would eliminate everything they fear, thus modernizing their boats. So let us get away from theory and review briefly the practical and proven advantages of draft control by means of spars.

To begin with, a skipper, using rigid spars, is stuck with whatever suit of sails he bends on. No matter how good a weather guesser he may be, that suit of sails can only be really efficient on one point of sailing, either close hauled or free, but never both. He may hold his own with rigid spars on one point of sailing, whichever it happens to be, but the flex ng will run away from him on the other.

When close hauled, for a boat with rigid spars to hold one with flex spars, the wind must be steady and the draft in the former's mainsail must be just right for wind of that velocity. If puffy, the boat with flex spars will gain on every puff or between puffs, as the case may be, since the draft in that sail adjusts itself to the velocity of the wind. If there is a decided change of weather during the race, the skipper with flex spars, regardless of what sail he is using, is in a better position to cope with that change. Furthermore, the skipper with flex spars faces less of a mental hazard in deciding what sails to use. It is an important decision, of course, in championship competition, but it really resolves itself into guessing whether it will be very light going or very heavy. If it's anything between, whichever sail he decides upon will take care of the situation reasonably well.

Then too, flex spars have another advantage that is seldom mentioned. If the sail does not set perfectly or the draft is not just where the skipper would like it, this can be corrected to a great extent. I do not mean that an impossible sail can be made into a perfect one, but minor difficulties can be handled, whereas on rigid spars the sail has to be sent back to the sailmaker to be re-cut.

Next comes the question of economy. With flexible spars, two suits of sails are sufficient. The life of the sail is much longer, because it is not constantly being pulled out. On rigid spars, a drafty sail, after one season, is usually too flat for light air use. That means a new full draft sail the next year, while the flat sails begin to accumulate and are of no use to the owner. I have had drafty flex mainsails, which after three or four years of use, had almost as much draft left in them as when they were new. Assuming even that you lost a mast each year, which is an absurd assumption, still flexible spars would be an economy, since a suit of sails today costs more than twice as much as a mast. As I have explained, however, by using a little common sense, there is no reason why you should ever lose a mast. There is no good reason, therefore, why anyone should hesitate about flexible spars, unless he feels that he does not have sufficient nautical knowledge to deal with this more scientific element of yacht racing.

By the time the 1938 World's Championship was held at San Diego, California, flexible spars were pretty much in general use throughout the world. It was a series marked by very light air. This time, Pimm, with the same team of von Hutschler and Weise, was not to be denied. While the German boat won the title, it did not run away from the rest of the field, as it had done the previous year. Harry Nye, who seemed to be more proficient in the art of spar flexing than anyone else in the western hemisphere, won the first and last race and was only beaten by two points. Those two, however, had a big edge on the rest. Pimm was in the money every day and Harry's Gale only missed once. Jim Cowie and Niles Martin managed to squeeze in a first and second respectively, in the third race, while the two leaders were having a private scrap of their own. Otherwise the series was pretty cut and dried, except that it proved that von Hutschler was not invincible.

A horrible thing occurred in the second race. The power boat that was supposed to shift the home stakeboat for the finish (it should have been done for the first round) failed to show up. Pimm won by a minute and a half, so there was no question about that. Then all hell broke loose. Some boats passed between the committee boat and the stakeboat, some just left the stakeboat on the proper hand, as per instructions, and others did both, crossing one way and then swinging around and crossing the other. Poor Pop Corry, who was I.R.C. chairman, almost had kittens. It was impossible to keep track of what was going on. By rights, the race should have been called no contest and been re-sailed. It was feared, however, that such action might cause international complications, as a visitor was the winner. The contestants were most cooperative and agreed that the best plan was simply to take each boat's time, as it first crossed the line, regardless of which side of the stakeboat it passed It was not what the writer would consider a legal solution, in fact compromise decisions of that nature are all wrong, but it in no way affected the final results.

The big cup made its first trip across the Atlantic and was raced for at Kiel, as the clouds of war began to gather on the horizon. Once again it was Pimm, but this time by a more decisive margin. Straulino, of the Italian navy, was runner-up, ten points behind von Hutschler, and another German entry, Dr. Hanson, of the local Kiel fleet, was third. Wege-forth, 1937 champion, was the best among the U.S.A. entries, being a poor fourth, twenty-five points behind the winner.

The series was sailed under very trying conditions. Rumors of war caused quite a number of scheduled entries to withdraw at the last moment. There were several disqualifications, described by an eye witness, as resulting from fouls of the most flagrant sort—skippers taking wild, crazy chances. This was probably due to the nervous strain under which many were laboring. After a knock down and drag out opening race, calms made two double headers necessary. Without the last double header, the series never would have been finished, for the Holland, British, French and American entries received notices from their consulates to leave for home immediately. German and Italian skippers and crews were under orders to report to their units, but given a forty-eight hour leave to complete the series. It is a great pity that Europe's first World's Championship had to be raced under such conditions.

From an account written by Elizabeth Miller (now Mrs. Robin) the final reception was something never to be forgotten She states, in part, "It was also the hour of realization that we are, and always will be, an association of people who admit no prejudices and who stay until the dark hours strike for the sake of sportsmanship." Outside communications were cut off, cables were not accepted and telephone service was discontinued, but the Star class stayed to the bitter end. Many present were already in uniform. Toasts were drunk with solemn eyes, and friends, who within a short time, might be facing each other on the battlefield, parted with unspoken thoughts in their hearts

Everyone was unanimous in their praise of the courtesy and hospitality which was extended impartially to all visitors.

As might be expected of so methodical a nation, arrangements for handling the event were perfect down to the smallest detail. There is one thing which must be said of the German and Italian fleets before the war. To them rules were something to be observed and carried out to the Nth degree. They did not just scan through them, as do fleets in so many localities, and then promptly forget what they are supposed to do. The fleets of those two countries, and it was more or less characteristic of all European nations, always filed their forms on time and made them out properly. We never had the slightest bit of trouble with them. There was never any excuse about not understanding instructions because they were in English, because they put men in charge of such matters that could read and write English.

The one discordant note was struck at the annual meeting. It was the aftermath of a rhubarb, which had been brewing since spring, between Hubbard's South Coast Co.· and the measurement committee. The two could not see eye to eye as to the proper interpretation of a limitation rule governing the contour of the hull. It was much too technical and complicated for me to attempt to explain. The governing committee was obliged to step in, in an effort to adjust the matter, as there was much to be said for both sides. It was at about this time that the U.S. entries were leaving for Germany. Barney Lehman, who was employed by South Coast and generally recognized as its delegate at large, stopped in at the central office, while passing through New York, and had lunch with me. He had been instructed to bring the matter before the meeting. I asked him not to, as it was practically ironed out in a manner that would satisfy Hubbard. It was much too involved to attempt to discuss with delegates who spoke different languages.

Although officers were being elected by ballot, the annual meeting still had the power to amend rules. Enrique Conill, vice-president, was to have been chairman, but he, as well as all French continental entries, were ordered at the last moment not to leave the country. Pop was the I.R C. chairman, which was all right, but the meeting made him chairman of the meeting and that was all wrong. He was not an executive officer. Some delegate, I believe from Holland, brought up this measurement problem. Barney must have discussed this, as he was racing in Holland the week before and no other Europeans knew anything about it. Everyone began to shout at Pop in half a dozen languages. A resolution was introduced to do away with all measuring rules. Pop, who had no idea what it was all about, heard everyone shout, believed that some sort of motion had been carried and so ruled. Most of those there did not know what it was all about either. The one who saved the day was von Hutschler, who was acting as secretary. The minutes he sent in were so garbled that the G.C. could not make any sense out of them. Obviously that was intentional, as Walter can write English perfectly It gave us the out we needed. We quoted a few lines of that indecipherable jargon and stated that, as much as we regretted it, whatever amendment had been passed was all Greek to us and we could do nothing about it. Actually we did not know what it was at the time. There was never any repercussion. The whole thing had been adjusted and the few who did know what they had voted for, probably realized what a crazy thing it was. Imagine any sort of racing class without measurement rules!

There are many stories floating about after every World's Championship, but probably never were there quite as many as after that one. Most were of a pretty serious nature, among them, however, were some amusing ones Hitler had invited Pop to be in a parade to be held at Berlin and, war or no war, Pop was determined to go. If he had done so, he most likely would be there yet. Liz and the others had to practically drag him out of Germany He had converted all his dollars into marks, so when he reached Norway he did not have a red cent. The border was closed and no country would cash his marks He went over in the bridal suite, as a guest of the North German Lloyd and came back on a tramp in what amounted to steerage.

It is said that at one party, in a private home, Pop shocked all the guests by asking for butter. There was a dead silence. Then the hostess, a most gracious lady, called the butler. The shades were drawn. She went to the safe, worked the combination and produced one small pat. By so doing she risked being confined in a cencentration camp for the duration.

All foreign Stars reached their home ports safely. Those that went overland by trailer, were given a military escort to make sure that they would have no trouble in crossing. The American Stars were put on fishing boats and sent to Norway, from whence they were eventually shipped to the U.S. on a tramp steamer. The World's Championship trophy was salvaged by von Hutschler. He got out on the last steamer that left Norway before all ports were closed—so again the Star class was lucky, for otherwise we would never have seen the trophy again. Some may wonder why it came back to America, since von Hutschler won it that year. The rules provide that the same fleet cannot hold the event two years in a row. That was one little item the Germans must have overlooked, as it would have been very simple to have had him transfer to another German fleet. Under the circumstances, however, the place had to be determined by the total point score for the past three years—and there is where Wegforth's fourth place counted. It gave San Diego enough points to get the 1940 series.

Once again the title event went back to the west coast of North America, where it remained for two years. In 1940 the Cowie brothers, sailing Rambunctious, were the winners. They startled the Star world with a big roached mainsail, the like of which had never been seen before. The sailmakers had sworn on a stack of Logs (the Log being the Star owner's bible) that the length of the battens would always govern the roach. They had assured us that that it would be impossible to make a mainsail with an excessive roach, because it would collapse. Well Cowie's sail did collapse—but what of it? It collapsed each time the boom crossed the cockpit, but all Jim had to do was give the boom a shake and it flipped right back into position again. That sail threw a bomb shell into camp. Some rule had to be adopted, and quickly, to prevent that sort of thing. There were many suggestions, but we finally came up with an across sail maximum measurement. This was taken from a mid-point between head and tack and head and clew. The sail is measured on the floor, with the wrinkles brushed out, but not stretched. It is not a too accurate measurement. Some day we may devise a better method of governing both roach and draft. For the present it at least serves the purpose, as we care nothing about a slight variation of an inch or two.

The 1940 series was a three way battle between Jim Cowie, Bob White and Woodie Pirie, who finished within three points of each other in the order named. Needless to say, with Europe at war, no entries came from across the Atlantic. Freddie de Marigny, representing Nassau, made his international debut, a none too impressive one, as he finished last. But after that, did he improve—and fast! Coached by Walter von Hutschler for a few months, he proved to be an apt pupil. From an also-ran, within a year, he moved right up among the top flight skippers of the class.

Here is a bit of news, which very few members of the Star class even knew. Walter von Hutschler would have been second vice-president of the I.S.C.Y.R.A. in 1940, except for the fact that a whole flock of votes for him came in more than a month after the ballots were counted and the results of the election announced. Some may think that there should have been an extension of time, because of the war, but there were votes for von Hutschler received in time, and so would the rest had they been mailed in time. There is seldom a year in which there are not political situations in some part of the world If the counting of the annual ballots was postponed for such causes, the results of the elections never would be known.

When the 1941 World's Championship was sailed at Los Angeles, the United States was not yet at war, but everyone knew that it was simply a matter of time before it would be. Many of the younger skippers had been called into selective service. Had it not been for Charlie de Cardenas, the event would not have been international as no other entries came from outside North America proper. The fact is there were only thirteen entries, the smallest field since 1923. We were already cut off from most of the European countries. Italy, somehow managed to send in its 1941 dues. We also had an application for charter from a new fleet in Austria and a request for six numbers. Those were the last communications that came through from any of the warring countries on continental Europe.

George Fleitz won his first gold Star that year for the Los Angeles Harbor fleet, the old fleet having resumed its former name. Harry Nye was runner-up and Barney Lehman, in spite of one disqualification, placed third. Rascal, with which Frank Campbell had been winning everything in sight for a couple of seasons, along the Eastern seaboard, did not seem to take kindly to the long Pacific swells. Frank brought her in fourth, fifteen points behind the winner, and another myth about a so-called "unbeatable million dollar Star" exploded. That being the second consecutive year the event had been held in the fifth district, it had to shift location according to rules. Harry Nye, on aggregate points for the past two years, took the event to Lake Michigan. No eligible fleet had competed for three years.

So ended twenty-three years of between war racing in America. Europe, which became Star minded in the early thirties, had only enjoyed eight years of it and the progress made by European skippers in such a short time was really remarkable. Germany's Star supremacy was from 1936 to 1939 inclusive Except for Bischoff's Olympic victory, ironically enough, Germany's other major Star honors were won by proxy, that is by a Brazilian sailing with the Hamburger fleet.

CHAPTER XII

THROUGH WORLD WAR TWO

COULD THE STAR SURVIVE another world war? Stars were valued possessions. They would not just be abandoned to rot on the beach, which had been the fate of so many small one-designs twenty-five years before. Owners would store them away carefully, with an eye to the future. It was safe to assume that only a very small percentage would be destroyed as a result of the war. The membership was our real concern. If the war lasted many years, and it seemed like an endless one, we would have to deal with an entire new generation of owners. Could the spirit of the Star class ever be re-kindled? Could we ever weave these new owners into the smooth running world-wide organization of the past?

The association was already divided in half, geographically and numerically. Then Pearl Harbor was bombed and all our far east fleets destroyed. Aside from North America proper, a fleet in Cuba and one in Venezuela was all that was left.

Enrique Conill, European father of the Stars, had been missing for over two years. Last reported in invaded France, no one knew whether he was alive or dead. Adrian Iselin had replaced him as first vice-president. Then came the hardest blow of all. Samson Smith, our international secretary, followed in the footsteps of his illustrious forefathers (including Admiral Sampson, of Spanish war fame) and joined the navy. Parkman Yachts was sold. The days of plenty were over and the I.S.C.Y.R.A. was on its own.

This seems like the logical place to interrupt my story and tell the reader what Sam Smith did for the Star class. Everyone knows that he was primarily responsible for starting Star fleets on small inland lakes, thereby creating a fertile field for future development. But he did much more than that. It has never been hinted at in print and few, if any, realize how much Sam contributed toward the growth and prosperity of the Star class.

When he heard that Joe Parkman was going to retire, Sam bought the business lock, stock and barrel. He wanted to keep the last of the popular priced Stars on the market. He also wished to prove that one did not have to own an expensive custom built Star to win. That idea was once again curtailing Star production in the U.S. Sam never made a nickel out of Parkman Yachts, in fact he lost, but he accomplished what he set out to do for the Star class.

Yes, I was involved in a minor way. I held a small block of stock and received little more than a nominal salary to handle sales. An inquiry addressed to the I.S.C.Y.R.A. was never solicited. This was not mentioned at the time, as no one would have believed it. Our best friends thought that Sam and I were taking advantage of our association jobs to make money. If so much space is devoted to Parkman Yachts, it is because those five years were crucial ones.

Sam dictated Parkman Yacht policy. He did quite a bit of advertising and exhibited a Star for several years in the New York motor boat show. Those who had given up building Stars, evidently thought Sam was coining money, as they started in again. There was a wave of competitive Star building and more Stars were built in the U.S. than during any other five years. Each new Star meant a new member and the dues began to roll in.

Sam made the first I S.C.Y.R.A central office possible. He sublet half Parkman Yachts' office space to the association at a low rental He allowed his office staff, of four, to spend about eighty per cent of their time on I.S.C.Y.R.A. work. That was when running the association became a big business in itself The point had been reached where the Star class could not otherwise have been held together. Because of the small operating cost, the I S.C.Y.R.A. showed a big profit at the end of each fiscal year. That was when it built up the surplus that carried it through the war and still remains as a nest egg. Sam's loss was the association's gain. He really contributed more, in his indirect way, to the I.S.C.Y.R.A.'s future security than any other one individual, yet it went unnoticed and unappreciated.

Now let us continue with the conditions brought about by world war two. One fleet secretary after another was called to the colors. He would turn his portfolio over to someone else, who would soon follow suit. It became impossible to keep records. Finally the majority of the fleets in the U.S. followed the suggestion of making one of the fair sex responsible for the bookwork, regardless of membership qualifications. After that a semblance of order was restored.

Boys, old men and noncombatants strived valiantly to keep the fleets in North America alive, and in most cases, were successful. Yachtsmen were quickly developing into good naval officers Washington wanted small boat racing encouraged, provided it did not hinder the war effort People realized that it was a good training school and also provided mental relaxation for those not in uniform. This time public opinion was on our side and that helped a lot.

While necessary restrictions only put a few fleets completely out of commission, they affected almost every fleet on coastal waters. Unable to sail over their regular waters, many fleets were forced to race in small narrow bays and harbors, which in normal times would not have been considered fit for a course.

The greatest trouble was caused by channels and mined areas within the territory of a given fleet, which could only be crossed at certain times under specified conditions. Members of the same fleet, located on opposite shores and adjacent harbors, could not race against each other at will. This gave such groups an excuse to apply for a separate charter, which was usually granted, thereby creating a precedent. Western Long Island Sound is probably the best example. The territory of that one fleet was divided among three. Rules have always required that Stars on the same body of water, which normally race together in open regattas, be in one fleet. From then on, however, charters were granted on the slightest pretext and without regard to distances It is difficult to express an opinion, as some of these offshoot fleets benefited and some did not. Nevertheless, such subdivisions are contrary to the intent of the rules and this practice should be curbed before it is overdone.

During the war years, however, the Star class had a number of lucky breaks. The first came when it was able to obtain a smaller central office in the same building, as office space was then almost impossible to find. This time the I.S.C.Y.R.A. signed the lease and what had been Parkman Yachts became the subtenant. The writer was general manager of the old plant, renamed Star Marine, and Tom Parkman remained as superintendent. Although the parent company, which had bought a number of small factories to convert to war work, had half a floor of office space downtown and an office for me, it allowed me to stay in the I.S.C.Y.R.A. office and paid half the rent. That was due to the influence of Claud Launay, a member of the Paris fleet. It not only helped financially, but enabled me to keep a weather eye on Star work.

It was about that time that Miss Edith Glass came to the I.S.C.Y.R.A. direct from stenographic school. Between us we did the work of most of the Star officers and committees. Once Star Marine was converted over to making life boat accessories, supervising that work was easy. It was second nature and I could do it while thinking of other things. Of course I no longer had time to sit and chat with visiting Star members. The volume was light and Miss Glass was able to learn the routine work from the bottom up. The reader, however, must not get an idea that this routine work was simple To properly record a member involved eight, or more, operations, including the cutting of four coupons from the registration form and sending them to four different departments. That was only one of many routine jobs and one mistake in the system would mix the records all up. Today Miss Glass is corresponding secretary of the I.S.C.Y.R.A. and a most efficient one.

There were some Star officials that did double duty. Charlie Lucke was one. He was in the navy, but at night continued to hold down his job as editor. Much of this was probably done by his wife Barbara, who was just as good a Star skipper as her husband. News was so scarce, however, that Starlights skipped its first monthly issue in nineteen years. For a couple of years there were only seven or eight issues annually. The Log was already in the hands of the printer, when the war broke out, but after that it was cut to the bone—a couple of pictures, cheap paper and only absolutely necessary information. The Association lost money for the first time and adopted a policy of strict economy, only providing members with such essential service as could be expected under existing conditions.

Two special classes of memberships were created for the duration; life and service. Life memberships provided a working capital for 1943 and saved us from dipping into our reserve. While this created a liability of a sort, that would have to be taken care of somehow eventually, it answered our immediate needs. Service memberships enabled those in the armed forces to receive Star literature at about cost. They wanted the Star class to survive, in order to have something to come back to. As a matter of fact, service dues were largely responsible for our being able to carry on during the war.

Some, mostly outsiders, thought that the boys in uniform should have been sent Star literature gratis. To have done that would have taken practically all our invested surplus. That was profit earned during the good years and made possible by dues from Star owners all over the world. It was their money. Because the central office and most of our officers were in the U.S. did not give us the right to spend it only on those in the service of our own country. During the war H.R.H. Eugenio di Savoia and Admiral Goetting were re-elected vice and rear commodores respectively each year. Italian and German fleets were granted leave of absence and retained the same status as those in the allied countries. Had headquarters been elsewhere, we in the U.S. would have expected like courtesy. The I.S.C.Y.R.A. is an international sports organization and its policy has always been to show the same fairness to friend or foe alike.

At the 1942 annual meeting in Chicago it was agreed that no changes would be made in the rules until the war was over and a representative number of members were again able to express their opinions. That meeting also voted away its own power to pass amendments. From then on the meeting was only to act as a clearing house and sift out crack-brained ideas. If a proposed amendment was approved by the meeting, it was to be submitted to the membership on the annual ballot. Just to make sure that a change could only be made by a substantial majority, Don Bergman's suggestion that a two third vote be required, was passed. The meeting further voted to discontinue the point system, for deciding the locality of the World's Championship, until transportation facilities became reasonably normal again and other continents could send entries. It was clearly understood, however, that this should not prevent Charlie de Cardenas from taking the next regular World's Championship to Havana. Win, lose or draw, before the aggregate point system was suspended, Havana was entitled to the next regular series.

Because of the foregoing, the '43, '44 and '45 meetings amounted to little more than informal discussions and practically no business was transacted. The annual meeting still had the power to elect commodores and in '45, perhaps because it had nothing much else to do, it ran amuck and elected a whole flock of vice and rear commodores. A limit was placed upon such officers the following year, otherwise commodores would have been worth a dime a dozen.

One must not get the impression that only a very few Stars were built during the war. On the contrary, there was scarcely a country in which some were not produced. In Italy nearly one hundred new Stars were built for Lake Como and about forty new ones in invaded France, for what had been the Paris fleet. These boats were raced under local numbers, usually prefixed by an "O." We knew nothing about this, of course, until the war was over. Through the efforts of such loyal members as Messers. Chambrieres, Whitechurch, Peytel, Fassini-Camossi, Tay, Poggi and others, whose names escape me at the moment, records were kept of these boats, and local Star organizations of a sort were preserved. Most of the time they were not able to contact each other and their work made post-war reorganization much easier.

There was quite a bit of Star activity in neutral European countries. We knew that new boats were being built in Sweden, because of radiograms received requesting numbers. The same was true of Switzerland, where Star racing was being revived. Number taxes could not be paid, but fleet secretaries, in many instances, opened local bank accounts and deposited collections, which were to be transmitted later. The most of these European fleets, however, were only token ones. By this I mean that they consisted of only three un-named members, just to keep their charters active. The most outstanding example was the Salamis fleet of Greece. Its three members actually paid their dues throughout the war. Niarcos, who had an office in New York, saw to that. The three members were King Paul, Queen Fredricka and Niarcos.

The one exception was the fifteenth district, made up of fleets in Spain and Portugal. In the past those two countries had shown very little interest in the Star class. In 1941, however, they showed such activity and started so many new fleets, that this new district was formed and it was the only one in Europe that held Blue Star Championships during the war years. Because of their bulk, it was impossible to send regular forms by air mail and everything had to be handled by letter. While the records were a little garbled, those boys paid their dues and managed somehow to get the money through to the central office.

When North Africa was liberated, Star owners in Algeria and Morocco immediately requested a separate district of their own. They were on a different continent from the fleets in the south of France and entitled to it. The sixteenth district, with seven fleets, therefore, became official in 1944 and Tunisia became a part of it later. It started under difficulties. It had Stars, but could not get new sails or fittings.

After the attack on Pearl Harbor, all Hawaiian yachting was suspended. The membership, however, remained intact and corresponded quite frequently with the association. Unfortunately that did not apply to the rest of the Pacific theater of war, where our loss, especially in membership, was catastrophic.

Always small in fleets, although wide-spread in area, the Eleventh District was practically wiped out. District secretary Spackman, of Australia, and his assistant Jangelie, of Java, were lost during the early stages of the war. Melbourne was the only fleet left. The entire section, from Australia to the mainland of Asia, was like a rudderless ship, until Barton Harvey took over. He was gradually able to restore order to the chaos that had existed.

The Japanese carried off the best Stars at Manila, no trace of which was ever found. Among them was Herc Atkin's Jubilee, a winner of the Cup of Cuba, Atlantic Coast and four Sound Championships. Herc was confined in a concentration camp. Jim Rockwell, who had represented the same fleet in several World's Championships since 1927, was imprisoned in the office of the Manila Electric Co. Five G.I.'s launched a Star in the dead of night and escaped. These and many other rumors reached our ears, which later proved to be surprisingly correct.

Eleven British yachtsmen were racing Stars (not new ones) at Shanghai and were organizing a fleet when the war broke out. That is indeed a lost fleet, as nothing has ever been heard about those Stars or their owners. Fred Tracy, the most notable of all isolated members, built the first Star in China. This was Me Sing (meaning American Star) It made the front page even before it was completed. In the 20's a typhoon leveled the shipyard at Hong Kong, while the boat was still in frames, but the embryonic Star was unscathed. Fred returned to the States some time before the war, but the whereabouts of Me Sing is unknown. The same is true of two isolated Stars that were at Ceylon. When peace was declared, the Yokohama Bay fleet was no longer in existence. In other words, World War Two extinguished all Star activity in the Far East.

The forty new Stars built at Rio de Janeiro were the last of the war babies. The fleet received its charter in 1945 and the push and go of those Brazilian yachtsmen sparked Star development in South America. Lake Maracaibo was actually the first fleet on that continent. Made up of English and Americans in the oil business, it was very active locally. Most of its Stars were and still are the ones I helped Rudy Cunard collect in 1930 and they were not new then. The Titanic efforts of Chester Crebbs, a most efficient district officer, failed to awaken native Venezuelan interest, much less that of the countries to the south.

To go back still further, the first Star in South America was the Fay, named after the Federation Argentina of Yachting. Its launching at Buenos Aires was witnessed and cheered by thousands. Then all interest in the boat waned. Eight Stars were later imported from Finland. For some reason (probably club politics) the owners would not play ball with the I.S.C.Y.R.A. and remained as an outlaw group until quite recently.

The World's Championship was not interrupted by the war. It was continued as a skipper series, but that is a story in itself and will be told later. The Canadian northwest held its Blue Star event in the same manner during the war years. The twelfth inland lake trailer district tried to revive its championship in a similar way in 1945, but was only able to complete two fluky races on Lake Sunapee.

The 1942 Mid-Winters was the last of the Silver Star title events. The Cup of Cuba was won by Charlie de

Cardenas that year. That was fortunate, as it was able to remain in Havana until competed for again six years later. U.S. entries were more than lucky in getting their Stars to Havana and safely back home. Just at that time German U-Boats began to prey upon shipping along the Atlantic coast of North America. The sinkings became so numerous that the Spring Championship, scheduled for Nassau, had to be cancelled. New Orleans, which held the event on alternate years also cancelled for the duration.

The championship of the newly formed Fifteenth District, composed of fleets in neutral Spain and Portugal, was the only major series held during the war years, which was not affected in any manner. Skippers sailed their own Stars in the Atlantic Coast and Great Lakes Championships. The same applied to the latter's Green Star novice title. Entries dwindled and were mostly confined to nearby fleets. The few other annual fixtures that were still being attempted, were held under trying handicaps.

Adrian Iselin won the Atlantic Coast Blue Star in 1945. That was a feat of historic importance. His only other Blue Star was won twenty years before, the first time that event was ever held. Furthermore he won it with the same Star, Number 202, the Ace. The Ace is now entering its thirtieth season of racing and still going strong—so is Adrian. That shows what can be done with a Star, if properly taken care of.

Out of respect for George Corry, the office of commodore remained vacant until the end of 1944. Like his famous father, Adrian belongs to the immortals of yachting. He was elected commodore for 1945 and served for two years.

The pearl jubilee Log was published before the fate of Enrique Conill was known. When he was finally able to get away from invaded France, he eventually found himself aboard a steamer with a bunch of Spanish Star members. They recognized him from his photo in the Log. That was the first time Enrique saw the thirtieth anniversary Log, which had been dedicated to him. He became commodore in 1947 and also held office for two years—but that is getting a little ahead of our story.

When the war ended in Europe, the central office was swamped with requests for the most recent Log. Many old members, who had been out of touch with developments for seven years, wanted to bring themselves up-to-date. That sudden termination of hostilities had not been figured upon and our surplus of the 1945 issue was exhausted within a couple of months.

The I.S.C.Y R.A. had managed somehow to pull through five difficult years. Insofar as work and complicated problems were concerned, however, those years were child's play in comparison to the reconstruction period that followed.

CHAPTER XIII

THE FOUR SKIPPER SERIES

Due TO TRANSPORTATION DIFFICULTIES, the World's Championship was held as a skipper series four times. It was the only way it could have been held during those war years. Skippers brought their own sails and used them on whatever local Star they happened to draw for each race. Early in the spring of 1942, we knew that shipping priorities and gasoline rationing would prevent entries from taking their own Stars. To ease the minds of a few, who were skeptical about the patriotic angle, we wrote to Washington and were advised that such races would not interfere with the war effort. Then we went ahead with our plans.

The Star class was lucky again. Harry Nye had brought the '42 Gold Star event to Chicago on aggregate points. It was probably the only spot in the world, at that time, where enough Stars were in commission to make such a skippers' series possible. Furthermore, there were no special navigation restrictions on Lake Michigan to seriously bother us. Much thought was given to the method of drawing for boats, in order to eliminate the element of luck insofar as possible. Since the system devised, to the best of the writer's knowledge, has never been used by any other class, it should be described.

The required number of Stars were divided into two groups, A and B, the former being presumably the faster boats. A couple of spares were provided in each case. This had to be done by a local committee, familiar with the reputation of each boat. Age could not be the basis, as some old Stars are in better condition and reputed to be faster than new ones. A line was drawn through the middle of the entry list, which is printed in the numerical order of the skipper's own sails A coin was tossed to determine whether the upper or lower half should draw the A boats for the first race. The second day it was reversed. For the first four races, therefore, each entry drew an A boat twice.

For the fifth and final race, the entries were re-grouped. The half having the highest total point score became the championship division and were entitled to A boats. Hence the leaders did not have to suffer any real or fancied handicap, by having to draw for a boat of questionable reputation. The other half was known as the eliminated division and drew for the B boats. None of them had a chance of placing among the first three anyway.

Drawings were at ten o'clock a. m. daily. No one could sail the same boat twice, nor his own, if in the pool. If either happened on the last draw, then the boat was exchanged with the first skipper that drew and so on down.

Those four skipper series proved beyond the shadow of a doubt that winning depended upon the man and not the boat The same skipper did just about as well with a B as he did with an A boat. If the boat played any part, it was a negative one. You could not blame the skipper, if something broke, for the condition of another man's property. Sails were a factor, but good skippers always have good sails. Ability counted and anybody in the know could come pretty near naming the winner in advance, as usual. If a dark horse came into the picture, the records show that he was a potential champion, just coming into his own and continued his winning ways after the World's Championship was re-

stored to normalcy. Breakdowns and disqualifications affected the score now and then, but skippers run into the same
hard luck when racing their own Stars.

To those from coastal areas, Chicago was like old times.
The streets were brightly lighted at night. If there was a
food or gas shortage we did not notice it. We spent a glorious carefree week in Chicago and the war seemed very far
away. Headquarters were at the Columbia Yacht Club, a
converted lake steamer, tied up to one of the municipal docks.
It was only a short distance from the Blackstone, where most
of us stayed.

I was there as a contestant, with my wife as crew. That
was a welcome change We did poorly, but the gout and not
the boats I drew, was my alibi. When I placed in the middle
of the first race, I only had it in one foot. The following day
it was in both and I could not enter the next two. We tried
the fourth one, sailed in a thick fog. We had a backstay
jamb at the start. I could not get up and help. To avoid a
foul, I tried to go about without headway, and put the boat
in irons. Once we got started it went like the very devil, but
we were far behind and only caught six boats. We only started
in two races out of the five, but at that we did not finish last
in the series.

That Star was one of Nye's Gales, later re-named Gusty,
and I am not apt to forget it. Because of my feet, I could
not get out of the cockpit. A young fellow had to bend on and
take off the sails for me. The bolts, which held the floor
boards, had never been filed flush with the nuts. They
chewed off the entire seat of my pants and shorts, leaving
nothing but bare skin. I went back to the Blackstone on
crutches, with a sweater tied around my waist backward, as
a rear guard Soaking wet, we waited in the lobby for an
elevator, with pools of water spreading around our feet. It
was at the height of the cocktail hour, but no one seemed
to mind They just smiled and tiptoed around the puddles.
We were not told how to dress, or use the garbage elevator,
when going to a race and return. That is the nice thing about
staying at a hotel with a long established reputation. It

knows when to make exceptions, without fear of criticism, and does not pester its guests with small-minded regulations.

Speaking of correct attire, Ben Weston once told me a true story worth repeating, although it had nothing to do with Chicago. A prominent movie actor was strutting through the yacht club, which he had recently joined, all dolled up like Mrs. Astor's pet horse. Ben was a very good friend of his and thought he would appreciate a little well-meant advice.

"You should have black buttons on your yachting coat," Ben said, "only paid hands wear brass ones."

"Brass hell!', exclaimed the indignant actor, "those buttons are made of twenty-four carat gold."

Getting back to the series, Sterling Potter, of Santa Monica, won the first two races. That means, of course, that he sailed an A boat in one and a B boat in the other. He also won the last race, but not the series. Harry Nye, the odds-on favorite, annexed his first Gold Star by his consistent performance. In the fourth race, Nye was second, but Potter fell back to ninth, and that decided it. Tom Scripps, representing San Diego, was third in the series. Paul Smart won that fourth race and was the only other winner besides Potter and Nye. The racing was rather cut and dried. Except for the foregoing, there were very few highlights afloat.

Buddy Ibsen, another Santa Monica Star skipper and former district officer, served on the I R.C. by day and played in his own show at night. The theater was only a block from the Blackstone. He reserved a block of seats and the Star group saw the rollicking comedy, as his guests, on the night of the first race.

The stellar role at Chicago, insofar as class history is concerned, was played by Charlie de Cardenas. His entry kept the event international. His son, Carlos, Jr., was the youngest crew that ever competed for the title. Charlie suggested continental vice presidents that year, but action was deferred for the duration. The series was required to leave the continent of North America the following year, but conditions made that impossible. The meeting, therefore, voted to discontinue series points, as of 1943. Charlie, however, accum-

ulated enough points at Chicago, plus those of the two previous years, to take the World's Championship to Havana,
as soon as transportation would permit.

It should be explained that Cuba was then within the
territory of a South American Star district Cuba and the
Bahamas were not shifted to the Third District, located in
the southeastern part of the United States, until a couple
of years after the World's Championship was sailed at Havana.
The Seventh District originally consisted of fleets in the
West Indies and one at Maracaibo, Venezuela. Eventually
most of these small island fleets folded and the Star class
began to spread in South America. Had Havana and Nassau
been shifted before the Star class began to develop on the
mainland, there would have been no Seventh District left.
I just want to make it clear that Havana was legally entitled
to hold the World's Championship in 1946 and that it was
not due to any technicality.

The late John Pirie handled all advance arrangements
and did the lion's share of the work on the I.R.C. John,
although better known as his brother's crew, sailed Stars
since he was a little boy and was himself among the best
skippers in the class. It was our first skipper series and had
it not been for John's efficient management, it could have
easily resulted in a terrible mess.

The 1942 World's Championship was the last that Pop
Corry attended. His heart was light and gay. He enjoyed
every minute of it. Pop was the official chairman of the I.R.C.
and spent every afternoon on the committee boat. Dressed in
his full commodore's regalia, he was at every entertainment
and danced until the wee hours. The next morning he was
the first at the Columbia Y.C., where he sat and sipped black
coffee, while awaiting the draw. I am sure it was the sort
of farewell that he would have wanted.

In 1943 the G.C. had to select a fleet equipped to hold
a skipper series. It could not ask Chicago to do so twice in
a row The Great South Bay was willing and seemed to be
the best bet, although it did not have enough Stars. There
were several neighboring fleets, who were able to get suf-

ficient gas for a short haul, that trailed over one or two Stars each. Jack Wood, then a lieutenant in the Coast Guard, towed down two more from the academy at New London. They saved the day. At that we were always skating on mighty thin ice.

It was no easy matter to divide the few available Stars into A and B groups. To make it worse, the local boats had never raced against a number of the imported ones, nor had some of the latter competed against each other. In many cases there were no comparative records to go by and it was all pretty much guess work. Horace Havemeyer's Gull, formerly Frank Campbell's Rascal, was a real poser. Its phenomenal record on the Sound and the fact that Horace had won the Atlantic Coast title with it that year, seemed to place the boat in a class by itself. The Coe brothers, of West Jersey, drew Gull for the first race and solved the problem very quickly. In a tune up spin, they carried away the mast before the race started. That left us with only one spare.

Headquarters was at the Bay Shore Y.C. Regardless of the wind, all races were started about one hundred yards off shore. That was because the committee boat, Bill Picken's cruiser, could not obtain any more gas and had to stay put. Jack Wood's little power boat, of course, was not rationed. Otherwise, I do not see how the marks could have been placed. So again the Coast Guard came to the rescue. Adrian Iselin was to have been chairman of the I.R.C. He was called home, due to an emergency, the night before the opening race. Ted Everitt, the only other major officer present, automatically became chairman. The other four I.R.C. members had to be elected from the floor. Around half a dozen Stars were owned by competing skippers. Since they were not allowed to sail their own boat, or the same one twice, that complicated the draw daily. Yes, there were many obstacles to surmount that year, but they managed it somehow.

Once more I was there as a contestant and beginning to like it. I doubt if most contestants realize how lucky they are. When a race is finished, their worries are usually over until the next morning. An official, however, is always on call. His troubles and responsibilities start the day before the first race and are not over until the loose ends are cleaned up, the day following the last race, and he boards the train for home.

Bay Shore was no longer the quaint little rural village of my boyhood. A few things, however, remained unchanged. Some of the party boats, among those at the dock, were the same. Engines had been installed and spars removed, but the names and those of their captains (sons and grandsons of the original ones) were the same.

Many of us stayed at the renovated Courtland House, another old landmark. It had a modern ship's bar, where we spent much of our leisure time. One evening we returned with sopping wet sails. It was still raining and there was no place to dry them. The management shooed the regular guests out of the reception room and let us hang them up in there. What more co-operation could one ask?

A dinner at the hotel, the night before the first race, and another at the club, on the last night, were the only formal entertainments. There were some impromptu cocktail parties, of course, but the rest of the time we were on our own. There were no prearranged functions, which we had to rush back and get dressed for after each race. It was a welcome change, which the boys liked—I know that I did. Yes, I raced each day, finished around the middle and that was just about where I belonged.

Charlie de Cardenas was again headline news. With two firsts and a third under his belt, he drew the Star that was leading in the boat score and entered the final race with a three point lead, a heavy favorite. After a reach and a run, he hauled on the wind in third place. The two ahead of him did not have enough points to be dangerous. He elected to follow them up in under the shore. It had paid off on a previous day, but it was clearing and the fitful easterly was getting ready to shift. His real rivals split the moment they rounded and tacked out in the Bay. They held the wind until it died and began to swing clockwise. Charlie did not cover. He sailed into a soft spot, fell back to eleventh and lost both the race and the series.

One of the cardinal principles of yacht racing is to keep between your nearest competitor and the next mark. Charlie did not do it. Charlie was a stranger and could not have been expected to know the weather, but he could have covered the local skipper, Bill Picken, who was behind him. Charlie was inclined to blame the boat for being sluggish in light air, yet that same Star won the boat score two years later, in the lightest of all skipper series. The wind had shifted and, no matter what Star he had drawn, I do not see how he could have extricated himself from the predicament he was in. At that he saved enough points to place third in the series. Always a serious threat, it was the nearest Charlie has ever come to winning a Gold Star.

While the "grandpappy" fleet of them all was dwindling numerically, it still had a wealth of talent. Art Deacon won another world's title for Western Long Island. He did it the hard way, finishing third twice, but never worse than fifth. Art is one of the very few skippers that has ever won the classic by consistent sailing, but without taking a single race.

The late Bill Picken, sailing on his home waters, was runner-up It was the best World's Championship performance of his career. Bill was both mother and father to the Great South Bay fleet. His boathouse and hoist were available to all. Wherever he competed, good old jovial Bill was the life and soul of the party. A Picken Memorial Trophy is now raced for every Labor Day weekend at Bellport, Long Island Because of Bill's popularity, the event always attracts many entries, even from far distant fleets.

Cliff Baker, of Lake Ontario American, crashed into the hall of fame by winning the third race. Cliff is also among the departed. A few years later, having been advised that Star racing was a bit too strenuous, he bought a Six Metre and succumbed to a heart attack at its helm. Cliff was another of those likable fellows. During his Star years he covered a lot of territory representing his fleet, including Cuba and California.

The Rochester skipper made the front page the next day, the day of the big rains, but in quite another way.

Shaving it too close, he slammed broadside into the committee boat, when his keel caught on its anchor cable. Knowing he had fouled, as a number of people had finally pushed him clear, he started to withdraw, but was told to go ahead and race. Cliff was still laughing about it the next morning at breakfast. He could not understand why he had not been disqualified, nor could anyone else. When will committees ever learn to stop being softhearted? It only breeds disregard of rules and subjects them to criticism from the very ones they seek to please.

The 1944 skipper series was again sailed on Lake Michigan. I was not at Chicago that year and, therefore, only have hearsay information about the event. Shore activities were pretty much a replica of 1942 and so, to some extent, were the results.

Once again the same skipper won the first two races, one with an A and one with a B boat, again proving that it is the man and not the boat. In this case it was Gerry Driscoll, of San Diego, who also won another race, but he won the series. With an eight-point lead, he just played it safe on that last blusterous day to make sure of finishing in one piece.

Bob Lippincott was runner-up. The West Jersey skipper was on his way to fame, but attracted very little notice that year. Bert Williams placed third, winning the last race, in which his weight was an advantage. On that final day the Windy City really lived up to its name. There was such a sea that the race was started from the breakwater. Five entries did not even venture forth. The sixth non-starter had already withdrawn from the series.

That was the first year that Watt sails began to attract general attention. Driscoll used them, but Skip Etchells did also, when he made a clean sweep of the five Atlantic Coast championship races. Ed Ketcham duplicated this feat in 1947.

In 1944 occurred the end of an era in the Star class. On a cold, stormy night in early January, our grand old man passed away. Pop had been bedridden for nearly a year, nevertheless, it came as a terrific shock to the whole yachting world. There never has been and there never will be another Pop Corry. The class went into mourning and many displayed a band of black crepe across the Star on their sails.

The commodore must have foreseen the end. Shortly after his death we learned that he had given the Little Dipper away the previous year. The new owner, who was going to condition and race it, generously offered to present it to the association, if the latter paid the yard bills. That was taken care of by small contributions and the overage given to Ma Corry. The Manhasset Bay Yacht Club, located at Port Washington, Long Island, agreed to keep the Little Dipper. It was only fitting that Star. No. 1 should rest at the club, of which Pop was the number one member. The first Star built can be seen there today, where it stands as a tribute to the yachting career of Commodore George A. Corry, the most beloved and never to be forgotten of all Star owners.

The Stamford Yacht Club, which did not have a single Star of its own, was our host for the fourth and last of the skipper series. It was a picturesque headquarters and Stamford gave the boys everything but wind. It was a good thing it was the last series of the sort, as I doubt very much if we could have held another one successfully.

Most of the Stars used were provided by the Central Long Island Sound fleet, although neighboring ones contributed a few. Fearing a shortage, we offered a boat score prize as an incentive, but it did not help very much. Few, if any, name Stars were among those in the pool. No equipment had been replaced for four years and, like the one-horse shay, many of them began to fall apart at once. It could not have been due to inexperienced handling, as the skippers were among the best in the class; nor to wind, since there was none. After each race, a launch from the local shipyard towed away a number of Stars, which had to be repaired. We never knew until the next morning how many of them would be ready and could be drawn for that day.

The war was just over. Gasoline restrictions had been relaxed somewhat, but practically no powerboats were in commission. We were allocated a small Coast Guard boat, without which it would have been almost impossible to manage. There was only one stakeboat available, hence a government buoy had to be used instead of the other. It was no easy matter to establish a standard Star course using a fixed mark. That was a grueling series for the contestants and a nerve-wracking one for the race committee, which never knew where it stood and which taxed its ingenuity to the utmost. Last minute arrangements had to be improvised constantly to make a race possible and to complete the series

Each morning there was a veritable epidemic of complaints about the boats drawn. Some were justifiable and some due to force of habit. The bolt rope of the sail the skipper wanted to use would not fit the grooves. Turnbuckles were frozen and he could not adjust the shrouds. Fair-leaders were stationary and he could not properly trim his jib, etc. The I.R.C. was forced to get tough. If a Star was sailable, the skipper had to do the best he could with it, or stay out of the race. We could not give him another boat, as we had none. The situation was getting out of hand.

There was never enough wind to get any of the scheduled races started until late afternoon and the entries did not get back to their moorings before dark. Had there been a little breeze, the starts would not have been delayed. The I.R.C. had been over-lenient for three years, because of the difficulty a skipper had in getting another's Star ready to race. They were beginning to take advantage of that. When the majority were at the line, a few were always missing. They knew the race would not be started without them and were just taking their own sweet time about coming out Usually the Coast Guard boat had to be sent back to the harbor for them and that took another half hour. Yes, it was high time that that sort of racing came to an end.

Three different skippers won the first three races, namely: de Cardenas, Cowie and Etchells. Burnham took two seconds, otherwise a different skipper was among the first three each of those days and it was anyone's series. On the second evening, the light southerly was steady enough for a windward and leeward course—the only one of the week.

It was overcast on rest day, with a really nice sailing breeze. The I.R C. wanted to hold a race, but the boys were tired and insisted on having the day off. On Friday it was raining and blowing great guns from the east. Ordinarily there would have been a race, as the heavy weather boys have as much right to their weather as the drifters. Considering the condition of the boats and the fact that there were not enough power craft to serve as a rescue squad, it would have been too dangerous to risk. It moderated in the early afternoon, but many of the entries had wandered off and could not be found.

We held a double header the next day, hoping to complete the series on time. The start was bright and early, but after two hours no one had rounded the first mark and the race had to be called off. Stars had to be changed for the afternoon race. A launch was sent back for sandwiches and beer. The I.R.C. did the drawing. A flat calm made it possible for Stars to tie up all around the committee boat. Contestants stepped from one to another, until they found the one they were going to race. Then came hours of waiting. Several times little overshots caused us to start giving signals, but they always died out.

The mooring breeze sprang up even later than usual. The sun was already sinking in the west, when in desperation we gave them a reaching start. The leaders were not quite holding their own with the time limit at the end of the first round, but the wind was freshening somewhat. Through the glasses we were just able to see the first Star round the last turning mark. There was no moon and it was black as pitch. The breeze had just hauled enough to make that last leg a dead beat, instead of a long and short one. We kept our searchlight trained on the line stakeboat. The Coast Guard tied up alongside. Its searchlight was waved vertically to call attention to the line. We had run out of liquor and had to wet our whistles with soda pop. Of course no one swallowed any, just gargled with it. It was a very weird experience. We could not see twenty feet away and did not know what was going on, as the minutes ticked away.

That was the only night finish in the annals of the World's Championship. With five minutes to go, we began shouting through a megaphone, to find out if any Star was within earshot. An answering hail came out of the ebon void. It sounded far away and wanted to know how much time was left.

"About four minutes, can you make it?"

"Yes, I think so."

With more than a minute to spare, Bert Williams' sail cut the beam of our searchlight. A gun barked and the race was official. Malin Burnham flashed across a few moments later, again finishing second. Then came a regular photo finish between Ceb Lee and Skip Etchells. While you can only see the yachts for a couple of seconds, numbers can be distinguished more clearly and close finishes judged more accurately by searchlight than by day. Cebern won his gold chevron by inches, but there was no question about it. Every now and then a ghostly apparition would loom up and the lookout shouted, "boat," a jiffy before it streaked across the line. After seventeen Stars crossed, there was a long pause. No hails were answered and we weighed anchor and returned to the harbor.

It was Saturday night, the night of the final banquet. The club was crowded, when we finally got back, and the improvised bar at the end of the dance floor was a welcome sight. The Star contingent monopolized it for awhile and then went to the Star table just as they were. It had been a long, long day. The contestants had been in their Stars for nearly fifteen hours and, because of the early start, some had not shaved since the morning before. The witching hour of midnight struck before the first course was placed before us. The cordial Commodore Beck was M C., but only daily prizes could be presented. He and the other Stamford flag officers did everything possible to care for our needs during that week.

The final race was sailed on Sunday morning in a puffy northwester That was lucky, as it was blowing a full gale by early afternoon. Skippy Shaw went A.W.O.L. to complete the series and was probably thrown in the brig for doing so. Bob Lippincott rounded up and said he could not keep the mast in the boat he had. He asked for a postponement, while he went back for another, but the request was denied. It was tough on Bob, as it did him out of a chance of placing third, but he was thirteen points behind the leader and could not have won. In any event, we had to get that race started before all those boats fell apart. Bud Jahncke had jib trouble and did not start until five minutes after the rest. The New Orleans skipper picked up a lot of boats to finish fifth and win the Distant Fleet trophy.

Ted Clark and Bert Williams parted their main halyards before they even reached the first mark. Charlie de Cardenas was first around it, but was misdirected by some youngster, who was a guest on the marker yacht. He should have paid no attention, but by the time Charlie found he was holding much too high for the next mark, he was no longer ahead. In trying to clear a jammed mainsheet, Harold Halsted fell over. The crew did not see it happen and the boat went sailing off by itself. An unidentified motorboat passed and someone threw a life ring. It hit Harold and promptly sank. He was picked up about twenty minutes later by the Coast Guard and a serious accident narrowly averted.

Jim Cowie started with a four point advantage over the field. The 1940 champion, of gigantic roach fame, was expected to win again, but he too had sail trouble. Jim managed to repair it, however, and finished seventh, to become runner-up. Skip Etchells finished ninth and, with Lippincott out of it, was an easy third in the series.

Malin Burnham, who crewed for Driscoll the previous year, won the race and gave San Diego another gold Star. Considering the weather and condition of the boats, Malin turned in a superb performance. Whether sailing an A or a B boat, he finished second or better in every race but one. He and Lowell North, his crew, were then in their teens. They still are the youngest combination that has ever won the title.

The last race was a sort of anti-climax. Prizes were hastily presented on the club lawn, while the newly crowned champions were still wet and shivering from the traditional ducking. We were all glad that fateful series was over. Those four years should have taught everyone a lesson, but it was quickly forgotten. Within a couple of months, owners and prospective owners were again discussing the relative speed of Stars by different builders. Even the most inexperienced secretly believed that he could win, if he only had the right Star. It will be ever thus and perhaps it is a good thing, as it helps hold the interest of the rank and file. Otherwise those with latent talent would probably become discouraged and drop out before giving it half a chance to develop.

CHAPTER XIV

STAR INSURANCE

THERE IS A REGULAR STAR POLICY. It covers all racing risk, including damaged sails, makes the president of the I.S.C.Y R.A. the final arbitrator and even has a picture of a Star boat printed upon it. To the best of my knowledge it is the only policy ever written around the needs of and for a special class of racing yachts. Many years ago, through the persistent efforts of Donald Walker, an insurance company was finally persuaded to issue that policy. The idea, of course, was to obtain a lower premium by having all Star members place their insurance with the same firm. In those days the Star was the only class with a big enough organization to make such a thing possible.

Don was then an active Star skipper and still is an enthusiastic member. It was not a commercial venture with him, but a hobby. It was his contribution toward keeping down the cost of owning a Star. In recognition of that the association made him Star insurance officer. He must have settled every claim satisfactorily, as no complaint was ever lodged with the association, at least not during the twenty-five years I was president. He saw the Star class through its various stages of development, including the experimental period with flexible spars. In fact the Star policy reimbursed many members for spar flexing experiments that did not pan out.

The association has grown and, I fear, the new generation of members do not fully understand the above. An increasing number have been placing their Star insurance with some friend or relation—we all have one that is a broker. When this is called to their attention, they say, "Why not? I can get the same rate." Of course they can, as the Star policy establishes the rate. What they cannot seem to grasp is that the company that issues the Star policy cannot maintain a low rate unless it receives a sufficient volume of business to warrant it. The premium has already been increased slightly and I just hope that they wake up to the fact that they are cutting their own throats before it is too late.

The writer realizes that the average reader will not be interested in this short chapter. The Star policy has played a small part in the history of the I.S.C.Y.R.A., otherwise it would not be included in this story. Like transportation rates, etc., it is just one of the many things that those at the helm have studied and worked on for years, to protect and further the interests of Star members, so as to make the I.S.C.Y.R.A. what it is today.

The Star policy did not apply to a skipper series. Don, however, arranged to have the same insurance company cover the 1942 World's Championship at ten dollars per boat. The association charged each skipper an entry fee of a similar amount, but forgot about the twenty-five dollar minimum claim clause. There were quite a number of minor claims for scratches, lost cleats, etc. Collectively they mounted up and the association felt it should make good. There were large ones too and the company lost.

The next year Don would not touch that sort of insurance with a ten foot pole. Reeve Bowden obtained another company that was willing to do so and at the same as the year before. Benefiting from experience, we jumped the entry fee to fifteen dollars. A mast was carried away and, if I recall correctly, a whisker-pole was lost at Bay Shore. At Chicago, in 1944, no damages were claimed, major or minor, so the insurance company must have made out all right.

Then Don decided to step into it again—and he sure did. That was the catastrophic skipper series of '45, when practically every Star used had a yard bill against it. Other claims, and large ones, were filed later. Poor Don, he just picked the wrong years. His principals took a whale of a shellacking. It's a strange thing, but those who try the hardest to be good Samaritans usually get the worst of it. By increasing the entry fee, the association made up for the first year and ended in the black.

CHAPTER XV

WORLD'S CHAMPIONSHIP MECHANICS

THE WORLD'S CHAMPIONSHIPS ARE THE CORE, the sun of the solar system around which the Star class revolves. Being the first annual world-wide championship in the history of yachting, Star members had to develop their own method of conducting it. They also had to work out the system of eliminations leading up to it, so that every Star skipper had an equal chance to qualify and compete for the title each year. This story would not be complete without a summary of the mechanics involved. Most of them originated with the Star class and some are still only to be found in the Star class. The same methods, as applicable, are used in lesser Star championships.

As soon as a World's Championship is over, preparations for the next begin. The place is determined by the point system. The date depends upon local weather conditions, although it is usually in late August or early September. The person selected to handle advance local arrangements has a difficult and most responsible job. He becomes a sort of chairman ex-officio of other local committees, in charge of transportation, housing, entertainment, etc. He is the contact man between the host fleet and the central office. That reduces errors, which would probably result from dealing through various channels.

Necessary forms are sent to fleet secretaries at a very early date. Challenges are usually required by the first of July. They indicate the approximate numbers of entries to provide for. Entry forms must reach the central office twenty days before the opening race, or sooner, that the eligibility of yachts, skippers and crews may be checked, and score cards printed by the host fleet. Copy of the race circular is checked in New York and often printed there.

The home fleet must furnish the daily prizes. During the first week in July, it is sent a check in the amount of all W.C. taxes and interest received during the preceding twelve months. The association buys the series prizes. Now I am going to let the reader in on a top secret. It usually buys those prizes by weight. Old junk? Not at all. Silver is silver, whether melted and cast again or one hundred per cent renovated. I defy anyone to tell the difference, because there is none. This practice has enabled the association to obtain much finer sterling trophies and for much less money than it would have paid for so-called new ones, even at a wholesale price. I know, as I bought these series prizes for twenty-seven years. At one time we bought them through a purchasing agent, for a very big firm, a friend of Pop's. He received a larger trade discount than any club, but those prizes were not nearly as good as the ones given today.

Series headquarters must provide a private room for the I.R.C. hearings and a bulletin board. Many other things must be done locally and at the central office, which I will not bother to mention, as this chapter deals with matters pertinent to the World's Championship and seldom, if ever, found elsewhere.

Due to the large number of entries these days, several measurers are kept busy for two or three days, before the series, checking masts, sails, rudders and keels. Oddly enough, a number of violations are found each year, which the skippers themselves did not know about. Measurers also have the right to check any integral part of the hull, which obviously does not conform to specifications or shows signs of having been altered since the certificate was issued.

The races are conducted by the I.R.C., consisting of five Star officers, automatically selected in order of rank. Except for the probable chairman, no one really knows what ranking officers will be present and eligible, by reason of not being contestants, until the I.R.C is ratified by the annual meeting, held the afternoon before the first race. You can only be sure that the event will be run by qualified Star officers and not by some local club R C, which cannot be expected to be versed in class rules or Star championship procedure. The alternates are selected in the same manner. Then all other series officials are approved. Mark and course officials work in pairs. One, in charge of the boat used, is recommended locally and the other is a visitor from another fleet All have to sign a pledge, agreeing to strictly enforce rules, investigate alleged violations, regardless of protests, etc. This system tends to prevent collusion, partiality and softheartedness.

Typewritten instructions, often consisting of several pages, are given to all series officials. Much time and study is given to revising these instructions annually. If it was only a question of telling them what to do, they could be printed, but it is even more important to warn them against what not to do. Each year some little errors crop up that have not happened before. They usually go unnoticed and seldom cause any damage—but they could. I have always made a careful record of such incidents to prevent any repetition These revised instructions, in my opinion, have done more than any one other thing to continually improve the management of the event, by gradually eliminating faults.

The morning of the first race is a hectic one for the I R C. Having just taken over, it has to check every detail. Required paraphernalia must be there and must be put aboard the boat that is going to use it. A couple of items have usually been mislaid and have to be replaced in a rush The measurers have not yet reported on a few spars and sails. Everything happens at once. Spectators pour into the club and the clatter of voices becomes deafening. The chairman is bombarded with questions and constantly interrupted by phone calls, greetings from old friends and other irrelevant matters. There are always a few skippers each of whom feels that he has been a victim of circumstance and is entitled to some sort of special dispensation. Everything is always adjusted, however, before the I.R.C. has to leave headquarters.

The chairman is invariably called upon to make several emergency decisions, without time to confer with the rest of the I.R.C. In matters connected with the mechanics of the race, he must use his best judgment. Often, however, this applies to answering questions and granting last minute requests. In the latter case, I have always adhered to a fixed policy. If the slightest doubt exists in your mind, "no" should be the answer. Then you can never be wrong. Anyone has the right to change his mind later, after sleeping over a problem. I have always warned other Star officers against being stampeded into a spontaneous "yes." If you make a mistake because you did not take time to think it over, you are quoted and a precedent is established, even if you did not have authority to make a ruling. Eventually it has to be corrected, of course, but the damage has been done and you subject yourself to a lot of justifiable criticism.

If a start, with a windward first leg, cannot be established from the probable starting line, the committee displays code N and moves the committee boat to the selected line. As soon as it has anchored, the marker yachts come alongside and are given the distance and direction for placing their mark After the stakeboat is anchored and an official put aboard of it, the marker yacht takes its station. That is about seventy-five yards behind the stakeboat and in a line with the course the competing yachts must sail. It displays a large white flag to make it easier for skippers to spot the mark There is a red and yellow cylinder, about four feet by two feet on the upright of each rounding stakeboat. That combination of colors was recommended by an expert as the most easily discerned against any background. In other words, all these seemingly minor details are the result of intensive study. Mark officials watch for fouls. They also time and record the order of rounding. These records are given to the I.R C. and, since most fouls happen near a mark, are often valuable in establishing the facts connected with a protest.

As soon as the marker yachts have been instructed, the I.R.C. establishes the starting line. Here again we have learned from experience that a club work boat, with power, has many advantages over the conventional stakeboat. It can place itself more quickly and accurately than a launch can place a stakeboat. If it drags at a critical moment, the engine can be started and it can hold its position for a while, at least long enough to bridge the emergency. Such a boat will accommodate several officials. They can watch for fouls on all sides and see the number on the sail of a Star making a premature start. One man in a dinghy, being bounced around in a seaway, cannot be expected to have eyes in the back of his head, or do everything that should be done at the same time.

After the start, the I.R.C. immediately shifts the line mark to the proper position for the end of the first round and finish. Again having a mark with its own power is a great advantage. At least it obviates the risk of having a launch go off and not return in time to shift the mark. That has happened.

Courses are given by sliding numerals and letters, painted on cardboard, into a signal frame. Full sized code flags are also painted on such slides. In very light air they can be seen, whereas a real flag would hang limp on the halyard and could not be distinguished. The I.S.C.Y.R.A. owns its own signals and ships them from one locality to another.

The I.R.C. then prepares for a dress rehearsal at the end of the first round, with everything except the gun. That is especially important the first day. Whistles and cheers from spectator boats make such a din at the finish, that it can be very disconcerting to a comparatively new official and cause him to make mistakes. He must know how to do his job almost automatically On the last day, with a gun for each Star to finish, it's pandemonium, but by that time the I R.C can do its work blindfolded.

Finishes are handled pretty much the same as in any yacht race. A couple of the I.R.C. write down racing numbers in order of finish. One, who stands near the timer, writes down the times only. Ordinary ruled yellow pads are used. A vertical line is drawn near the left-hand margin. The horizontal rulings are numbered from one to the total number of entries. They indicate the position of finish and make checking easy. The man who sights the line, blows a mouth whistle, as each Star crosses. He makes no attempt to decipher racing numbers but concentrates upon judging which bow hits the line first. He has two assistants who spot the racing numbers as the boats approach. In a close finish, once the order has been judged usually by the color of hull (or by referring to the near or far boat) they furnish the correct number. When there is a break, the judge says, "Rest. How many boats?" The timer stops counting the seconds and, writing down the results, states the number on the left-hand margin of their pads. Two or three others, with no specified duty, also keep track of close finishes, just in case of any disagreement.

Once the I R.C is ready, the recording committee is organized. It consists mostly of wives of the officials Five thin legal sheets, with carbons between, are inserted into a portable typewriter. This later becomes the official record, subject to protest. It is dated and the chairman supplies the time of start, wind and course. The positions, starting with one, are typed close to the left hand margin. Then the other columns are headed: yacht's number, fleet, skipper and Star's name, if there is room. After the first race, there are three columns for points—previously won, won that day and total.

A liaison officer is appointed. He copies the racing numbers and time by looking over the shoulder of those writing this down When there is a break, he rushes back and gives his sheet to the recording committee, being sure to write the next position on his next sheet. One girl types, one reads these sheets, one locates the entry on the score card and gives skipper's name, etc. The typist announces the daily points won. A fourth girl adds them to the points previously won and states the total. The recording committee can keep up with the finishes and is always finished by the time the last Star crosses. Then the chairman checks with the official records, to make sure there has been no mistake.

When the committee boat contingent gets ashore, a typewritten copy of the results is immediately posted on the bulletin board and another handed to the press. The mark officials, who are usually waiting on the float, give their reports to the chairman. One of the I.R.C. remains at headquarters to receive protests, if any, and posts a notice of a hearing the following morning. The other officials can return to their rooms, rest a little, shower and dress for dinner.

Compare the above with the old method, when the I.R.C. had to figure out points and make several result sheets in longhand. After a long day, no one felt like working. It took a good half hour to corral them and get started. Even with a locked door, there were frequent interruptions. Press reports were delayed and everyone was kept waiting a couple of hours, often longer. A recording committee saves the I.R.C. a lot of time and work. To the best of my knowledge, it has never been tried, except by the Star class. Why? Because the average R.C. is prejudiced against trying anything new. When I first introduced the idea, the others on the I.R.C. were positive it would not work, until it was proved that it would.

Hearings usually start at nine o'clock the next morning. Alleged violations can often be settled the night before by a few questions, so that no hearing is necessary. All I.R.C. decisions are written and posted. All protests and reported violations on the previous day must be decided before officials and contestants leave headquarters for the next race. A skipper is entitled to know, before a race starts, which rivals he must watch.

The only hearings held in the late afternoon are on the day of the last race. On that day everyone is warned to remain at headquarters after the race, in case they are needed as witnesses. This is necessary since the final results must be known in time to present prizes at the final banquet.

The day after the series is over the I.R.C. is supposed to gather together all the paraphernalia belonging to the association, check it and get it ready to be shipped to the locality holding the next Worlds Championship. By that time, I regret to say, series officials feel that they have done all that should be expected of them. The job is left to some local, who does not tackle it for a couple of weeks, and several items are usually lost.

Let me add a recommendation to the foregoing. The chairman of the I.R.C., or any R.C., should have no prescribed duty, other than being general supervisor. No one can concentrate on one job and keep a weather eye on everything that is going on. A free lance chairman will gravitate to where he is most needed.

With a flock of boats milling about the line, the best officials are apt to have their attention distracted temporarily. Timers have been known to take their eyes off the chronometer at a crucial moment, upon hearing two yachts collide. An experienced committeeman can never be spared to handle the cannon, there should be two, in case of a misfire. If the trigger is cocked before the lower, the usually inexperienced cannoneer is apt to get excited and fire on the lower count. Do not laugh—I have seen it happen to some of the best club R.C.'s. These are the sort of little things that the chairman must constantly keep in mind and guard against. Many a mistake has been narrowly averted by a timely reminder.

A free lance chairman can answer hails and is really the only one with authority to do so. At the last moment he is often called upon to make a quick emergency decision. That would be impossible if his mind was occupied with some routine job. I have taken the line at the start and finish like the rest In recent years, however, I have found myself turning it over to another more and more, in order to be free to check something else. If two or more entries make a premature start, there is always considerable confusion. A lot of things have to be watched and done all at once and the chairman is held responsible. He must know his business, but he must also be free to give orders and see to it that everything is handled properly.

CHAPTER XVI

REORGANIZATION

LIKE THE MYTHICAL PHOENIX, almost while the echoes of the last gunfire were still reverberating, European Star racing arose from its own ashes. The first thought of every owner, after the war, seemed to be to get back in his Star European yachtsmen became much more boat minded. Former owners of much larger yachts turned to the Star. It was the only racing machine they could afford, the only class that offered them organized international competition. Any lingering doubts about reorganizing the class in Europe vanished immediately. The Star provided a nucleus around which yacht racing interest was revived in the old world, just as it had supplied the foundation for rebuilding the sport in the new world after world war one.

A rough inventory disclosed the fact that quite a number of European fleets, for several years, had been fleets in name only Their Stars had been bought by neighboring localities, whereas those that had belonged to service fleets, had found their way into civilian hands. This was chiefly the case in France and Italy. New fleets quickly replaced the old ones, but they consisted mostly of the same old Stars, renamed and sailed by new owners.

Four or five Stars were demolished when a shipyard, near Paris, was bombed. There is no record of any other Stars having been actually destroyed as a direct result of the war. Many were and still are unaccounted for, but there is no good reason to believe that they no longer exist. The largest group of missing European Stars, of course, were the pre-war Stars in Germany. West Germany has since shown some fleet activity and that country was represented by a Star in the '52 Olympics. Walter von Hutschler found the Pimm, when he accompanied the Brazilian yachtsmen to the '48 Olympics, as coach It was in good condition, just where he had left it, so he shipped Pimm to Sao Paulo. Other unaccounted-for European Stars are probably being sailed right now, mostly by new owners. There are various reasons why they may not have seen fit to contact the association. Except at a few Star centers, little is known about organized yachting throughout the Far East. The missing Stars in that vast area could easily be in the hands of owners who do not even know there is an I.S.C.Y.R.A Stars have disappeared before, only to appear again years later. In all probability most of the Stars presumably lost, strayed or stolen (I use the last word advisedly) will be heard of again, sometime, somewhere.

Annual reports piled into the central office. Almost every European fleet had a new secretary, who was not yet familiar with the system. Most of those reports were incomplete and not too accurate Numbers had been cabled and radiographed during the war to countries that could not communicate by mail, often on very meager information. Official numbers were allocated, through fleet officials, to Stars built in the war years, which had been racing under temporary local numbers All these things combined created many errors and duplications

Peace brought all the inactive Stars in North America and elsewhere back into circulation. The description of practically every other Star had to be changed, both in the permanent register and the printer's copy for the Log. The boat either had a new name, a new owner, belonged to a different fleet, or all three. With two thousand four hundred Stars, that in itself was a long tedious job. To make it worse, many of those changes had to be verified. Except for the carelessness of some builders and measurers, who had not seen to it that the number was cut or burned into the top of the keelson, identification would have been quick and a lot of time and effort would have been saved. Several lengthy individual letters had to be exchanged about nearly every doubtful case. It took almost two years to untangle the mess and restore the records to normalcy.

Every now and then unidentified Stars kept popping up here and there. They were war loot, carried off by the invaders It was done by both sides. Some may have been legally acquired for speculation, from a bona fide owner in need of cash. It was usually impossible to tell, as they had passed through several hands and no one remembered names or had former bills of sale. There never had been a number on the keelson of some, but there were also cases where the number had been intentionally obliterated. A pretty good guess could always be made as to the builder and approximate year built. If a Star, built about that time, was positively known to have been wrecked and destroyed, the boat was given that number. If any doubt existed, however, the number was prefixed by an X. Probably some owners did not like that. If you buy questionable goods, however, you must expect to be subjected to some inconvenience.

Virtually all the little three boat fleets were wiped out. That was a good thing. Except perhaps in the early years, when Stars had to be demonstrated, the baby fleet has been a perpetual headache. Three boat racing cannot sustain interest very long. When one Star was sold, the remaining two were not enough to renew the fleet's charter, which forthwith was revoked. Those minimum fleets were short-lived They either developed a locality within a year, or not at all. Where substantial fleets were developed, a charter could have been obtained with a greater number of Stars a few months later anyway. Those minimum fleets, which kept coming and going, only inflicted a lot of extra book work upon the office.

One of the most constructive rule changes made, during the reconstruction period, was to require a new fleet to start with five Stars. Thereafter, three could retain the charter. That provided a reasonable amount of competition and gave the fleet a little leeway, if it met with early adversities. Since then the I.S.C.Y.R.A. has scarcely lost a fleet.

European memberships continued to pour in, in ever increasing numbers. I said memberships—not dues. Funds were frozen in practically all of those countries. Fleet secretaries collected dues in the usual manner and certified to the fact that they had been paid by all members, whose green forms were filed. Those dues were deposited locally to be transmitted to the association when, as and if possible. European members, being in good standing, were entitled to the same service as all others. Logs, twelve issues of Starlights, membership cards, etc. had to be sent to all of them. The association, however, was receiving very little additional cash to take care of all this extra business. The situation created some pretty knotty financial problems.

Occasionally a district officer was able to get a special permit to transmit a portion of the accumulated dues. Sometimes a member over there had an account here, or the reverse, by means of which other part payments were managed. By various methods, the bulk of those fluctuating deposits eventually reached the international treasurer, but in some cases too late. In one instance the rate of exchange was fifty to one, when dues were collected, but three hundred and fifty to one, by the time the money was transmitted. In some cases associate dues only amounted to a small fraction of an American dollar and did not even pay for postage to that member. It became necessary to reduce the service to that class of membership, in such cases, to sending a membership card only.

It would have been too complicated to even attempt to figure the World's Championship tax deduction, of twenty-five cents per member, on European dues. Those balances were all mixed up with plans and buttons sold on credit. Part payments were received at indeterminate periods of even amounts, say one hundred dollars. There was no way of telling how many dues, of each class of membership it represented, or how much could not be applied to dues at all The association, therefore, made another rule change. It just deducted five per cent from all European remittances received within the twelve month period. That was simple and it worked out about the same.

Life members presented another knotty problem. At fifty dollars each, they had paid roughly four thousand dollars That sum tided the association over a crisis, but left it with about eighty members to carry for an indefinite number of years Securities, in the amount of the principal, would have to be set aside, so the interest would take care of that class of membership. The association-owned bonds would have produced one dollar and twenty-five cents per annum for each member, which would have been a losing proposition. It bought approximately four thousand dollars worth of common stock, making the dividends exempt from World's Championship tax. The annual yield per member was then about equal to an associate's dues. Perhaps it was not the most conservative move imaginable, but it was the only answer. The association's common stock, therefore, is a sort of separate trust fund, established to provide for the life memberships.

The creating of continental vice presidents was approved at the 1948 meeting and subsequently passed by the membership Like district secretaries, when that office was started, they were next to useless for a couple of years. Then they were renamed international vice presidents and given specific duties.

Through the same procedure, a three-man judiciary board was created the following year. Its members were to serve for three years, one to be appointed annually. Its duty was to decide appeals and interpret obscure class rules, also to make necessary changes in existing rules to conform with any passed amendments. Most of its decisions have been on very controversial issues. They have usually dealt with the somewhat doubtful intent of a class rule. Only those who have lived with the rules, who are familiar with their origin and history, are really qualified to service on the judiciary board.

As a result of that same meeting, the names of candidates for commodoreships were put on the ballot. That eliminated the last chance of any spontaneous act by the annual meeting, which might be contrary to the wish of the membership. The amendment also provided that the two vice and three rear commodores could not be chosen from members on the same continent. It made for a more wide-spread distribution of the honorary officers.

Again at Chicago, in 1950, the machinery was set in motion to give the association an international president (distinct from the executive one) and continental committees. These committees consisted of the first and second vice presidents on each continent, with the one international president acting as chairman of each. Their duties were to sanction events, grant charters, decide territorial disputes and supervise Star activity on their respective continents. The constitution states, however, that such officers have no jurisdiction over finances or the routine business of the I.S.C.Y.R.A. Thus international officers came into their own and, with definite duties to perform, became an asset.

Carlos de Cardenas, unopposed, was elected and still is international president. He has a thorough knowledge of rules, has raced in more major Star championships in various parts of the world and has been in the class longer than any of the present chief executive officers. It was not right to bar members like him, because of their residence, from ever becoming president. On the other hand, the finances and general business of the association must be handled at its central office. The executive president and the four other major executive officers, who form the governing committee, frequently meet in person and have to do most of their own work. It is necessary, therefore, that these officers be selected from qualified members in or near New York City. The

I.S.C.Y R.A. has solved that problem by having co-presidents, of equal rank, but with different duties.

The greatest menace to sports organizations is the tendency of members to elect a popular hero, without giving any thought as to whether he is qualified for that particular type of job. The amendments engineered by those three annual meetings were intended to prevent that sort of thing. They made it possible for Star officials to specialize in a given field of endeavor, so that each did not have to be a jack-of-all-trades. They also made it possible for the membership to elect a deserving popular hero to an equally high office.

There is nothing complicated about the present form of Star government, if one tries to understand it. Both presidents and commodores are elected by the entire membership. Voting for continental officers is restricted to members on the continent in question and district officers to those in each district. Fleets elect their fleet officers in such manner as they see fit, but the names of candidates do not go on the annual ballot.

The I.S.C.Y.R.A. is run by three separate and distinct groups of officers. There are (a) the executive group, who handle the finances and business of the association, the districts and the fleets; (b) the international officers in charge of continental activities; and (c) judiciary branch, in charge of appeals and interpretations. This setup will reduce the work of the major officers and take care of continued growth, provided qualified members are elected and appointed, also provided none of them attempt to usurp the powers of others.

Under the able management of Anchyses Lopes, South American vice president, Star activity on that continent has flourished It is still in its infancy, of course, but an annual Silver Star Championship has already been inaugurated and there are fleets in four countries: Venezuela, Brazil, Argentina and Chile. Rio de Janeiro has entered the World's Championship ever since 1946 and each time it has done better than the year before.

The international vice president of Africa, Yves Lorion, has added a fleet in Tunisia to those in Morocco and Algeria, bringing the total to eleven.

There has been a marked revival throughout Australia and the islands of the Far East. International vice president Harvey's efforts have resulted in four fleets in Australia alone. U.S. navy officers established a Yokosuka fleet, on Tokyo Bay, Japan. It was expected that some of the Manila Stars would be found there, but such was not the case. Most of their Stars were of German build. Nothing more has ever been heard from Yokohama or Batavia, but the charter of the Manila Bay fleet has just been renewed.

The exploits of Jean Peytel are too well known to bear repeating. Star development throughout Europe, of which he is international vice president, has been tremendous, even extending behind the iron curtain. There are now thirty Star fleets in Italy alone.

At this writing, in the spring of 1953, North America has seventy-four fleets to seventy-two in Europe. Both have seven districts, making it about even. Dave Dunigan, however, probably had the most troublesome job of all the international vice presidents, as North America holds many more sanctioned events than any other continent. A number of them became regular fixtures long before the Star began to take root elsewhere. Sanctions have to be renewed annually. Some were found to have changed character during the years and had to be given lower classifications. There are always a few new requests for sanctions, which seldom are entitled to the rating their sponsors feel they should have. In North America, all this passed through Dave's hands. While not of vital importance, it took time and explaining.

International officers are a new branch of the organization, hence the amount of space devoted to them. The governing committee made no secret of the fact that it did not especially approve of these officers. Every now and then it ignored them and handled some matter itself, over which international officers had jurisdiction. That naturally caused friction and occasional flare-ups between the two departments.

The same thing happened at times to the measurement committee. The governing committee would take over, on the slightest pretext, apply the measurements itself, send out conflicting orders and practically grant or refuse a certificate. That also caused confusion and dissatisfaction. If a technical committee did not do its work properly, it should have been replaced. Even if the constitution is a bit ambiguous on the point, it never intended that an executive group should handle the work of those appointed because of their specialized knowledge.

If this is to be an authentic story of the Star class, the bad must be included with the good. The writer is not criticizing the zeal of that governing committee. It probably worked harder than any other the association has ever had. That was the trouble—it worked too hard. It tried to do the work of all its appointed officers and committees, as well as that of some over which it had no jurisdiction. That either made others mad, or they just sat back, shrugged their shoulders and said, "O.K., then, you go ahead and do it for me." I sincerely hope and have every reason to believe that that temporary phase of internal squabbling is over.

Incidents that occurred in the '50's cannot be considered part of the reorganization period, although some were the outgrowth thereof. After the war, when ceiling prices were lifted, the cost of running the association began to soar. Being dependent upon its literature and forms, printing bills, which were about double, became the largest item of expense. Rent and other costs also went up. Dues in the western hemisphere were increased, but that only served to stem the tide somewhat. It became very difficult to make both ends meet and still is.

Administrations since 1948 are to be complimented upon enacting many needed improvements. For one thing, a new I S.C.Y R A banner was adopted. It consists of the two hemispheres, with a red star between, on a blue field The old banner was white and bordered with many little red stars, one for each fleet The number had to be changed all the time and fleets became too numerous to make this practicable.

Taking a page from the book of some other organized one-designs, strips of canvas labels were sold to sailmakers.

A label had to be sewed on all jibs and mainsails to make them legal. Sail plans are copyrighted and have always been sold under a royalty agreement. Under the old method, keeping track of the number of suits made annually was difficult and complicated. Now sailmakers have to pay royalties in advance, which makes it much easier for all concerned.

The association has a circulating library of motion picture films, which includes every World's Championship ever held and a few other important events. The early ones were in black and white, but the more recent ones are in color. Peck Farley, Jr., son of the never to be forgotten Peck, handled this department most efficiently for a number of years. Reels could be obtained by any fleet for a short period. Current ones were booked far in advance, so duplicates were made for use on other continents, in order to avoid long delays.

The two hemisphere emblem is now obtainable on a small piece of dark cloth. This most recent innovation is for use on blazers and similar jackets, worn around yacht clubs, or on semi-dress occasions. The latest report is that they are most popular and selling very well. These and a number of other minor improvements and innovations had added to the prestige of the association, but have not materially increased its revenue.

In the humble opinion of the writer, there is only one way to alleviate the present financial problem. Members in the eastern hemisphere are still paying dues on a pre-war basis. If they can find a way to increase their dues to half the amount paid in the western hemisphere, which was originally the case, the association will no longer have to keep wracking its brain to keep out of the red.

Star production in North America has been at a very low ebb since the war and still is. Higher labor and material has naturally increased the cost of a new Star. The demand has been as great as ever and people had the money, but ordering new Stars has been limited by another factor. Unless a prospective buyer could get a boat from the name

builder, then in vogue, he was convinced that it would be
useless to order one from any other builder, as he could
never hope to win a race. The said name builder could only
complete around a dozen of these especially custom built
Stars each year. While some others were built, his capacity
practically governed the continent's output. Conditions are
now a little better, as there are two or three name builders,
but production is still far below normal.

The price of a new name Star has been running around
two thousand five hundred dollars and up, depending upon
extras. That is not exhorbitant, considering the circumstances.
The name builder tries to get his Stars into the hands of
expert skippers, who will enhance their reputation. The de-
mands of such skippers are very exacting. Much time must
be given to little details and finish, which means a high
overhead. He is furthermore entitled to a reasonable profit
for the reputation of his Stars. The public does not realize
that it cost him time and money to gain that reputation. The
least little thing will cause public opinion to switch, so you
cannot blame him for trying to make a little hay while the
sun shines.

There have been a few small family shops right along,
which have been able to sell new Stars, and good ones, from
fifteen hundred dollars to seventeen hundred dollars. Such
builders usually own their own shops, live on the prem-
ises and are helped by sons or brothers. They do not charge
for their own labor, on an hourly basis, against the boat, nor
pay the relatives, who live with them, on that basis either.
Their overhead is low and they have to sell their Stars at an
attractive price, in order to get a few local orders, as they
are scarcely known fifty miles away.

Skippers of average ability and those wishing to place
a group order have been very foolish not to patronize one
of the cheaper builders. His few Stars have never been sailed
by enough expert skippers, in big events, to establish a wide-
spread reputation. He must be an experienced commercial
builder, however, or he would not be in that business. There
is very little difference in speed between two well built

Star hulls. The average skipper, even a pretty good one, can do just as well with one of those cheaper Stars. When he becomes a potential champion, if ever, it is time enough to talk about getting a Star from a name builder. Then, perhaps, when he knows what to do with it, it might prove to be an advantage. Buying a special bat and glove will not put a minor league player into one of the big leagues over night. It is exactly the same idea, but I realize that I am only wasting my breath in trying to explain it.

Fortunately for the Star class these conditions did not apply elsewhere. No super deluxe name builders have developed on other continents. Buyers demand good Stars, but price is also an essential consideration. If the builder wants the order, he has to sharpen his pencil. The result has been competitive building and an ever-increasing output of new Stars.

A new Star in Europe costs many more francs, or liras, etc. than it did before the war. The increase, however, is about proportionate with all other increases, including the average buyer's salary. Hence it is not much more of a financial problem for him to buy a Star now than it was before the war.

Shortly after the war was over, I received an interesting letter from a European builder. He claimed that he could dehver a new Star in New York for five hundred dollars, transatlantic freight and insurance paid. To the best of my knowledge, he was never given an opportunity to prove it. Even with import duty added, it would have been dirt cheap, but neither he, nor his Stars, were known. No one was willing to gamble, even at that price, which is an example of the North American Star buyer's frame of mind.

About the same time, I was informed through a reliable source, that a good new Star could be bought in Brazil for about the equivalent of eight hundred American dollars. I cannot vouch for its authenticity, but have every reason to believe it was correct. There would have been nothing odd about it, as good Stars could be bought around here for that price until the start of the war. Joe Parkman, whose Stars had quite a reputation, sold them even cheaper than that, until he sold out at the end of 1936.

The war was over. It was high time to begin breaking in younger officers. In the fall of 1945, governing committee members agreed among themselves to drop out gradually, as replacements were found. Harold Halsted was then serving his first term as vice president, but had been treasurer since 1940 He was favored to succeed me and become president for a time. All this had to be contingent upon nominations and elections. Because they had to meet frequently at the central office, the choice of candidates was virtually restricted to members living near New York City. The ones we recommended, therefore, were seldom opposed.

Sam Smith went first, followed by Ted Everitt and Al Wakefield. Al, who started racing Stars in 1918, was an exception to the general rule. He lived near Cleveland, but came to New York a couple of times each month and was able to work with the governing committee. He was also the last of the third vice presidents. I withdrew at the end of 1948 and Harold took over. Charlie de Cardenas was elected vice president. He was thoroughly qualified, but too far away to be on the governing committee. The same had once been true in the case of Enrique Conill. It was fundamentally wrong. The purpose of such an executive officer is to be an understudy to the president, conversant with current issues and able to preside in his absence.

During the transition period, a number of the younger members were invited to meet with the governing committee. Naturally they had no vote, but we wanted to hear their comments and judge of their qualifications. There were some shifts, as we could hardly have been expected to hit the jackpot the first time. Proper replacements were obviously found, or the changeover could not have been made in three years.

The next administration did away with any systematic search for young prospects. Young men, I was told, were too busy and could not be depended upon to assume the required responsibility. Tim Parkman was in his early twenties and working his way through law school, when he was elected, yet he found the time to become one of the best secretaries the I.S.C Y R.A. has ever had. Most of our officers were young men in those early years. The association was the only one of its kind and we had no precedent to guide us. If young men could be responsible then, there is no good reason why they cannot be now. There should be plenty of capable ones, but they have to be found. Suppose they do make a few mistakes, what of it? The advisory council was created and given the power of veto for the sole purpose of preventing any impetuous acts of young governing committees, which might prove harmful.

Certain Star officers should definitely be older men, if qualified ones are obtainable. An older man, generally speaking, is more level-headed and commands greater respect, but not always. The point I am trying to make is that, excluding teen agers, likely prospects should not be discriminated against just because of their youth. There are many more comparatively young Star veterans than old ones. Star knowledge is important, but being a good skipper has nothing to do with being a good official. How is a younger man going to gain the experience, unless given a chance? Certain Star jobs, of the understudy type, are practically earmarked for young men. I refer to assistant district secretaries, second international vice presidents, etc. The majority of the executive officers, who automatically serve on the governing committee, should also be young men. That involves highly specialized training. They have to start young, because only one out of many will survive and eventually become executive president.

The Star class is now more than half again as big as its pre-war peak. It is not apt to stumble across another Sam Smith, who will provide it with an entire office force. The association cannot afford to pay its officers. Because of their other business activities, they can only devote a portion of their time to Star work. The responsibility is no greater, perhaps not as great as in the past, but there is much more work to be done. It stands to reason, therefore, that there must be many more officers, that the work must be more widely distributed and more or less specialized, if it is to be done at all. At that, there is plenty of work for all, young and old alike, without anyone seeking more, or having to tread on the toes of another. The continued success of any international organization depends upon harmonious co-operation between its leaders.

CHAPTER XVII

ONE-DESIGN

THE TERM ONE-DESIGN, except perhaps in a broad sense, does not mean identical. It simply classifies a group of yachts built from any given set of plans, as against a class consisting of yachts of various designs. Wooden hulls and spars are made by hand. No two are, or ever were, *absolutely* identical It is only a question of how small a unit of measure is used before some differences can be detected. Boatbuilders are not watchmakers.

Stars are built all over the world and under all sorts of conditions, mostly by professionals, but some by amateurs. Specifications have to be translated into many languages and figures given in the nearest metric equivalent. The same materials are not obtainable everywhere. Some countries prohibit the importation of certain foreign materials. Even at an excessive cost, Stars could not be built in those places unless the closest local substitute was made optional. The Star is international It cannot specify American materials not obtainable in other countries, nor other products if not obtainable here. These combined circumstances are bound to cause some trivial discrepancies.

If it is any consolation, the club one-designs of old, built right in the same yard, probably varied just as much as Stars built at opposite ends of the earth. Small boats were then very unimportant. They were not measured with the painstaking exactitude of today. When completed, the designer gave them a casual inspection. He did not try to check and report trivial variations. If the group conformed to his plans, to all intents and purposes, he pronounced the boats O K. That was usually done before the prospective owners drew lots for their boats. They were mostly cheap little boats, the contract being given to the lowest bidder. The best of builders could not have afforded too much time to their construction. The public, however, took it for granted that those boats were identical throughout and that idea has remained in the minds of many.

The answer to the above is invariably, "I mean alike within reason." That is just the point. What is within reason? For Stars, it is defined by the I.S.C.Y.R.A. table of limitations. It fixes the over and under tolerances allowed in a Star. Many people will not agree with these figures, but that is because they do not know the problems and conditions involved. All I can say is that these tolerances have been very carefully studied. The advice obtained from impartial designers has always been that boats built within those tolerances could have no material advantage one over the other. In any event, Star measurement rules are made by and for Star members and we do not care what outsiders may think.

Why quibble about a few pounds, when there is such a great difference in the human weight aboard the boats, which cannot be controlled? Sails change size and shape each time they are used and if wet or dry. There are very drafty sails and very flat ones, big and little ones, with respect to linear dimensions, and all intermediary stages to be found on yachts in every class. They keep on changing constantly and the differences are tremendous. Sails are a component part of the boat. They can only be governed in a rough general manner. Even if everything else was absolutely identical, which is impossible, there would be wide differences between cloth sails. Everyone knows that the sail is a sailboat's driving power. Why then make such an issue of fractional hull discrepancies? At best the hull can only account for a very small percentage of the relative speed of boats in a one-design, or nearly one-design, class.

We had to learn the hard way, by actual experience. We first became aware of hull variations during the Star national championships of 1922. Those boats were in accord with the specifications sent out by the designer, but lo and behold the specifications were not exactly alike. It has been said that Gardner ran out of mimeographed sheets and dictated several new sets from memory. It is much more likely that he intentionally made a few minor changes, believing them to be improvements, which would make the boats better suited to conditions in the localities where they would be sailed. It was the sort of thing expected of designers in those days. Bill had no way of guessing that the Star would become a world-wide standard and no reason to maintain uniformity.

In the winter of 1922-23 the Star association wrote its own specifications, ironing out all known kinks. Bill Gardner approved and agreed to make them official henceforth. Among other things, they provided that all Stars built before 1922 would be given a blanket certificate. That was common sense, since no one knew then that there would be inter-fleet events and no Stars had been built with the idea of beating those in another locality. In fact, very few were aware that there were Stars in other localities.

Fred Teeves was then our one and only measurer. He and the executive committee drew up our first table of limitations. Fred and the secretary-in-chief (myself) had the only two official copies. Builders were advised to adhere to plans, as tolerances would not be made public and were only enough to cover unavoidable inexactnesses in normal building practice. It meant nothing, but the builders were satisfied. It was a tossup as to whether Gardner or Herreshoff was tops. Many people considered William Gardner the foremost designer in the world. They had the utmost faith in him and believed that an exact replica of his lines would result in the fastest Star. No one even thought of trying to beat Gardner at his own game, within the obviously fractional limitations.

Eye trouble forced Bill to retire, but his firm still owned the plans It charged fifteen dollars for a set and a like amount for every Star built from that set, after the first one. It had great difficulty, however, in collecting the royalties it was entitled to The Star was only one of the innumerable small classes designed by Bill Gardner. The firm was most friendly and co-operative, but it made its money from very much larger yachts The time and effort necessary to check upon Stars built was not commensurate with the income derived. The I.S.C.Y R.A bought the plans and had them copyrighted. It started by charging ten dollars for working drawings and imposed a five dollar number tax on each Star built. Builders had been reticent about divulging how many Stars they had sold and to whom, not wishing to pay a fifteen dollar royalty. The owner insisted that the builder pay the tax or paid it for him, as he could not race his boat without a number. Both parties gained. William Gardner and company took in a lump sum, which amounted to more than it could have collected in royalties in several years. The I.S C.Y.R.A. more than paid for the plans the first year and has derived a small income from them ever since.

The 1927 annual meeting, held at Warwick, R.I., voted to publish the limitations. It was argued that a builder was entitled to know how far afield he could stray I believe the resolution was prompted by the curiosity of the delegates, but it did not matter Keeping the tolerances a top secret had already served its purpose. Enough Stars had been measured for us to know how close a builder could stick to the lines, if he really tried As might be expected, the average amateur was not quite as accurate. We could not be too strict and discourage home building, but from then on we tightened limitations and added new ones. I know that limitations eventually had to be published, but it was kind of a pity.

Henceforth certificates were carefully scanned and victories often attributed to some minor discrepancy. Neither Gardner nor any professional designer had to do with the modern Star rig In fact, Gardner's only connection with the short Marconi was negative, an experiment which was a failure

The reader has probably noticed that a white boat looks somewhat larger than a black one of the same size. The optical illusion caused by the boot top, if any, on a Star is much more deceiving. For example, a Star without any, looks chunky and heavy, whereas a curved one makes the hull appear sleek, slim and light. This is most noticeable when two Stars are side by side out of water. Straight, high, low, narrow and wide boot-tops cause a lesser optical illusion. That is what started the first wild rumors about variations in Star hulls. It is needless to say that outsiders were chiefly responsible. Had they seen two Star hulls that were painted the same, they could not possibly have detected any of the minor variations that then existed.

While it was generally known, in a vague way, that some discrepancies existed in all one-designs, publishing the Star limitations was the first official acknowledgement and it made everyone variation minded. It started a mild epidemic of surreptitiously boarding another's Star, in an attempt to find out what made it click. Those who did this without the owner's permission, did not want it known that they had trespassed and said nothing. There was one notable incident, however, that caused quite a fracas. A U.S. skipper unofficially measured Ratsey's Irex after the races in Havana. Whatever he said was probably greatly exaggerated. The jist of it was that Irex did not measure in. The arguments became so widespread and vehement that a hearing was ordered. In the meantime Irex had been returned to City Island and was remeasured by Fred Teeves. A few ranking Star officers were there as witnesses Fred used templates, the taut wire base line was not yet in vogue Templates were checked with the plans and applied to the hull. They fit like a glove. Irex was one of the most correct Stars ever built.

The hearing was attended by many. Testimony revealed the fact that Irex had been measured with a piece of string and, if I remember correctly, over its shipping cover. Faced with the remeasuring facts, the one who did the measuring admitted that his methods were perhaps a little inaccurate and he escaped with a reprimand. It resulted, however, in two rules being passed. One, a fifty dollar deposit would have to accompany any protest involving the measurements of a Star holding a certificate. Two, any statement, which could not be proved, reflecting upon the validity of a certified Star was, thereafter, to become grounds for suspension. While altered Stars have been remeasured by order of the proper authorities, no fifty dollar protest has ever been filed. If anyone has ever said, without proof, that a Star was not entitled to its certificate, it has never reached my ears.

Remember that all this happened before builders began to experiment with round and flat bottoms. These experiments were made possible by one of our old measurement committees misinterpreting the contour tolerance. It was originally one inch total, meaning that if the contour was, for instance, one-quarter of an inch under the three-quarters of an inch over, or any fractional variation totaling one inch, it was O.K. The said committee interpreted it to mean one inch under or over at any point which was twice what was intended. Probably those who framed the tolerances did not word this too clearly. Three years elapsed before we woke up to what was going on. A great many Stars had been built, measured, obtained certificates and been raced. It was too late to make a change. Had this affected only one or two boats, something would probably have been done about it, but it affected many and we had no idea which type of bottom might be the fastest. Had a change been made that was not retroactive, it could eventually have meant that some old Stars would become unbeatable and ruin the intrinsic value of others. It would have been making a mountain out of a molehill, for after all the variation is comparatively minor, although twice what was intended, and there are still two schools of thought on the subject

Now let us consider what advantage can be gained by the contour tolerances, if any. I am not expressing my personal opinion, but that of technical experts who should know. Theoretically a rounder bottom should be faster in very light air and one flatter than standard should point better and be a bit faster in a strong breeze. In like manner a perfectly standard contour should win a mixed weather series on points, while those who gambled on either extreme are taking a shellacking. The only thing is that it does not work out that way. The athwart and fore-and-aft contour tolerances are not great enough to offset a skipper's lack of skill. Somehow the good boys always seem to be in the money, unless they get caught with the wrong sails. Sails that are much too drafty for a blow, or much too flat for light air, are a real handicap.

The I.S.C.Y.R.A. has never attempted the impossible. It recognizes and has maintained practicable uniformity among Stars. No retroactive changes are ever made that would deplete the class, or inflict a sudden and severe financial loss upon a substantial group of its members. Its chief aim is to carry out the intent and purpose of one-design racing. It looks upon a one-design yacht as an accessory, governed by reasonable restrictions, much as a bicycle in a bicycle race. It is primarily interested in making winning depend upon the ability of the human competitor. It has never prevented the individual from using his ingenuity in improving the appearance and speed of a Star in such a manner that it could be copied, at little cost, and benefit the Star class as a whole. Had it not been for this policy, the Star would still be the crude little gaff rigged boat of the past, so outmoded that in all probability the class would no longer be in existence.

Ability in yacht racing includes more diversified attributes than any other sport. The skipper must be a skilled helmsman. He must know sails, how to treat them and keep them efficient. He must be a good judge of weather, speed and distance. He must know the rules and racing tactics and be able to act instinctively, as he who hesitates is lost. He must have the knack of training his crew and perfecting team work, since he cannot always depend upon having the same crew. Having some of these attributes is not enough. A really good skipper must possess them all.

There is such a thing as being too technical. Technically minded skippers have been known to turn the helm over to the crew while making a number of minor adjustments. By the time they got the boat going the way they wanted, so many yachts had passed them that they were never able to overtake them. The average skipper spends entirely too much time in beautifying his boat and messing around with minor improvements. He would do better if he devoted that time to improving his racing technique. Only those who have already become potential champions can afford to waste time on minor details. Such details in themselves cannot contribute enough additional speed to overcome the superior skill of the better skipper.

The most important thing of all, of course, is to possess that rare sixth sense of tune. Except for a few fundamentals, it cannot be taught. It has to be inborn. No one can buy speed anymore than he can become the world's best violinist, just because he can afford to buy a Stradivarius. If I have said some of these things elsewhere, they bear repeating, as many people have the wrong conception of the real purpose of one-design yacht racing. It was never intended as a means of equalizing ability, since that can never be done. Winning or losing between skippers of equal ability depends upon who has the fewer unlucky breaks. That is true of all sports, whether individual competition or team play. Otherwise championships would all end in a tie.

In yacht racing the mediocre skipper has a better chance than the average competitor in any other sport I can think of. No one can always predict wind shifts accurately. If a skipper knows that he is outclassed, or is hopelessly out of it and has nothing to lose, if he splits with the pack, he will on rare occasions pick up a favorable slant, or wind shift, and win an individual race. Such practice is certainly not recommended No one can improve himself doing that, or hope to win a series. In no other sport, however, does that element of rare luck exist.

The Star class has something more than that to offer the mediocre and even the very poor skipper. It offers him world-wide friendships and a life long interest There are other ways in which he can become popular and even prominent, which have nothing to do with his ability as a racing skipper.

CHAPTER XVIII

MODERN STAR HISTORY

Half GALES AND MOUNTAINOUS SEAS, broken ultra fragile masts, bruised ribs and a glorious time, marked the 1946 World's Championship. The classic was held in late November to avoid the hurricane season and give shipping every chance to return to normal. Havana has an exotic charm all its own and that was a special occasion. The war was over, the boys had the wanderlust and skippers were once again to sail their own Stars. We had almost forgotten what a Star in proper racing condition looked like. The highly polished hulls and gleaming rigs we saw at Havana were a sight for sore eyes. What a difference there was between them and the war weary appearance of so many of those semi-derelicts of the previous year.

Competing Stars were moored off the boathouse on the Almendares A flock of the club's professional sailors did the heavy work. Star skippers are not accustomed to having someone else even rub down their boats. A few stags stayed at the boathouse and another handful at the Havana Yacht Club itself (official headquarters) which was a good two miles down the coast. Everyone else had rooms at the

Hotel Presidente, a like distance from the river, but in the opposite direction. It became a sort of secondary headquarters and a bulletin board was put in the center of the lobby. All results and notices had to be made in triplicate, one for each place.

The distance between points was an obstacle. Those who had been there before rented a car and chauffer in advance of their arrival. The rest had to find a taxi and try to make the driver understand them. When everyone was leaving the hotel at once, it was not as easy as it sounds.

No boat could anchor more than a short distance off shore, because the bottom fell away to an incredible depth. It was impossible to provide a starting line of proper length for twenty-eight entries The stakeboat was on the fringe of the outer break and gave practically no room to jockey at that end of the line. Its position, however, was accurate, being off the foot of a street, shown on the chart and easy to locate.

We would have had the same trouble establishing a standard course, except for the northeast trades. They favored us for the first four days. The locals anchored a red and yellow spar buoy to the northward of Morro Castle. They called it a shoal ledge, although it took about two hundred fathoms of steel cable and a huge concrete block to hold it at the carefully plotted spot. The buoy was two and one-half miles due northeast of the line, making a perfect windward and leeward course.

In the mornings the winds were light and variable. There was only a gentle ground swell on the gulf. Shortly after the noon hour the northeast trades settled in and increased steadily. The boys thought it was blowing over forty at times, and it did seem so, but the weather bureau, which is supposed to know, recorded the highest velocity as twenty-eight miles per hour. A swift Gulf Stream set was running against the wind and closer to shore than normal. It sharpened those long swells and topped them with white caps. It is safe to say, insofar as the sea was concerned, it was the most rugged World's Championship ever sailed.

The Cuban navy furnished two eighty-five-foot sub chasers, one of which was used as a committee boat. The set ran with such force that it held it broadside to that wind and sea. The I.R.C. and its helpers were rolled about as much, perhaps more, than the competing skippers.

The disappearance of the red and yellow buoy, on the morning of the first race, caused considerable excitement. A tug captain, who knew that no buoy belonged there and assumed it went adrift, towed it, concrete block and all, back into the harbor. The local yachtsmen had to plant it again in a hurry, which was no easy task.

The Simoes brothers were our real worry. They were bringing their Star up from Rio on a tramp, which was behind schedule No one supposed that it could reach port in time. The navy was ready to send out a seaplane at dawn, intercept it and fly the boys to Havana. That would have forced the I R C to decide whether they were entitled to sail a local Star, under the emergency substitution rule, until their own arrived. Such a dispensation would have created a precedent that might have caused a lot of trouble the following year, but more about that later. The tramp just made it. The Star was rushed to the boathouse and the Brazilians started Within one hundred yards of the line, they carried out the mast A spare mast was hastily rigged and they came out again the next day. That mast went out a few seconds before the start. It had been made clear to everyone that skippers were responsible for the condition of their rigs and equipment, so no postponement could be ordered.

Harbor signals were devised especially for conditions at Havana and given from the committee boat, anchored in the mouth of the Almendares. It was just a step from the boathouse, but Stars had to be towed there at the hour the drawbridge opened. Most of their crews were put aboard later. A most efficient young Cuban had the newly created job of harbor official His speedboat circulated among the Stars, as he urged laggards to hasten When the "hoist sail" was made, all mainsails went up. About ten minutes later, when signaled to do so, the Stars sailed out of the river. It was only about two hundred yards from the inlet to the line. The idea, however, was to let contestants wait in sheltered waters, until everything was ready, as sometimes there were unavoidably long delays. It worked so well, that the system was used thereafter.

An unfortunate occurrence marred the start of the first race. A moment before the gun, the other sub chaser loomed up about fifty feet in front of the line. Willie Rivero, who operated the loud speaker, shouted at it in Spanish. It was probably a good thing that those yelling in English were not understood. It began to swerve away, then something went wrong Suddenly it began to back at full speed toward the approaching Stars. It all happened instantaneously. Several Stars managed to keep clear. Bob Rogers could not The crash split Gusty's jib and he was forced to withdraw. Cameramen were aboard that chaser and they always try to get too near a sports event. The officer in charge cannot be blamed, however, as there were also a few local dignitaries aboard. I have no idea who they were, but if a young navy officer disregards the wishes of some important personage he is apt to find himself wearing a gob's uniform the next day It was my own fault that he did not receive more explicit instructions in advance From then on he proved both efficient and helpful.

There is not enough space to relate the kaleidoscope of incidents that happened during that knock down and drag out series, so I must confine myself to a few highlights. The first four winners were Etchells, Knowles, Fleitz and Nye. The windward and leeward course record, which had stood since 1924, was broken three times. That was due, I presume, to the strong current, which lee-bowed the Stars on the beat None could be held off before that sea and wind, they would have yawed too much Hence they tacked downwind. Luffing gradually, they worked in toward the beach, where the head current was deflected by the shore line Then they would jibe and, with booms to port, head for the stakeboat. If they made it, they could round without jibing again. If not, it meant two jibes, risking the mast, or the time lost in trying to go about twice.

Although warned, few, if any, strengthened their rig. I cannot recall of any wire shroud, even the thinnest, parting under the strain. Most of the casualties were caused by light fragile fittings, especially aloft. They could not withstand the sudden jerks caused by that terrific pounding. Tangs and spreaders broke, or pulled out. Masts performed unbelievable gyrations. Some were lost and some saved. I saw Barney Lehman's bend at an angle of about forty-five degrees, but he kept it in. Harry Nye was not as lucky. He lost his on the last run of one race, but drifted across nineteenth, with a bit of sail fastened to the remaining eight-foot stub. He came back, with another mast, and won two days later.

The trades did not put in an appearance on the day of the final race. Instead, we had a light southerly. It was a weather-breeder, the forerunner of one of those northers. A three times around course was established, with the line off the Malacone. It was not a perfect isoceles triangle, due to anchoring conditions. That was Bob Lippincott's race from start to finish. George Fleitz finished fourth, to win the series for Los Angeles. Bob White, with a second was runner-up and Durward Knowles placed third. It was a good thing it was over, as the following day the weather really started to tune up.

An impromptu meeting was held at the vacant end of the hotel veranda, to discuss the advisability of formulating rules to strengthen the rig. It became rather heated. The taxi drivers, out in front, saw the red ribbons worn by our minor officers and thought it was a communist gathering. They notified the police. Evidently the hotel management explained matters, since nothing happened.

This account would not be complete without mention of Rafael Posso. He was commodore of the Havana Y.C. and vice commodore of the I.S.C.Y.R A. Possito, the Beau Brummel of Cuba, did not look a day older than when I first met him in 1926 Ever the gracious host, he is the most thorough detail man I ever knew. Without any written notes, he can remember the most trivial thing, if only mentioned once, and every item is always ready, afloat or ashore.

The evening entertainments can only be described as exquisite They were confined to formal and semi-formal dinner dances. These were not the conventional banquets of cold storage chicken, canned peas and mashed potatoes. Each meal, at which two or more wines were served, was different. The cuisine was excellent, the music was good and the company agreeable The youngsters might have preferred the hot dog and jazz entertainment. The majority, however, enjoyed that more genteel form of relaxation, after a turbulent day afloat. The writer, of course, is prejudiced in favor of that colorful isle and its sunny people.

Durward Knowles, of Nassau, won the '47 gold Star. Hilary Smart (to be heard from in '48) was runner-up, while Dick Stearns (who had been setting the Great Lakes afire) came into international fame, by placing third. George Fleitz, the Los Angeles defender, did not finish in the money, sailing his new Wench.

For California, with few local fleets, to attract twenty-one entries was quite an achievement, especially in a lame duck year. It was that all right, as the event had to leave, not just the continent, but the western hemisphere.

By adding fifty-seven points to his fleets previous total, Duarte Bello took the World's Championship to Cascais. As it turned out, that Portuguese fleet need not have sent an entry to protect its lead, but no one knew that in advance.

There actually was another European entry. The skipper must have been under the misapprehension that borrowed boats were still allowed, if one's story was good enough and his almost was. A local Star was assigned to him to sail until his own arrived, but it never would have. He had the name and number O.K. and the Star was supposed to be aboard a freighter, delayed by bad weather in the Canal Zone. Oddly enough there was such a freighter, but no Star was on its manifest. That could have been an error, due to it having been shipped on deck. The skipper, however, made one slip He claimed half ownership in a Star owned by a European fleet officer The latter cabled that the Star was still in Europe, the skipper, while a member, had been ın the U.S.A for over two years and was not a part owner of the boat. The entry was rejected. An apologetic letter was received from the said fleet, disclaiming any knowledge of the deception and stating that the pseudo skipper's fleet membership had been revoked.

A semi-local Star arrived the night before the first race, but no entry had been filed. Had it been accepted, the skipper's eligibility would have been challenged under the six month's transfer rule. He was then registered as belong-ing to another fleet. That rejection was another wise move on the part of Jim Cowie. Since then there have been no questionable entries.

Nineteen hundred and forty-eight was quite a Star year. With most of the major events in Europe, Puget Sound held a Silver Star Championship of North America. Charles Ross, of the home fleet, was the winner. He sailed Cete, the first Star ever built in that locality. On their way from England to Portugal some stopped off at San Sebastian, Spain, for its big international series. It was won by the French skipper, Stephan.

A partly built club, at Cascais, was completed. It pro-vided a sort of shore headquarters, with lockers, showers and a bar. The contestants, however, lived in hotels at nearby Estoril.

Wınd, plenty of it, was the outstanding feature. A September date had been selected, as the locals claimed there would be gentle breezes, but they were all wet. The wınd faırly screeched. After midnight of the first race, it whıstled down from the Sonoras. Four Stars parted their moorıng lınes and drifted to sea—Africa next stop. In the early houıs of the morning, the minister of marine sent planes ın search Knowles' Gem II was located fıfteen miles out. All four were eventually towed back to port, pretty well batteı ed. The wınd showed no sıgn of abating and the day's race was postponed.

Lockwood Pirie won the serıes by a single point, but ıt was not as close as it sounds. Woodie had already beaten Italy's premier three times. Had there been a tie, he would have won anyway. Hence all he had to do was prevent two more Stars from finishing between them. Straulino, naturally, was runner-up. The Smarts were a poor third, some twenty-five points behind the leaders. Sturrock, of Melbourne, was the first and only bona fide Australian entry. Like de Cardenas, he was a heavy weather favorite; both had withdrawals and their point scores were not impressive.

For some unknown reason, the annual meeting ratified a ten-man I.R.C., although the constitution specifies half that many. Aboard the Santa Maria, the committee boat furnished by the navy, blue ribboned Star officers were so thick that they were tripping over each other. That, and the conflicting lunch hour of the crew and inadequate ground tackle, for the line stakeboat, delayed some of the starts. Otherwise chairman Enrique Conill did a good job.

On one of the off days, the Portuguese staged a bull fight. Cebern Lee, proficient at the art of throwing the bull, was a volunteer toreador. I neglected to mention that only bull calves were put in the arena. Lee could run. He beat the calf to one of the safety niches. It was already occupied by three other neophyte toreadores and there was no room. No one seems quite sure whether he, or bull junior, was the most amazed and frightened. Jean Peytel also tried it. He would gracefully side-step the animal's rush, bending at the waist. Evidently it was in anticipation of the plaudits. Whereupon the calf would turn and playfully butt him in the stern. I state on good authority that, during the remainder of his stay, Jean ate his meals off the mantelpiece.

And what meals they were! Everyone agreed that Portuguese hospitality outdid Havana's—so did its wind, but it came from the land and the Stars did not have to plough through such gigantic seas. It was tough going, however, and only five of the twenty-four entries (from eleven different nations) completed all the races. I wonder what Adler thought of that Yes, Sig was there, combining the past and the present. He will be remembered as one of the team of Adler and O'Brian, who sailed the Canis Minor in the early teens. The pioneers of the gaff rigged days finished a race, come hell or high water. The idea of sailing back into the bay, so as to race another day (which many did) may be all right, but it never won a major championship.

There was so little water on Lake Michigan in 1949 that the World's Championship had to be held off the Chicago Y.C., some twenty-five miles down the coast. That was because Stars could not get in or out of Wilmette harbor. At the meeting, before the first race, it was unanimously agreed that if Nye won (he did) it would not prevent the event from being sailed off his own fleet the ensuing year. That action was unnecessary. The rules already provided that the series could remain in the same district, not the same fleet, for two consecutive years. The Chicago Y C is not within the territory of the Wilmette Harbor fleet.

Due to that last minute change in venue, another organization had already reserved the space indoors. The annual meeting, therefore, was held in the open air. From what I gather, it was rather a slam bang affair. No one knew who had a right to vote and who did not. Halsted and de Cardenas, between them, managed to get through it somehow. Reeve Bowden flew out to chairman the I R.C. It had no recording committee that year, hence worked late every evening.

Lowell North and Woodie Pirie sailed as if they belonged in another league. North finished first in four races, but did not win the series, being disqualified the second day. Pirie met the same fate before the starting gun the first day. The disqualifications occurred at the line, where everything was right under the eyes of the I.R.C. Both Stars, because of their speed, caused endless G.C. arguments throughout the winter.

By consistent sailing, Harry Nye won his second gold Star and second ducking in the lake—an old Star custom. Bob Lippincott was runner-up, once again attracting little attention, although he won the fourth race without the help of any disqualifications. Stan Ogilvy took third series prize.

The 1950 meeting was orderly. Charlie de Cardenas presided, while Paul Smart acted as secretary. A roped-off section was reserved for delegates and proxies. They stood, when voting, so there could be no mistake in the count. I was again chairman of the I.R.C. We were all quartered at an hotel, two long blocks away from the club.

Bob Lippincott, of West Jersey, put on the most spectacular performance. He broke his mast a couple of hundred yards from the finish and drifted across the line, under a jury rig, for a ninth. Then he won the series, being the first to have ever done so with a broken mast in one race; nor was Bob protested for not displaying his racing number. Believe it or not that happened to a yacht finishing in a squall under jib only—but not in the Star class. Nevertheless, the rules state that the racing number must be displayed. Now there is a kink for the sea lawyer to mull over.

If anyone thinks that Lake Michigan is a mild little pond, they have another think coming. It blew hard in every race and there was actually a surf pounding on the shore. There was only one exception, the Saturday morning race, held then to avoid conflict with the club's regular regatta. A club is perhaps favored with an international event once in a lifetime, but nothing must interfere with that regular weekend regatta, no sir! The fact that those early morning light airs might completely disrupt the results of a series was not considered, yet it almost happened.

Twin Star put so many boats between it and Sea Robin, at the end of the first circuit, that it seemed as if Woodie would again wear the crown, if they finished. Then something happened, which even the contestants do not know about The haze lifted and we saw stakeboat number two. It did not bear correctly, making the leeward leg about half a mile too long. We phoned its mark officials, who could see number one, to move it the required distance. No Star had as yet rounded. The course was exactly the same, but the right length. It was perfectly legal, the same as replacing a mark gone adrift. Had it not been done, the race would never have been finished. That would have spelled trouble. The Coast Guard had other commitments for the morrow.

Tito Nordio, of Trieste, won within the stipulated three and one-half hours. Lippincott, coming from nowhere, beat

Pirie, who became runner-up. Skip Etchells had the third highest point score. A different skipper won every race, against that field of forty-one, beating the previous year's record by a single entry.

Bob took the opener and Durward won the second race, but the Bahaman's jubilation was short. Returning to the club, he discovered that his locker had been purloined. All his valuables were gone, including his return ticket to Nassau. We learned later that there had been other locker pilferings that year.

After winning the third race, Agostino ran into his usual bad luck Friday. It was one of those cold gray days; half a gale with intermittent rain and big seas. Starting that race with a substantial lead, he broke a shroud. Lowering the jib, the Italian used its halyard to keep the mast in Merope. It worked, but with mainsail only, he fell back and finished twenty-ninth. It was the only race in which Straulino did not finish third or better. Except for that one mishap, he would have won the series easily. Etchells won. North, whom they feared in light air, strangely enough made his best showing, getting a daily third.

That same day some well-meaning person lowered the red cylinder, to save it from further punishment. It had remained up throughout over one hundred international races and was in sad need of repair. In fact it should have been replaced Lowering it had never been an official signal to contestants and it was not mentioned in the race circular. It simply meant that course and mark officials could go home. There were seasoned officers handling those jobs. Suppose the weather mark had been picked up and towed in, what then? The race would have been called and the I.R.C. accused of trying to give those down in the ruck another chance It was unnoticed, except by a few on the committee boat, but that seemingly harmless act might have caused a lot of criticism.

Another minor blunder occurred at the start of the final race. Because of the way it lay, the line flag was placed on the stern of the committee boat Our recall officer could not see it from inside the pilothouse and stood on the bridge. The bosun was inside with instructions to sound the whistle if told. It was close, but no one was over ahead of the gun and I so signaled from deck Our officer said O.K. and walked away. The bosun thought he meant that it was O.K. to pull the whistle cord and did so. A few skippers looked back, but none tried to return. If one had, he would have lost many places in that light air.

Incidentally Nye did not qualify that year and Bert Williams was the defender. Some people thought a start was postponed to give him time to reach the line, but they were mistaken. Kathleen had already been accounted for, but Bert had lowered his mainsail to adjust something. Some locals began to yell, "Wait for Williams." The I.R.C., however, was watching the wind, which had hauled. It postponed the start in order to shift the stakeboats. Otherwise there would not have been a windward leg.

The only criticism that reached my ears was that starts were delayed too long and they were. Let me state here and now that it was no fault of the I.R.C. Even had the courses been in that harbor, there would have been unavoidable delays. Why? Because the I.R.C. seldom was able to get away from the float before the time the first signal should have been given. People simply do not realize that a race cannot be started until, at least, the weather mark is anchored, and placing it takes time. Delays were caused by conflicting shore arrangements.

The I.R.C. had to dispose of all pending cases before the day's race. It did not get to the mess hall until a few minutes after noon. There was always a long line at the buffet lunch table and three or four rows waiting for the bar to open. Yes, some wanted a drink, after a long morning's work, before boarding an arid Coast Guard committee boat. The help, having been kept up late the night before, would not start earlier, nor could you blame them The I.R.C. had no priority. It does not seek special favors, but it's absurd for spectators to rush out to the line and wait for the officials who start the race to get there.

After the first day, I suggested postponing all signals one hour, but the majority did not wish to interfere with local arrangements. Another solution would have been to bring sandwiches, ice and glasses to the committee room. There probably always will be a certain amount of conflict between race management and shore activities. It usually starts at the annual meeting.

Some commodore decides to throw a cocktail party the same day. His emissary drifts in late in the afternoon. He takes a seat, bites his nails and squirms. When he can stand it no longer, he gets up and says, "Gentlemen, you must break this up or you will offend your host. The commodore and his friends have already been kept waiting nearly an hour."

That does it. Chairs are pushed back and people begin to leave. Some delegate, anxious to submit his motion, shouts it at the chairman. Only a few hear it, due to the confusion. Everyone yells, "Yes. Now let's adjourn."

How can such hasty action be curbed? Do not schedule any parties on the day of the annual meeting. It's the only day in the year that Star fleets meet, through their accredited representatives and they have lots of business to transact. It is useless to warn the one throwing the party, as he soon forgets that warning. Just do not have a party. A second session is legal, but no longer practical. Most delegates and proxies are also contestants. They treasure their day of rest and do not wish to spend it at a meeting.

The foregoing is not said in the light of criticism. Entertainments are necessary to make a World's Championship a success. Naturally the hosts feel their responsibility and wish to do a good job. A little forethought, however, will avoid a lot of quite unnecessary trouble. This statement is made simply to explain those delayed starts. Except for these few little things, which the average person probably never noticed, the 1950 Chicago jamboree was grand.

The waters of Bob Lippincott's West Jersey fleet were not suitable for a standard course. Hence the 1951 championship was held at Gibson Island. It is a beautiful spot. Like

Havana, however, the focal points are a little too far apart. The writer expected to chairman the I.R.C., but a broken leg and the purchase of a house in the country prevented. Dave Dunigan, international vice president elect of North America, did the honors and made a fine job of it.

These happenings are so recent that they are known to most sailing fans. It is, therefore, only necessary to skim the surface and perhaps mention a couple of incidents not generally known to the yachting public.

The most important feature of the 1951 World's Championship was its all time record of forty-nine starters. That is a slew of yachts to handle on one gun in any race. It gave rise to a flock of suggestions about restricting the number of entries to one from a district, etc. Anything of the sort would be a great mistake. Many fleets, who know they have no chance of placing, send an entry to meet the crowd, gain experience, take back useful information and attend the annual meeting. To change that would undermine the organization. Furthermore, districts would begin to split, just as large fleets have been doing, to gain an extra entry. Pretty soon the same condition would apply again.

If the number of entries become unwieldy, say forty-eight or more, split them into two divisions, by lot. Let the first three races be qualifications. After a rest day, start all over again with three more races. The fifty per cent with the highest score in each qualification group to constitute the championship division and race for the gold Star. The remainder could start fifteen minutes later for consolation series prizes. Do away with special prizes, such as the invaders, which no longer serves any real purpose. It involves one more race, but could be handled within a week. Financing daily prizes should not be too difficult. It is better than the odd and even number type of qualification and would not kill the incentive of all fleets from gathering annually. Maintaining the esprit de corps is the all important thing.

There were the usual complaints about delayed starts. Some people do not realize that the steamship channel, off

Gibson Island, is so narrow that the Coast Guard cannot divert commercial shipping. A course between it and land would have to be sailed three times around. It would also bring the yachts too close to the beach. Dave had them towed out three miles and started the races on the other side of the said channel. That and light, fluky airs caused some unavoidable delays. Anyone can be a good second guesser, but Dave used his head. Had a long tow scrambled the results of a race, or a Star run aground, then there would have been justifiable cause for criticism.

Skip and Mary Etchells won. Mary was the first girl crew that ever won a Star world's title. Dick Stearns, of Chicago, was only beaten by one point, while old Prof. Ogilvy, who is always among the leaders, wriggled in third.

Straulino won two races, but fate again deprived him of a gold Star, this time through no real fault of his own. He made a premature start at the end of that long line and did not hear the recall. By the time the course launch overtook him and brought him back, he must have been about half a mile behind that record breaking field and his '51 chances were shot. Unless a loud speaker can be hooked up to the committee boat's electric plant, the committee might just as well use the old time cards with numbers. Those little portable battery amplifiers are no damn good. The human voice through a megaphone carries further in a breeze.

The big event had to leave the continent, but not the hemisphere. It amounted, however, to the same thing. Rio de Janeiro had only a theoretical chance of taking the series to Brazil, if the European entries fell on their faces and failed to finish in several races. Duarte Bello, of Cascais, again took the event to Portugal on aggregate points and that involved a most unpleasant incident. I do not like to air our dirty linen, but it is better for people to know the facts than formulate ideas of their own from a few half truths, which may have been overheard. The worst of it is that everything was caused by a misinterpretation of rules by our own chief of the measurement department, which certainly put the association on the spot. While rather involved, I will attempt to cover the essential facts from memory. I may be a bit foggy on some of the details, but at least I know that I am correct as to the principles and rules. Bello had every reason to believe that the boat he took to Gibson Island was a bona fide Star, since it had a certificate. While he had his own ideas about the contour aft, he did not try to beat the rules. He discussed the matter with our measurement committee chairman before the boat was built and received the latter's O.K.

We have many certified measurers all over the world who are constantly taking the physical dimensions of Stars and sending same to the measurement committee, which grants or refuses a certificate. To speed up and simplify the work, the association supplies these measurers with measurement blanks. On the blank is a rough outline of a Star. As I recall it, measurements at three key stations were mandatory. The dimensions were entered after the corresponding key letter on the form. It was assumed that if the contour was correct at these three stations it would be correct throughout or otherwise noticeable. If noticeable, the measurer was instructed to check and report, as the rules require that a Star be as per plan. That rule, a basic one, is what caused all the trouble. The boat did not look like a Star aft of station seven. Many noticed it and the I.R.C. had it remeasured. Aft of station seven it was not as per plan and was barred from competition. The I.R.C. had a perfect right to take that action. Errors are possible and its first thought must be to protect the interests of the other World's Championship entries.

Our measurement committee chairman contended that the key stations shown on the measurement form superseded the plans. Why that form is not even mentioned in the rules. I am not even sure that it is to scale. It's simply an aid. Bello was given a substitute boat, as he most certainly was not to blame. Perhaps he did better with it than he would have with his own. Anyway he accomplished his purpose. The I.R.C. also made a mistake. It overstepped its authority ın ordering the boat rebuilt. Its authority ends twenty-four hours after the series. Bello entered an appeal, but he did so almost nine months after the time limit and it was not allowed. That Bello had to suffer for another's mistake may sound cruel, but if that boat had been allowed to race, it would have created a precedent that would have been most harmful to the Star Class.

And now we enter Europe's golden age of Stardom, the three consecutive years that the World's Championship was held on that continent and the last phase of Star history that can be covered by this book. I was not present and the average reader probably knows the net results as well as I do. I shall confıne myself, therefore, to a very brıef summary of what happened and let the tabulated score speak for ıtself insofar as the details are concerned. Perhaps I may be allowed a few comments on how these three years have affected the Star class. To my mind they were most beneficial. Few realize how many records were broken, records whıch will probably stand for many years to come.

This most recent era started with the 1952 Olympics, won by Straulino and Rode. The story is told in chapter eight. Having shaken their jinx, the Italian commanders went on to win just about every championship in Europe. In '52 and '53 they made grand slams, capturing the World's, European and Italıan titles. That in itself is a record which will be dıfficult to duplicate. They almost did it again in '54. I predicted for some years before the majority seemed to grasp the fact, that Agostino Straulino had more potential championship ability than any other skipper and was the man to watch, if he ever got going. My prophesy came true, but I am getting a little ahead of myself.

Quite a number of Olympic entries shipped their Stars from Helsinki to Lisbon. The European contingent had to compete for the championship of that continent, also off Cascais, the week before the big event. Merope romped away with the 1952 World's Championship. Bob Lippincott, the gold Star man of '50, was a poor second, finishing twenty-five points behind Straulino. There is another record that may stand for some years to come. The world's title has never been won by such a wide margin of points before. Duarte Bello placed third on his home waters.

The 1953 series was sailed off Napoli beneath ominous Vesuvius that towered in the background. Straulino won again, but only by four points, over—guess who—the ever persistent Duarte Bello. Nordio, of Trieste, was a poor third. Since under our rotating rule the same fleet cannot hold the event for two consecutive years, the location had to be decided on aggregate points and it went back once more to Cascais. Now that really is remarkable. Three times Duarte Bello took the World's Championship back to Portugal by aggregate points. He had the help of Capucho in '46 and '49 and of Tito in '50, but Bello was the anchor man each time and sewed it up. The third time he did it single handed. Here you have a record for both a fleet and a skipper, which I doubt will ever be matched again.

The World's Championship having been held in Europe for three consecutive years, it had to leave the continent after 1954. Habana and Nassau were practically tied on aggregate points, or to be more exact, de Cardenas and Knowles were tied. An entry from the U.S. might take it with an outright win, but that seemed unlikely. Lippincott took quite a beating in '52 and the best U.S. entry only placed eleventh in '53. That an African, Australian or South American skipper could win outright was not even considered.

What actually happened, and I guess everyone knows it by now, was that Charlie de Cardenas at long last achieved his life's ambition and won a gold Star. Charlie competed in his first World's Championship twenty-five years ago. He has not entered every year during that quarter of a century, but he has been in more World's Championships than any other Star member. Sharing the honors, of course, was his oldest boy, Carlos, Jr. The latter made his debut as crew in the event twelve years ago, when he was only knee high to a marlin spike. Charlie had no intention of messing around with any aggregate point nonsense. He just went out and did it up brown with four firsts and one second, coming within a single point of a perfect score. And there indeed you do have a record, for no one has ever done it before.

Our international president's victory was without a doubt the most popular of all victories. It was also one of the greatest things that could have happened for the class. Fair, fat and over fifty, Charlie proved that the younger element can be beaten. It should lift the morale of many an old timer, who was becoming discouraged. Furthermore Charlie is a Simon pure. It will stop all that nonsensical talk about only those being connected in the sail or boat building business being able to win. Charlie was wined and dined all over Europe and if he ever survives the reception planned by Habana it will be a wonder.

Before I forget, Durward Knowles was runner-up and Agostino Straulino placed third. I have been told by President Smart that the courses could not have been better and the races were run perfectly. Our European brothers outdid themselves for three years in efficient management and lavish entertainment. Those fellows came to the U.S.A. for many years. They probably felt that the odds were overwhelmingly against them because there were so many American fleets entered. It was high time that they held the World's Championship for the time limit allowed by the rules. The event was much more international in character than in the past, because of the many fleets from countries that were within a reasonable distance. The record breaking entry of 1951 was not approached, but that is unimportant. There was no longer the feeling that two fleet entries from a given country should team up and help each other. Nothing in my humble opinion could have been more beneficial for the Star class than those three years. This brings us up-to-date, with fabulous Habana to look forward to in 1955 and with a greater fraternal feeling existing throughout the I.S.C.Y.R.A. than ever before.

EPILOGUE

POP CORRY ONCE SAID, "George, some day you'll be the old man of the Star Class." That was long ago, but he was prophetic. It's incredible how the years roll by. He is gone and I am serving my sixth term as commodore and understand that I have been nominated for a seventh. No one can ever fill Pop's shoes, so I am tackling the job from a different angle, which I hope may prove helpful.

I have been re-appointed to the judiciary board for another three years, still being chairman because of my seniority. I have lost my key man, Stan Ogilvy, who was elected executive vice president. My two associates are now Ted Clark and Owen Torry. I also have a most able alternate in Howard Walden. We do not have as many appeals and requests for interpretations as in the past. It's spasmodic, but important work, which is not very exacting. To be qualified, however, one must have a thorough knowledge of Star rules, their intent and purpose. Most appeals are the result of some words that are accidentally missing, or which were left in, due to an oversight, and never brought into accord with some more recent and basic amendment. Hence the appeals we do get are complicated.

Once again I have been named on the seven man U.S. Olympic yachting committee, in charge of Stars. It only involves a few months of concentrated work every fourth year. My real job in connection with the Olympics has been of an underground character. Most members think the Star has been automatically placed on the program each time, but that is not so. There have been powerful interests opposed to us and few realize by what a narrow squeak the Star has finally been put on the Olympic program at the very last moment. It has meant many very lengthy letters to establish contact with influential persons in various countries and to explain to them, usually through a third party how they should vote and why. All that, I believe, is behind us. I am happy to say that the Star is included for the 1956 Olympics in Australia. It should be, since of all yachting classes, it comes the nearest to conforming with Olympic principles.

I am now officially retired and have a house at Bellport. It's a little country town on the south shore of Long Island, about thirty miles east of where I spent most of my boyhood. I say officially retired, because actually I am helping my wife run a tiny store in the village, which is only a couple of hundred yards from our home. Most of the customers are of the fair sex. I can just picture myself saying, "Stow the gab kiddo and buy that red blouse, it'll look damn good on you." So I am kept in a back office and take care of the buying and the books. Between ourselves it's the hardest job I ever had.

I am thankful that we no longer live in the city. Out here one knows one's next door neighbor and, after the summer folks leave, everyone you pass on the street. They are friendly people, who speak my language. I could no longer stand the hustle and bustle of the city. It's no longer the little old New York I once knew. For all of me they can give it back to the Indians. I go there on a buying trip a couple of times a year and stay as few hours as possible. For example, on my last trip a wholesaler said to me, "I can tell that you are not a native New Yorker by the way you speak." That got my goat, so I replied, "Not only was I born on Manhattan Island, but so were all my forefathers back to the days when it was called New Amsterdam. The trouble with you, my boy, is that you probably never spoke to a genuine New Yorker before."

We have a fair sized and active Star fleet, with headquarters at a small yacht club three blocks from my house. I do not go there very often. I do not intend to race again, because I know that I would get the hell walloped out of me. Star skippers improve every year and I have been inactive since 1948. If I were a younger man I would practice what I preach, but I could never hope to catch up now. Unlike Pop Corry, I am not interested in just sailing for the fresh air. I get plenty of that anyway and besides I am too busy Saturdays and believe me I need the rest on Sundays. Although asked, local race committee work is out. Judiciary board members are ineligible. It's a good rule, because even if excused from voting, the very fact that a J.B. member was on an R.C., whose decision was appealed, would influence the others on the J.B.

All I do now is mostly by mail. I still hear from a few old timers, but their letters are becoming few and far between. It's to be expected. Time marches on. I have lived to see my dreams of 1916 come true and am content. Harold Halsted is building a house here. Ted Everitt and Reeve Bowden live here. It seems that this joint is rapidly becoming an approved spot for putting aged ex-officials of the Star class out to pasture.

If other organizations could only develop the international comradeship of the Star class, this troubled world would be a more peaceful place to live. As Stan once wrote in Starlights, "The first forty years are the hardest." The foundation has been laid. The most important thing for those at the helm to do from now on is to keep the I.S.C.Y.R.A. out of club or national politics and the Star class will rise to undreamed of magnitude. Why the surface as yet has not even been scratched. Star development on four continents is still in its infancy. There are plenty of localities in Europe and North America left where successful fleets can be developed, but those in power must keep right on pitching. I devoted the greater part of my life to the Star class. It's in just as capable hands now and I know it will continue to be—all power to its continued growth and success.

World's Championship Results

> Abbreviations, etc Dsa—Disabled   Dsq—Disqualified   DNS—Did Not Start   Wdr—
> Withdrew   Ch—Chairman   B—Builder   *—Defending Fleet   0—No points, reason not given

1923—ON WESTERN LONG ISLAND SOUND

Skipper	Crew	Yacht	Fleet	Daily Finish					Pts
W Inslee	R Nelson	Taurus	W Long Island Sound	1	2	1			23
H Wylie	E Ratsey	Astrea	English Bay	4	1	2			20
R Walton	L Carey	Doris	Central Lake Erie	3	6	3			15
W Wood	W Wood	Ara	Narragansett Bay	2	4	7			14
E Walker	G Curry	Kangaroo	New South Wales	5	5	5			12
F Bedford	W Bull	Peacock	C Long Island Sound	6	3	6			12
B Weston	G Waters	California	Southern California	Dsa	7	4			7
H Waite	F Lord	Ursa Minor	E Long Island Sound	7	Wdr	Wdr			2

Winning yacht No 1 B—Ike Smith, Port Washington, N Y , 1911 Races conducted by Club
R C 's Ch Meeting—G A Corry Ch I E C —G W Elder

1924—ON WESTERN LONG ISLAND SOUND

Skipper	Crew	Yacht	Fleet	Daily Finish					Pts
J Robinson	A Knapp	Little Bear	*W Long Island Sound	6	1	1	1	2	44
B Comstock	W Gidley	Rhody	Narragansett Bay	2	3	5	2	1	42
B Weston	R Schauer	California	Southern California	4	4	2	6	4	35
W Inslee	C Byram	Sonny	Gravesend Bay	1	2	4	3	DNS	34
W McHugh	F Bedford	South Wind	C Long Island Sound	3	5	3	4	DNS	29
N Kenney	J Miller	Porpoise	Chesapeake Bay	8	7	7	Wdr	3	22
L Bainbridge	E Gibb	Sayonara	Peconic Bay	5	8	6	5	Wdr	20
R Purvis	R McLennan	Stella Maris	English Bay	7	6	8	8	DNS	19
H Watterson	L Carey	Audrey	Central Lake Erie	Wdr	9	9	7	DNS	9
H Waite	F Lord	Dot	E Long Island Sound	9	10	DNS	DNS	DNS	3

Winning yacht No 61 B—Ike Smith, Port Washington, N Y , 1915 Races conducted by Club
R C 's Ch Meeting—G A Corry Ch I E C —G W Elder

1925—ON WESTERN LONG ISLAND SOUND

Skipper	Crew	Yacht	Fleet	Daily Finish					Pts
A Iselin	E Willis	Ace	*W Long Island Sound	1	1	9	1	2	66
G Phillips	C Davis	Auriga	English Bay	3	2	2	6	1	61
R Schauer	E Gillett	Movie Star II	Southern California	4	6	2	6	3	59
B Comstock	W Gidley	Rhody	Narragansett Bay	6	3	Wdr	5	1	49
N Kenney	T Kenney	Porpoise	Chesapeake Bay	8	4	4	3	Dsq	45
W Inslee	A Webb	Sonny	Gravesend Bay	5	9	1	4	Dsq	45
F Bedford	W McHugh	Maia II	C Long Island Sound	7	5	3	Dsq	5	44
J Jessop	J Sykes	Windward	San Diego Bay	11	10	5	7	4	43
E Blouin	E Rau	Talita	New Orleans	2	7	10	8	Dsq	37
H Dowsett	C Dillingham	Hokulele	Hawaiian Islands	14	12	7	9	7	31
L Bainbridge	E Gibb	Sayonara	Peconic Bay	9	11	8	Wdr	8	28
R Walton	W Fraizier	Doris	Central Lake Erie	10	8	11	Dsq	DNS	19
P Holden	G Chappel	Hildy	E Long Island Sound	13	Dsq	13	10	Dsq	12
M de Sena	G Alamilla	Aurrera	Habana	12	Dsq	12	Wdr	Dsq	8
W Hyde	J Brewster	Cooperstown	Otsego Lake	15	Dsq	DNS	Wdr	9	8

Winning yacht No 202 B—Owner, 1924 Races conducted by Club R C 's Ch Meeting—
G W Elder Ch I E C —G W Elder

1926—ON WESTERN LONG ISLAND SOUND

Skipper	Crew	Yacht	Fleet	Daily Finish					Pts.
B Comstock	W Gidley	Rbody	Narragansett Bay	1	1	6	1	3	73
D Starring	F Bedford	Ardara	C Long Island Sound	7	2	1	3	4	68
H Fisher	H Denhie	Dona Bertha	San Diego Bay	5	5	2	2	7	64
L Bainbridge	E Gibb	Sayonara II	Peconic Bay	6	9	3	6	2	58
W Inslee	C Byram	Sonny II	Gravesend Bay	3	4	5	4	DNS	52
R Schauer	T Parkman	Movie Star II	Los Angeles Harbor	2	3	9	Dsq	5	47
V Darlinson	W Boice	Alya	West Lake Erie	8	7	Dsq	5	6	42
W Hubbard	W Hervey	Tempe II	Newport Harbor	12	10	4	10	9	40
G Elder	R Finlay	Iscyra	*W Long Island Sound	14	11	12	8	1	39
E Bouin	O Humphreys	Talita	New Orleans	4	6	14	12	15	34
H Dowsett	J Woolaway	Hula Star II	Hawaiian Islands	9	12	10	7	14	33
R Walton	J Fraser	Doris	Central Lake Erie	10	8	13	11	13	30
F Silva	F Villapol	Lisa	Cienfuegos	15	14	7	9	11	29
J Gorrin	A Bru	Gavilan	Habana	13	13	8	14	8	29
F Clancy	W Meurer	Scrapper	Detroit River	11	15	11	13	10	25
L Curtis	Mrs Curtis	Nor' Light	Massachusetts Coast	16	16	15	15	12	11

Winning yacht No 143 B—Baxter, Pawtucket, R I, 1923 Races conducted by Club R C's
Meeting—G W Elder Ch I R C—P E Edrington

1927—ON NARRAGANSETT BAY

Skipper	Crew	Yacht	Fleet	Daily Finish					Pts.
W Hubbard	R Edwards	Tempe III	Newport Harbor	6	1	6	3	3	†71
F Bedford	B Cunningham	Colleen	C Long Island Sound	1	2	3	12	1	71
H Smith	W Henderson	Mackerel	Chesapeake	2	7	1	4	5	71
B Comstock	W Gidley	Rbody	*Narragansett Bay	4	3	2	9	4	68
E Bogardus	R Purvis	Hoku	Hawaiian Islands	7	6	9	1	6	61
A Iselin	E Willis	Ace	W Long Island Sound	3	5	4	11	9	58
E DeMoe	H Elliott	Dream Star	Lake Michigan	8	14	10	2	2	54
E Blouin	S Jahncke	Talita	New Orleans	11	12	5	7	8	47
V Darlinson	J McInnes	Alya	West Lake Erie	12	10	11	5	7	45
D Roberts	B Hutchinson	Ruth	Peconic Bay	10	13	7	6	15	39
L Curtis	La Curtis	Nor Light	Massachusetts Coast	13	11	13	10	10	33
J Gorrin	M Riva	Gavilan	Habana	9	8	8	Wdr	Dsq	29
A Goesle	T Parkman	Ben MaChree	Gravesend Bay	Wdr	4	14	8	Wdr	28
J Rockwell	M Minnigerode	Limbas	Philippine Islands	14	9	17	13	11	26
J Miller	G Miller	Tom Boy	Hampton Roads	5	Wdr	15	Wdr	13	21
E duPont	A Randall	Clytie	Delaware River	15	15	16	14	14	16
D Colyer	J Parsons	Yankee	E Long Island Sound	16	16	12	DNS	12	16

†Sail-off, triple tie Winning yacht No 423 B—Owner, 1927 Ch Meeting—G W Elder Ch
I R C—G W Elder

1928—OFF NEWPORT HARBOR, CALIFORNIA

Skipper	Crew	Yacht	Fleet	Daily Finish					Pts
P Edrington	G Gray	Sparkler II	New Orleans	7	5	3	3	3	68
J Watkins	A Knapp	Okla	C Long Island Sound	12	6	1	2	2	†67
J Jessop	J Sykes	Windward	San Diego Bay	4	10	2	1	6	67
R Schauer	E Fink	Movie Star II	Los Angeles Harbor	3	9	5	9	1	63
F Robinson	D Robinson	Budsal II	Peconic-Gardiners	9	1	7	6	5	62
J Johnson	L Johnson	Undine	Chesapeake Bay	2	4	8	5	13	58
E Willis	S Cogswell	Ace	W Long Island Sound	1	8	Dsq	4	4	55
W Atwater	J Atwater	Minx	Great South Bay	5	7	9	8	7	54
B Hirst	G Woodward	Arrow	Delaware River	6	12	4	10	10	48
W Wood	W Wood	Ara	Narragansett Bay	7	3	13	4	9	47
W Hubbard	R Edwards	Tempe III	*Newport Harbor	10	2	6	Dsq	11	43
N Williams	A Williams	Lucky Lindy	Gravesend Bay	11	13	10	12	8	36
G Phillips	R Kerr	Auriga	English Bay	14	16	12	7	14	27
M deSena	R Gomez	Aurrera IV	Habana	16	15	11	15	12	21
E Bogardus	R Purvis	Hoku	Hawaiian Islands	13	11	Wdr	13	15	20
H Doulton	E Hayward	Skipper	Santa Barbara	15	14	14	14	16	17
C Smith	B Mitchell	Frisco Star	San Francisco	Dsq	17	Wdr	16	17	4

†Sail-off, tie for 2nd Winning yacht No 486 B—Joe Parkman, Brooklyn, N Y, 1928 Ch
Meeting—P E Edrington Ch I R C—H M Worcester

1928—AT NEW ORLEANS

Skipper	Crew	Yacht	Fleet	Daily Finish					Pts
G Johnson	C Johnson	Eel	Chesapeake Bay	5	4	1	1	1	108
G Gray	P Edrington	Sparkler II	*New Orleans	2	1	4	2	8	105
J Watkins	W McHugh	Okla II	C Long Island Sound	6	6	2	10	2	92
A Knapp	N Weed	Peggy Wee	W Long Island Sound	1	8	2	11	5	91
W Atwater	J Atwater	Sunbeam	Great South Bay	8	3	14	6	3	84
F Robinson	N Robinson	Budsal II	Peconic-Gardiners	Wdr	2	6	8	4	75
B Comstock	W Gidley	Rhody	Narragansett Bay	6	10	7	8	14	73
W Hubbard	R Webster	Tempe III	Newport Harbor	13	5	9	4	15	73
R Mann	G Worthington	Starlite	San Diego Bay	10	15	10	5	7	72
T Parkman	T Parkman	Fleet Star II	Gravesend Bay	9	7	7	14	13	69
S Dale	C Grover	Vixen II	Barnegat Bay	14	11	16	6	9	64
G Phillips	P Gordon	Chico	English Bay	3	12	13	18	11	63
R Bradley	C Howland	Majella	Illinois River	4	14	12	17	12	61
F Robertson	R Robinson	Juno	Delaware River	Dsq	Wdr	9	3	3	57
E Fink	P Worcester	Movie Star	Los Angeles	Wdr	9	5	10	Wdr	48
M Riva	C deCardenas	Mambi	Habana	11	18	17	19	10	45
R Anderson	B Wilder	Kausia	Hawaiian Islands	16	13	18	13	17	43
H Doulton	W Soule	Skipper	Santa Barbara	12	17	15	20	18	38
A Skeets	J Thorne	Alcyone	Barbados	15	16	22	22	20	25
W Judkins	J McDonald	Mille Tonnere	Mississippi Sound	Dsa	20	20	16	16	24
J Thomas	F Swan	Limbas	Philippines	18	21	21	21	19	22
E DeMoe	J Dennison	Dream Star	Lake Michigan	17	19	19	Dsq	DNS	17
J Miller	G Miller	Tomboy II	Hampton Roads	19	Dsq	Dsq	15	Dsq	9

Winning yacht No 56 B—Owner, 1928 Ch Meeting and IRC—G W Elder

1930—ON CHESAPEAKE BAY

Skipper	Crew	Yacht	Fleet	Daily Finish					Pts
A Knapp	N Weed	Peggy Wee	W Long Island Sound	1	3	7	2	4	98
W Hubbard	T Ditmar	Tempe IV	Newport Harbor	2	7	1	1	9	95
J Watkins	W McHugh	Okla II	C Long Island Sound	4	4	3	8	4	93
S Dale	C Grover	Vixen	Barnegat Bay	3	1	6	10	7	88
J Miller	G Miller	Flapper	Hampton Roads	17	2	2	5	6	83
G Gray	D Wuescher	Chico	New Orleans	5	15	4	4	5	82
J Johnson	C Johnson	Ripple	*Chesapeake Bay	6	5	5	3	13	82
E Poor	E Towl	Tsan	Peconic-Gardiners	7	10	14	16	1	67
C Ratsey	J Atkin	Joy	Solent	9	11	11	7	13	64
T Parkman	T Parkman	Fleet Star	Gravesend Bay	13	6	12	13	10	61
M deSena	R Gomez	Yuyu	Habana	16	8	9	21	2	59
R Bradley	F Bloom	Majella II	Illinois River	8	9	8	Dsq	8	59
J Rockwell	A Tigh	Lintik	Philippines	11	19	19	6	18	48
D Atwater	E Elsbree	Moonshine	Narragansett Bay	14	17	10	15	19	40
C Stewart	J Mason	Fawn	Elk River	19	16	21	17	12	40
H Halsted	P duGumoens	Chuckle	Great South Bay	20	18	20	11	11	35
H Doulton	W Soule	Emmeline	Santa Barbara	10	Wdr	16	9	Wdr	34
R Anderson	C Dyer	Nalu	Hawaiian Islands	15	20	15	14	17	34
F Manegold	M Nilson	Fram	Lake Michigan	19	16	21	12	16	33
J Peytel	J Lebrun	Startle	Paris	21	12	17	19	15	31
S Smith	Mrs Smith	Red Star II	Otsego Lake	18	21	13	18	21	24
E Kelly	J McClatchey	Licette	Cannes	22	19	22	20	20	12

Winning yacht No 455 B—New England Boat Works, Cos Cob, Conn Ch IRC and Meeting—G W Elder

1931—ON WESTERN LONG ISLAND SOUND

Skipper	Crew	Yacht	Fleet	Daily Finish				Pts
W McHugh	J Watkins	Colleen	C Long Island Sound	2	1	10	5	7	110
C Ratsey	S Elsbree	Joy	Solent	9	14	1	2	4	†105
E Fink	A McCrate	Zoa	Long Beach	8	5	8	4	5	105
C Pflug	J Pflug	Wings	Great South Bay	1	20	4	6	2	102
R Bradley	C Howland	Majella II	Illinois River	12	3	3	11	15	91
E Jahncke	D Wuescher	Dixie	New Orleans	5	10	2	7 Dsq	84
W Lyons	B Henderson	Vega	Newport Harbor	Dsq	6	14	3	3	82
S Dale	C Grover	Vixen II	Barnegat Bay	14	13	6	14	8	81
B Comstock	T Harris	Rhody	Narragansett Bay	3	12 Dsq	1	13	79
F Robertson	R Robinson	Juno	Delaware River	15	8	15	15	6	76
T Parkman	F Robinson	Fleet Star II	Gravesend Bay	DNS		5 Wdr	1	71
C Henderson	B Randall	Gar	Chesapeake Bay	4	11	11 Wdr	12	70
H Edwards	G Godwin	Winsome	Peconic-Gardiners	10	9	9 Dsq	10	70
J Miller	W Sellers	Flapper	Hampton Roads	7 Wdr	7	9	18	67
A Knapp	N Weed	Peggy Wee	*W Long Island Sound	6	2 Dsq Wdr	9	64
F Bottomley	H Dowsett	Menehune	Hawaiian Islands	14	7	20	10	20	64
W Soule	W Dickson	Barby	Santa Barbara	16	16	13	13	19	58
M Rhys-Price	P Doyle	Virgo	Lake Maracaibo	20	15 Dsq	8	11	54
J Downey	R Downey	Blue Mist	Lake Ontario	18	22	16	16	16	47
W MacDonald	J Parsons	Kittiwake	E Long Island Sound	Wdr	19	18	12	14	45
S Smith	H Grew	Natty Bumppo	Otsego Lake	11	21	12 Wdr	22	42
S Goss	M Hayford	Carol II	Lake Michigan	19	18	21	18	21	38
J McClatchy	P McClatchy	Lone Wolf	Elk River	17	17 Wdr Dsq	17	30
N Davis	M Sutter	Sea Beast	Nantucket Sound	21	23	22	17	24	28
E Gamba	J Lucke	Mabuya	Habana	22	24	17 Wdr	23	22
G dePiolenc	C LaCarriere	Darling	Paris	Dsa	25	19	Dsa	25	12

†Won sail-off Winning yacht No 333   B—Bear & Egerton, Glenwood Landing, N Y , 1926
Ch Meeting and I R C —G W Elder

1932—ON CENTRAL LONG ISLAND SOUND

Skipper	Crew	Yacht	Fleet	Daily Finish				Pts
E Fink	E Thorne	Mist	Long Beach	7	2	16	1	2	118
C Pflug	J Pflug	Wings	Moriches Bay	1	6	15	4	4	116
R Bradley	P Singer	Laura G	Illinois River	2	3	14	3	10	114
T Parkman	F Robinson	Fleet Star 3	Gravesend Bay	8	13	6	2	8	104
W McHugh	J Watkins	Colleen	*C Long Island Sound	17	8	5	6	11	99
F Robertson	R Robinson	Juno	Delaware River	21	5	11	10	3	97
S Dale	P Jenness	Spray	Barnegat Bay	16	11	8	11	6	95
E Hayward	W Dickinson	Howdy	Santa Barbara	9	7	12	14	17	88
L Meory	A Haire	Seeadler	Great South Bay	10	24	2	5	16	88
J Miller	J Atwater	Flapper	Hampton Roads	20	1	3	19	15	87
J McClatchy	Mrs McClatchy	Lone Wolf	Elk River	23	10	17	9	5	82
D Atwater	C Lawton	Moonshine	Narragansett Bay	5	17	26	18	1	79
J Herbulot	J Peytel	Tramontane	Paris	11	23	9	8	18	78
W vonHutschler	E Beyn	Ha-Eff	Norddeutsche	15	19	18	22	14	68
R Smith	J Smith	Lone Star	Galveston Bay	18	4	13	24	19	68
H Blake	M Blake	Dice	Peconic-Gardiners	6	19	21	25	13	62
B Vanderveer	S Vanderveer	Bandit II	W Long Island Sound	4	21	1 DNS DNS	61
P Raskob	M Shehan	Ripple	Eastern Shore	Wdr	16	7	15	9	61
H Dowsett	H White	Hula Star	Hawaiian Islands	14	20	23	7	21	61
G Waterhouse	W Metcalf	Three Star	San Francisco	25	14	22	17	7	58
E Kelly	K Phillips	Fouah Lieh	Cannes	24	27	10	12	22	52
J Cleary	E Rea	Sparkler II	New Orleans	19	15	24	26	13	50
W MacDonald	J Parsons	Kittiwake	E Long Island Sound	Dsq	12	19	19	23	49
C Ratsey	P Jasse	Joy	Solent	3	22	25	21 Dsq	46
A Ames	C Larsen	Lintik	Philippines	22	18	4	23	20	42
D S-Cullberg	K Millett	Swedish Star	Stockholm	13 Dsq	20	20 Dsq	35
S Smith	J Greenough	Red Star	Otsego Lake	12	26	27	23 Wdr	28
H Sherman	J Lucke	Sea Gate	Lake Maracaibo	Dsq	25 DNS DNS DNS	4

Winning yacht No 879   B—Purdy Boat Works, Port Washington, N Y Ch Meeting and I R C
—G W Elder

1933—OFF LONG BEACH HARBOR

Skipper	Crew	Yacht	Fleet	Daily Finish					Pts
G Waterhouse	W Metcalf	Three Star	San Francisco	3	4	7	3	1	67
E Thorne	L Thorne	Mist	Great South Bay	2	13	2	2	3	63
H Dowsett, Jr	H White	Chip	Hawaiian Islands	5	12	4	5	2	57
J Arms	M Sykes	Andiamo II	C Long Island Sound	12	6	3	4	4	56
A Iselin	E Willis	Ace	W Long Island Sound	10	1	6	10	5	53
H Beardslee	T Webster	Moira	Newport Harbor	8	3	5	9	9	51
E Fink	J Hayes	Movie Star II	*Long Beach	1	Dsq	1	1	Dsq	48
N Martin	T Cram	Phar Lap	Santa Barbara	9	5	Wdr	7	6	41
J Rockwell	W Lyon	Vega II	Philippines	11	14	8	6	7	39
P Shields	L Bainbridge	Gull	Peconic-Gardiners	7	10	9	12	8	39
R Smith	J Winterbotham	Neried	Galveston Bay	4	2	10	15	DNS	37
P Raskob	M Shehan	Ripple	Eastern Shore	6	8	12	11	11	37
C Kelley	R Summer	Seaward	San Diego Bay	15	7	DNS	13	12	23
J Cleary	H Graham	Sparkler II	New Orleans	14	9	14	8	DNS	23
C Ross	G Horder	Cene	Puget Sound	13	15	13	14	12	18
Mrs Balken	J Norwood	LaTortue	Villefranche	16	11	11	16	DNS	14

Winning yacht No 946 B—Dittmar, Newport, California, 1932 Ch I R C —H M Dowsett Ch Meeting—H M Worcester

1934—AT SAN FRANCISCO

Skipper	Crew	Yacht	Fleet	Daily Finish					Pts.
H Beardslee	M Lehman	By-C	Newport Harbor	1	1	4	1	1	72
J Arms	J Abberley	Andiamo III	C Long Island Sound	3	5	2	2	6	62
A Iselin	E White	Ace	W Long Island Sound	5	2	6	5	3	59
A Bown	B Sumner	Whitecap	San Diego Bay	4	4	5	8	7	52
J McAleese	H Peterson	Corinthian 4	*San Francisco	2	3	Wdr	6	2	51
H Meislahn	R Bowden	Sunbeam	Moriches Bay	6	7	1	10	10	46
G Gray	A Libano	Jupiter	New Orleans	Dsa	10	3	4	11	36
G Dillingham	H White	Mamo	Waikiki	10	6	8	12	9	35
L Pirie	S Pirie	Gemini	Lake Michigan	11	12	11	7	4	35
W Soule	W Baldwin	Barby II	Santa Barbara	12	8	12	3	14	31
E Thorne	L Thorne	Mist	Great South Bay	9	11	13	13	5	29
F Lippman	L Benzini	Pat Riot	Long Beach	Wdr	9	10	11	8	26
H Dowsett, Jr	H Dowsett	Chip	Hawaiian Islands	8	13	7	14	12	26
R Lamson	O Lamson	Alcor	Puget Sound	7	Wdr	9	15	15	18
Mrs Balken	J Fullerton	That's That	Villefranche	13	14	Wdr	9	13	15

Winning yacht No 1052 B—Douglass Canoe Co , Newport Beach, California Ch I R C — Sampson Smith Ch Meeting—H M Dowsett

1935—OFF NEWPORT HARBOR

Skipper	Crew	Yacht	Fleet	Daily Finish					Pts
H Beardslee	M Lehman	By-C	*Newport Harbor	1	1	4	1	6	72
A Iselin	E Willis	Ace	W Long Island Sound	4	2	2	2	5	70
G Waterhouse	W Metcalf	Three Star	San Francisco	10	5	1	3	1	65
S Pirie	L Pirie	Gemini II	Lake Michigan	6	4	8	4	7	56
M Shehan	C Johnson	Stardust	Eastern Shore	2	7	6	5	12	53
R Harris	B Harris	Vega	Moriches Bay	Dsq	3	10	6	3	46
N Martin	Mrs Martin	Phar Lap	Santa Barbara	5	13	5	9	8	45
A Bown	F Brown	Whitecap II	San Diego Bay	3	12	7	7	11	45
S Smith	F Robinson	Pathfinder	Otsego Lake	7	6	9	10	10	43
C Crebbs	F Laurie	Star Baby	Lake Maracaibo	11	9	11	8	4	42
J Arms	J Abberley	Andiamo III	C Long Island Sound	14	10	3	11	9	38
A McCrate	W McCrate	Zoa	Long Beach	12	Wdr	Dsq	12	2	25
M Musser	R Streeton	Pollux II	Hawaiian Islands	8	15	12	14	13	23
M Fahnestock	G Fahnestock	D Quichotte	Villefranche	9	11	13	16	15	21
C Ross	K Hine	Cene	Puget Sound	Dsq	8	15	13	14	18
J Kolisch	S Trumbull	Procyon II	Santa Monica	13	14	14	15	16	13

Winning yacht No 1052 B—Douglass Canoe Co , Newport Beach, California Ch I R C — J Webster Ch Meeting—G Waterhouse

1936—ON LAKE ONTARIO, AT ROCHESTER

Skipper	Crew	Yacht	Fleet	Daily Finish					Pts
A Iselin	G Horder	Ace	W Long Island Sound	4	4	2	9	2	159
H Beardslee	L Lehman	By-C	*Newport Harbor	1	2	5	10	6	156
H Halsted	W Halsey	Chuckle II	Moriches Bay	13	1	11	5	9	141
H Clark	J Clark	Sans Souci	Sandy Bay	9	9	1	3	5	140
N Martin	Mrs Martin	Phar Lap	Santa Barbara	5	18	7	11	1	138
P Shields	L Bainbridge	Jack Rabbit	Peconic-Gardiners	3	10	18	4	13	132
J Keith	E Phillips	Turtle Star	Santa Monica	18	16	4	1	12	129
R Symonette	B Kelly	Gull	Nassau	23	5	3	6	15	128
H Havemeyer	M Hayward	Vim	Great South Bay	17	12	1	10	14	126
J Arms	M Sykes	Andiamo III	C Long Island Sound	2	8	0	2	10	122
D Doeller	M Grosvenor	Restless II	Chesapeake Bay	15	14	6	13	17	116
M Shehan	P Shehan	Stardust	Eastern Shore	16	15	13	12	8	116
E Jahncke	Mrs Jahncke	Tempe III	New Orleans	12	19	8	22	3	116
H Nye	H Vested	Gale IV	Lake Michigan	24	3	17	16	16	104
W Stueck	R Childs	Altair	E Long Island Sound	7	17	15	14	26	101
F Swicker	E Lago	Guiding Star	San Francisco	Wdr	13	9	17	4	101
S Smith	Mrs Smith	Pioneer	Otsego Lake	14	6	0	7	18	99
J McClatchy	P McClatchy	Lone Wolf	Elk River	8	29	16	18	20	89
J Bloch	R Bernheim	Izard	Paris	20	25	10	19	19	87
D Steere	B Steere	Valiant	Nantucket Sound	6	7	0	0	11	84
W Calkins	H Christy	Red Head	Lake Ontario, U S	11	26	14	21	29	81
E Knevale	E Knevale, Jr	Fleet Star 3	Detroit River	10	21	0	25	7	81
S Wilson	C Miller	Fleet Star	Lake George	19	11	29	31	24	66
C Crozier	L Hoskins	Silver Slipper	Hawaiian Islands	26	20	19	24	27	64
W Grube	J Tallman	Neptune III	W Lake Erie	27	23	21	23	28	58
S Bell	P Upton	Bottoms Up	Paw Paw Lake	32	33	23	15	22	55
J Rockwell	W Rockwell	Nalo	Manila Bay	28	28	20	27	23	54
M Wegeforth	C Hoskins	Emmy Lou	San Diego Bay	21	22	22	30	31	54
R Laughlin	C Taylor	Tribly	S Lake Erie	25	32	0	26	25	42
R Miller	T Howard	Old Crow II	L Lake Huron	34	24	27	32	21	41
A Post	H Scofield	Loon	Seneca Lake	31	27	25	26	33	38
C Parsons	R Parsons	Bandit	Lake Keuka	22	30	0	28	30	34
G Patterson, Jr	L Patterson	Peggy Wee	Habana	30	34	24	29	34	29
Y Carney	A Young	Laura II	Gull Lake	29	31	28	33	0	24
R Patterson	T Howard	Osprey	L Ontario, Canadian	33	0	26	34	32	19

Winning yacht No 202 B—Owner, 1924 Ch I R C and Meeting—G W Elder

1937—ON WESTERN LONG ISLAND SOUND

Skipper	Crew	Yacht	Fleet	Daily Finish					Pts
M Wegeforth	E Phillips	Lecky	San Diego Bay	2	6	6	4	3	164
W vonHutschler	J Weise	Pimm	Hamburger	22	1	1	1	1	159
H Halsted	W Halsey	Chuckle III	Moriches Bay	1	7	21	2	10	144
H Nye	A Nye	Gale VII	Southern L Michigan	10	11	2	8	17	137
A MacCrate	W MacCrate	Zoa	Long Beach	8	5	20	7	9	136
C deCardenas	W Rivero	Kurush	Habana	5	20	8	14	6	132
S Smith	Mrs Smith	Pioneer	Lake Otsego	20	14	7	11	2	131
A Iselin	G Horder	Ace	*W Long Island Sound	3	29	5	13	4	131
G Clark	J Clark	Sans Souci	Cape Ann	12	3	22	10	8	130
C Stetson	J Arms	Windward	C Long Island Sound	11	12	11	9	16	126
P Shields	M Sykes	Jack Rabbit	Peconic-Gardiners	6	4	9	5	0	124
H Havemeyer	Havemeyer, Jr	Gull	Great South Bay	4	8	10	3	0	123
L Pirie	J Pirie	Gemini	Wilmette Harbor	15	2	3	0	12	116
P Wood	C Euler	Scarab	South Jersey	9	21	18	18	7	112
J Michael	F Graham	Roulette	West San Francisco	16	16	25	6	11	111
G Colwell	P Colwell	Hope	Narragansett Bay	7	31	26	12	15	94
M Lehman	S MacKay	Pasha	Newport Harbor	0	15	17	22	5	89
A Tietge	J Tietge	Nina	Puget Sound	19	9	16	21	0	83
F Laurie	W Nickel	A-L	Lake Maracaibo	21	30	27	17	13	77
P Melville	E Holden	Nani	Hawaiian Islands	13	28	31	15	26	76
M Perretti	B Bianchi	O Sole Mio	Sorrento	0	13	4	20	0	74
M Newman	E Jahncke	Chuckle II	New Orleans	0	27	15	19	14	73
C Parsons	Miss Parsons	Bandit III	Lake Keuka	26	17	28	23	18	73
H Wilmer	P Thomas	Aries	Delaware River	14	25	12	0	0	60
M Grosvenor	Mrs Grosvenor	Escape	Chesapeake Bay	23	19	24	0	23	59
J Todd	W Myers	Merry Widow	Eastern Shore	28	26	32	26	20	57

(CONTINUED)

(1937 WORLD'S CHAMPIONSHIP CONTINUED)

Skipper	Crew	Yacht	Fleet	Daily Finish					Pts
R Symonette	R Bowden	Zelda II	Nassau	17	24	34	16	0	57
Mrs Lucke	D Sayia	Eel	Barnegat Bay	27	0	13	0	21	50
W Stueck	R Childs	Altair	E Long Island Sound	18	10	36	0	0	47
C Steele	S Hager	Wab-Ben-O	L Ontario, Canadian	24	36	30	27	24	46
D Harris	A Prout	Dubbe	U S Naval Academy	25	25	35	0	19	44
P Upton	D Campbell	Ibis	St Joseph-Paw Paw Lake	0	18	14	0	0	42
A Tams	E Ellice	Eva May	Greenwood Lake	30	26	29	25	0	38
R Miller	T Howard	Old Crow II	Lake Huron	29	32	23	29	0	35
E Doyle	Miss Doyle	Turtle Star	Lake Ontario, U S	0	23	33	24	0	29
J McClatchy	J Doyle	Lone Wolf	Elk River	0	35	19	28	0	

Winning yacht No 1414 B—Kettenberg, Santa Barbara, California Ch I R C and Meeting—G W Elder

1938—OFF SAN DIEGO

Skipper	Crew	Yacht	Fleet	Daily Finish					Pts
W vonHutschler	J Weise	Pimm	Hamberger	2	1	3	1	2	106
H Nye	L Lehman	Gale	Southern Lake Michigan	1	2	5	2	1	104
J McAleese	F Graham	Mercury	West San Francisco	3	6	8	3	4	91
C Baxter	W Hubbard	Stormy	Newport Harbor	4	4	7	7	5	88
N Martin	Mrs Martin	Phar Lap	Santa Barbara	5	10	2	8	6	84
J Cowie	C Cowie	Rambunctious	Santa Monica	Wdr	3	1	4	3	81
S Ogilvy	M Shehan	Jay	W Long Island Sound	9	8	6	9	9	74
G Waterhouse	L Conn	Three Star 2	East San Francisco	13	9	4	10	8	71
D Mackenzie	L Donaldson	Sachem	Long Beach	8	11	16	5	7	68
C Ross	R Lanson	Cene Too	Puget Sound	7	12	11	14	10	61
E Ketcham	W Hayward	Draco	Great South Bay	12	7	9	11	19	57
V Doyle	J Boue	Lecky	*San Diego Bay	6	14	10	6	Dsq	56
C McNeely	R Scott	Star Dust	Barnegat Bay	Dsq	5	19	13	12	43
J Waller	N Batchelor	Black Roger	Nantucket Sound	10	15	17	12	Wdr	38
R Symonette	H Knowles	Nassau Star	Nassau	16	18	12	19	14	37
D Porterfield	No Report	Trece	Lake Maracaibo	11	16	18	18	20	32
R Day	W Day	Nomana	English Bay	15	13	22	21	13	32
J Clancy	B Cross	Sparkler II	New Orleans	18	17	15	20	16	30
C deCardenas	W Rivero	Kurush	Habana	20	Wdr	13	17	15	28
T Murray	J Murray	Seadler	Moriches Bay	17	19	20	15	17	28
G Crozier	P Withington	Yaca	Hawaiian Islands	21	21	14	16	18	26
C Baker	S Farnham	Peggy Wee	L Ontario, American	19	20	21	22	11	23

Winning yacht No 1420 B—Abeking & Rasmussen, Lemwerder, Germany, 1937 Ch Meeting—G'enn Waterhouse Ch I R C—G A Corry

1939—OFF KIEL

Skipper	Crew	Yacht	Fleet	Daily Finish					Pts
W vonHutschler	E Beyn	Pimm	*Hamberger	1	5	1	3	1	99
A Straulino	N Rode	Polluce	1st Div Navale	4	1	7	5	4	89
P Hanson	C Blankenburg	Maggel	Kiel	2	6	20	1	6	75
M Wegerforth	M Lehman	Scout II	San Diego Bay	5	2	5	17	7	74
J Weise	K Weise	Hasio	Berlin	10	3	3	8	13	73
S Ogilvy	T Fairbanks	Spirit	W Long Island Sound	3	7	2	10	15	73
D Salata	L Manineor	Castore	Regia Acd Nav	11	11	4	6	9	69
K Koppenhagen	Lt Karof	Pegasus	Marineschu'e M	8	14	11	7	3	67
Y Lorion	Chatord	Aloha	Alger	6	12	17	2	8	65
Oblt Esterer	Lt Kolbe	Bellona	Mar der Ostsee	Dsq	8	10	4	2	64
A Gaedtke	Poppe	Grunau	Muggelsee	7	4	8	Wdr	11	68
Peltow	Kopinzsch	Albatross	S d Luftwaffe	14	9	13	12	5	57
G Fagow	V Merani	Stella Diana	La Spezia	9	13	16	13	16	43
H Gumprecht	S Kerrison	Mona III	Norfolk Broads	16	10	9	11	DNS	42
M Ducrot	E Ducrot	Gloriana II	Palermo	12	Wdr	19	9	10	38
I Abberley	E Seay	Rhythm	C Long Island Sound	13	16	21	14	14	32
T Nordio	P Mitis	Axilla	Trieste	18	Wdr	12	15	17	26
A Maas	H Scholtz	Bem II	No Holland	17	Dsq	6	Wdr	DNS	21
D Albers	P Rohland	Bremen	Bremer	15	Dsq	18	16	18	21
Oblt Hissink	Lt Bertelaman	Perseus	M St Nordsee	Wdr	Dsq	14	Wdr	12	18
A Laurin	A Verne	Unn	Stockholm	Wdr	15	15	Wdr	DNS	14

Winning yacht No 1420 B—Abeking & Rasmussen, Lemwerder, Germany, 1937 Ch Meeting and I R C —G A Corry

1940—OFF SAN DIEGO

Skipper	Crew	Yacht	Fleet	Daily Finish					Pts.
J Cowie	G Cowie	Rambunctious	Los Angeles Harbor	1	6	1	2	2	83
R White	R Holcomb	Jade	West San Francisco	6	2	2	1	3	81
L Pirie	R Miller	Twin Star	Wilmette Harbor	5	3	3	3	1	80
H Nye	J Vilas	Gale	S Lake Michigan	3	7	5	5	5	70
M Lehman	C Baxter	Scout III	Newport Harbor	4	4	8	4	7	68
C Ross	R Ross	Cene	Puget Sound	7	1	7	7	9	64
W Sumner	J Watson	White Cap	San Diego Bay	2	5	4	0	10	55
L Dowsett	J Streeton	Roulette	Hawaiian Islands	9	9	10	8	4	55
W Picken	C Dominy	Fo Fo	Great South Bay	10	8	9	6	8	54
N Martin	Mrs Martin	Warlock	Santa Barbara	8	10	6	13	6	52
W Lewis	R Lewis	Lulu	Santa Monica	15	11	11	9	0	30
H B'oomer	J Anderson	Suzette II	L Ontario, American	11	12	12	0	11	30
C deCardenas	M Bustamente	Kurush II	Habana	16	13	13	12	12	29
H Uhler	R Pennhallow	Kuuipo	Waikiki	12	17	14	11	13	28
A Brown	R Wilkinson	Brownie	Lake Arrowhead	13	15	15	10	0	23
C Gasparich	W Luckert	Pagan	East San Francisco	17	14	17	14	15	18
J Smyth	W Hansen	Stella Maris	Gravesend Bay	18	16	16	16	14	15
A deMarigny	B McKinnie	Concubine	Nassau	14	0	0	15	0	9

Winning yacht No 1150 B—Douglass Canoe Co , Newport Beach, California, 1935 Ch Meeting
—Wm Picken, Jr Ch I R C —G A Corry

1941—OFF LOS ANGELES

Skipper	Crew	Yacht	Fleet	Daily Finish					Pts
G Fleitz	W Severance	Wench	*Los Angeles Harbor	2	2	1	4	3	58
H Nye	J Michael	Gale	S Lake Michigan	3	3	2	1	7	54
M Lehman	P McKibben	Scout III	Newport Harbor	1	1	3	Dsq	1	50
F Campbell	Mrs Campbell	Rascal .	W Long Island Sound	8	7	8	2	2	43
R White	V Benson	Jade	West San Francisco	5	12	4	3	5	41
C deCardenas	N Carrillo	Kurush II	Habana	7	4	6	10	6	37
W Sumner	R Sumner	White Cap II	San Diego	6	8	9	7	4	36
R Otter	W Otter	Step 'n Fetchit	Wilmette Harbor	9	6	5	8	8	34
W Lewis	R Lewis	Sioux	Santa Monica	0	5	7	6	9	29
T Hamilton	B Allen	Brownie	Lake Arrowhead	4	0	10	5	10	27
S Wright	J Forrington	Chief	Great South Bay	10	9	11	11	0	15
W Warren	L Cary	Guiding Star	East San Francisco	0	10	12	9	11	14
E Vynne, Jr	F Moegling	Cene	Puget Sound	0	11	0	12	12	7

Winning yacht No 1912 B—South Coast Boat Bldg , Newport Harbor, California, 1940 Ch
I R C —Leo Benzini Ch Meeting—Glenn Waterhouse

1942—ON LAKE MICHIGAN
(War-Time Skipper Series)

Skipper	Crew	Fleet	Daily Finish					Pts
H Nye	S Fahlstrom	S Lake Michigan	2	2	1	2	3	71
S Potter	E Douglass	Santa Monica	1	1	4	9	1	69
T Scripps	M Watson	San Diego Bay	8	4	2	6	2	63
P Smart	S Smart	C Long Island Sound	3	5	9	1	10	57
R Lippincott	S Lippincott	West Jersey	Dsa	6	3	3	4	52
C deCardenas	deCardenas, Jr	Habana	7	3	11	8	9	47
R Craig	B Bomboy	Lake George	13	8	7	5	6	46
I Cleary	A Nugon	New Orleans	5	11	10	7	8	44
F Raymond	M Raymond	Wilmette Harbor	12	10	5	12	7	39
P Woodbury	Mrs Woodbury	Cape Ann	4	7	14	Dsq	5	38
S Bell	R Hutchinson	St Joseph-Paw Paw Lake	6	14	6	11	13	35
E Austin	T Everitt	Great South Bay	11	9	12	4	15	34
R Boudeman	R VanPeenan	Gull Lake	10	13	8	13	11	30
I Dale	Miss Dale	Lake Ontario, American	15	12	13	15	14	16
G Elder	Mrs Elder	Gravesend Bay	9	DNS	DNS	10	DNS	15
H Beck	A Hamers	Central Lake Erie	14	Wdr	15	14	12	13

Best Boat Score No 1861, Rhapsody B—Parkman Yachts, Brooklyn, N Y , 1939 Ch Meeting
—G W Elder Ch I R C —G A Corry

1943—ON GREAT SOUTH BAY
(War-Time Skipper Series)

Skipper	Crew	Fleet	Daily Finish					Pts
A Deacon	P Roehm	W Long Island Sound	5	3	5	5	3	79
W Picken, Jr	J Forrington	Great South Bay	1	13	2	4	4	76
C deCardenas	G Carricaburu	Habana	3	1	10	1	11	74
T Coe	B Coe	West Jersey	4	8	7	3	6	72
H Halsted	R Bowden	Moriches Bay	2	12	8	7	2	69
H Driscoll	N Burnham	San Diego Bay	13	7	3	9	1	67
C Baker	N Castle	Lake Ontario, American	9	6	1	11	7	66
R Allen	J Smyth	Newport Harbor	Dsa	5	4	2	9	64
P Smart	V McHugh	C Long Island Sound	6	2	13	Dsa	12	47
H Brown	L Nelson	South Jersey	Dsa	4	9	6	14	47
G Elder	J Zimmerman	Gravesend Bay	10	14	12	8	10	46
T Clark	W Wilson	S Long Island Sound	7	10	11	Dsa	9	43
C Ulmer	Mrs Ulmer	East River	Dsa	11	6	12	8	43
E Raymond	F Rich	Wilmette Harbor	14	15	18	10	13	30
C Lee	E Vick	Seneca Lake	8	17	16	15	17	27
C Daniel	J Bolding	U S Coast Guard	15	9	14	Dsa	15	27
H Clark	M Kuehne	Cape Ann	11	16	15	14	18	26
C Shoemaker	S Daubin	U S Naval Academy	12	19	17	Dsq	16	16
J Douglas	L Stevens	Lake Maracaibo	16	18	19	13	19	15

Best Boat Score No 1951, *Flying Colors* B—Saybrook Yacht Yards, Saybrook, Connecticut, 1940 Ch Meeting—G W Elder Ch I R C —T T Everitt

1944—ON LAKE MICHIGAN
(War-Time Skipper Series)

Skipper	Crew	Fleet	Daily Finish					Pts
G Driscoll	M Burnham	San Diego Bay	1	1	6	1	5	86
R Lippincott	E Shive'hood	West Jersey	3	4	1	9	3	80
H Williams	A Nye	S Lake Michigan	6	3	9	5	1	76
W Picken, Jr	J Forrington	Great South Bay	12	9	3	2	2	72
H Halsted	P Maynard	Moriches Bay	9	6	2	7	8	68
B McKinney	C Brown	Nassau	13	7	7	4	6	63
W Hale	D Pierce	Cape Ann	4	12	5	3	0	56
D Bergman	C Floyd	Wilmette Harbor	Dsq	2	15	6	4	53
N Burrage	R Patterson	Lake Springfield	2	13	10	12	12	51
A Lawrence	Mrs Lawrence	S Long Island Sound	8	15	4	13	13	47
C deCardenas	H Duff	Habana	16	5	11	15	15	44
R Bottger	D Campbell	C Long Island Sound	15	8	16	11	7	43
C Lee	E Vick	Seneca Lake	5	14	12	8	0	41
R Allen	W Mitchell	Newport Harbor	10	10	Dsq	18	10	32
J Smyth	J Doody	Gravesend Bay	11	17	17	16	11	28
B Waddell	A Allardyce	Sarnia Bay	7	16	Dsq	10	0	27
E Nurme	M Amo	Detroit River	17	11	8	17	0	27
S Bell	R Moats	St Joseph-Paw Paw Lake	14	18	13	14	0	21
A Young	G Comer	Gull Lake	Dsq	Dsq	14	DNS	DNS	6

Best Boat Score No 1801, *Triton* B—Mystic Shipyard, Mystic, Connecticut, 1939 Ch Meeting—H C Halsted Ch I R C —C H Pajeau

1945—ON CENTRAL LONG ISLAND SOUND
(War-Time Skipper Series)

Skipper	Crew	Fleet		Daily Finish				Pts
M Burnham	L North	*San Diego Bay	2	16	2	2	1	87
J Cowie	W Krug	Los Angeles Harbor	6	1	5	6	7	85
E Etchells	Mrs Etchells	W Long Island Sound	8	13	1	4	9	75
R Allen	Rob't Allen	C Long Island Sound	7	5	9	15	6	68
W Hale	M Moulton	Cape Ann	9	3	11	8	11	68
E Jahncke	R Cross	New Orleans	12	14	3	13	5	63
H Shaw	R Jill	Gravesend Bay	15	7	6	16	4	62
H Williams	H Black	S Lake Michigan	10	12	4	1	Dsa	61
C deCardenas	G Carricaburu	Habana	1	17	17	11	3	61
T Clark	E Schelin	S Long Island Sound	11	2	8	7	Dsa	60
R Lippincott	S Lippincott	West Jersey	5	4	10	12	Dsa	57
C Lee	G Wilson	Seneca Lake	14	15	12	3	12	54
H Halsted	A Andon	Moriches Bay	3	6	16	9	Wdr	54
R Rogers	W VanArsdale	Wilmette Harbor	4	18	7	17	10	54
R Craig	B Bomboy	Lake George	19	10	15	5	8	53
W Picken, Jr	J Forrington	Great South Bay	18	11	14	Wdr	2	43
W Boss	B Boss	Narragansett Bay	13	8	18	10	DNS	39
B Waddell	G Barwise	Sarnia Bay	16	9	20	14	DNS	29
G Criminale	A Smith	Mobile Bay	17	19	19	Wdr	13	20
E Nurme	M Amo	Detroit River	Dsq	20	13	Wdr	DNS	11
T Ziluca	C VonDrusche	Adm Farragut Academy	Wdr	21	DNS	DNS	DNS	1

Best Boat Score No 2145, *Dandy* B—Parkman Yachts, 1942 Ch I R C and Meeting —G
W Elder

1946—OFF HAVANA
(Normal Conditions Resumed)

Skipper	Crew	Yacht	Fleet		Daily Finish				Pts
G Fleitz	W Krug	*Wench II*	Los Angeles	3	3	1	3	4	131
R White	G Holcombe	*Pagan*	West San Francisco	4	6	6	4	2	123
D Knowles	B Kelly	*Gem II*	Nassau	2	1	7	7	8	120
R Lippincott	R Levin	*Blue Star II*	West Jersey	14	8	4	2	1	116
H Nye	S Fahlstrom	*Pilot*	S Lake Michigan	6	19	11	1	3	105
C deCardenas	C Inclan	*Kurush III*	Habana	7	4	9	12	10	103
E Etchells	Mrs Etchells	*Shillalah*	W Long Island Sound	1	2	10	6	Wdr	97
J Lorber	E Leverich	*Scout*	New Orleans	9	9	2	9	21	95
C Ulmer	J Forrington	*Scylla*	East River	11	13	18	11	11	81
H Halsted	W Halsted	*Chuckle*	Moriches Bay	5	7	16	8	Wdr	80
J Capucho	J Crespo	*Capucho*	Cascais	13	14	5	Wdr	9	75
W Hutton	J Hutton	*Kittiwake*	Peconic-Gardiners	16	10	8	14	22	75
M Lehman	R Ziegler	*Scout V*	Newport Harbor	Wdr	5	3	Dsa	5	74
P Woodbury	W Trayes	*Flamingo II*	Cape Ann	17	18	14	13	20	63
H Wilmer	R Jones	*Aries II*	Eastern Shore	10	12	17	16	Wdr	61
D Morrell	Mrs Morrell	*Honey*	E Long Island Sound	12	17	13	19	23	61
C Dole	P Dean	*Flooy*	Waikiki	15	Wdr	19	5	19	58
C Baker	P Farley	*Zoa II*	L Ontario, American	18	15	Wdr	15	13	55
W Hodges	J McCrillis	*Nashira*	Lake Sunapee	Wdr	22	15	17	15	47
R Rogers	A Barber	*Gusty*	Wilmette Harbor	Wdr	21	Wdr	10	14	42
P Smart	R Allen	*Melody*	C Long Island Sound	Wdr	Dsa	12	Wdr	6	40
E Simoes	A Simoes	*Toro*	Rio de Janeiro	Dsa	DNS	21	18	12	36
G Driscoll	G Jessop	*Dream*	*San Diego Bay	Wdr	16	DNS	DNS	7	35
C Lee	R Allen	*Fifinella*	Lake Seneca	Wdr	20	20	DNS	17	30
G Criminale	S S Tam	*Little Dipper*	Mobile Bay	Wdr	DNS	DNS	21	16	21
I Smyth	D Campbell	*Viking III*	Gravesend Bay	8	Dsa	Wdr	Dsa	DNS	21
A deZulueta	Mrs Zulueta	*Conan Berri*	San Sebastian	Wdr	Wdr	Dsa	20	18	20
J Fiuza	J Gorinho	*Viking II*	Lisboa	Wdr	11	Dsa	DNS	DNS	18

Winning yacht No 2427 B—South Coast Boat Bldg , Newport Harbor, California, 1946 Ch
I R C and Meeting—G W Elder

1947—OFF LOS ANGELES

Skipper	Crew	Yacht	Fleet	Daily Finish					Pts
D Knowles	S Farrington	Gem II	Nassau	6	1	2	2	2	97
H Smart	S Ogilvy	Hilarius	C Long Island Sound	2	6	3	1	5	95
R Stearns	R Rodgers	Glider	Wilmette Harbor	4	3	4	3	4	92
M Lehman	R McKibben	Scout VI	Newport Harbor	10	8	9	6	1	76
G Fleitz	W Krug	Wench III	Los Angeles	1	4	5	Dsq	6	72
C Ross	R Ross	Cene	Puget Sound	7	13	11	4	3	72
T Scripps	C DeLong	Tom Tom	San Diego Bay	3	5	7	9	15	71
O Torrey	R Rich	Sugar Rabbit	W Long Island Sound	9	10	6	8	12	65
F Wooser	J McAleese	Can Can	West San Francisco	5	7	8	Dsa	8	60
D Bello	F Bello	Faneca	Cascais	18	9	10	5	11	57
R Lippincott	R Levine	Blue Star II	West Jersey	8	Dsq	1	Wdr	7	50
J Cleary	J Cleary, Jr	Sparkler III	New Orleans	12	12	12	11	13	50
P Miller	S Miller	Clear Sky	English Bay	11	Dsa	14	7	10	46
H Williams	C Ohgren	Kathleen	S Lake Michigan	Wdr	2	13	Wdr	9	42
R Cameron	J Tilton	Lochinvar	St Joseph-PawPaw Lake	17	14	15	12	16	36
F Rothwell	P Hagen	Pupule	Waikiki	13	11	18	Wdr	14	32
J Bracony	C Bittencourt	Buscape	Rio de Janeiro	14	18	20	10	18	30
H Burrall	W Smith	Rebel	Seneca Lake	20	15	17	13	17	28
C Borden	E Wehn	Risque	East San Francisco	15	17	16	Wdr	20	20
G Criminale	R Hires	Aquila	Mobile Bay	19	16	19	Wdr	19	15
N Marchuk	C Paul	Tomahawk	Illinois River	16	Wdr	Wdr	14	21	15

Winning yacht No 1976 B—South Coast Boat Bldg, Newport Harbor, California, 1940 Ch
I R C —James Cowie Ch Meeting—A F Wakefield

1948—OFF CASCAIS

Skipper	Crew	Yacht	Fleet	Daily Finish					Pts.
L Pirie	H Rugeroni	Twin Star	Wilmette Harbor	2	1	1	7	107	
A Straulino	N Rode	Polluce	Taranto	1	4	2	2	5	106
H Smart	P Smart	Hilarius	C Long Island Sound	4	7	6	12	10	81
S Ogilvy	G Daly	Flame	W Long Island Sound	6	Wdr	4	5	4	77
D Bello	F Bello	Faneca	Cascais	5	9	Dsa	6	1	75
T Nordio	L Manicor	Lusta II	Trieste	13	1	8	10	13	75
A Maas	E Stutterheim	Starita	No Holland	Wdr	10	5	4	9	68
A Sturrock	L Fenton	Moorina	Melbourne	8	17	3	Dsa	3	65
Y Lorion	A Chatord	Aloba II	Alger	16	15	7	3	14	65
E Mendonca	A Silva	Margabell	Vila Franca	7	5	Dsa	9	12	63
R Ciappa	C Rolandi	Legionario	Capri	15	8	9	7	Wdr	57
D Knowles	S Farrington	Gem II	*Nassau	3	12	Dsa	Dsa	2	55
A Costa	E Simoes	Bug	Rio de Janeiro	17	11	10	13	16	53
J Fiuza	J Gorinho	Espadarte	Lisbon	11	16	11	8	Dsq	50
C Ulmer	W Flynn	Scylla	East River	10	6	DNS	Dsa	8	48
D Salata	L Cattaneo	Vipera III	Lario	14	3	13	Wdr	Wdr	42
A Cosentino	A Morelli	Hydra II	Naples	Wdr	13	Wdr	11	11	37
C deCardenas	deCardenas, Jr	Kurush III	Habana	12	18	Dsa	Wdr	6	36
J Peytel	R Bernheim	Izard III	Paris	9	14	Wdr	Dsq	15	34
P Chancerel	J Saintenis	Fandango	St Germain	18	19	12	Wdr	17	30
P Montaut	Mrs Montaut	Fada III	Seine & Oise	Dsq	20	Dsa	14	18	20
T Allende	J L Allende	Duende	Santander	19	22	14	Wdr	DNS	17
R Elosegui	I Ganuza	Chiqui IV	San Sebastian	Wdr	21	WdrWdr	DNS		3
J Allende	E Aznar	Galerna	Bilbao	Dsa	DNS	DNS	DNS	DNS	0

Winning yacht No 1961 B—Karas Boat Yard, Chicago, Illinois, 1940 Ch Meeting—C de
Cardenas Ch I R C —E J Conill

1949—AT CHICAGO

Skipper	Crew	Yacht	Fleet	Daily Finish					Pts
H Nye, Jr	S Fahlstrom	Gale	S Lake Michigan	4	4	4	3	8	182
R Lippincott	R Levin	Blue Star II	West Jersey	8	3	6	1	10	177
S Ogilvy	O Torrey	Flame	W Long Island Sound	7	14	3	10	2	169
C Rogers, Jr	Mrs Rogers	Magic	L Ontario, American	3	10	7	16	4	165
L North	J Hill	North Star II	San Diego Bay	1	Dsq	1	2	1	159
W M Shehan	R Jones	Duchess	Eastern Shore	10	6	10	15	9	155
D Bever	C Voss	Luscious	Central Lake Erie	12	12	9	11	11	150
J Bennett	W Campbell	Sanderling	St Joseph-PawPaw Lake	11	7	15	4	22	146
F Wosser	K Ownes	Cancan	W San Francisco Bay	9	8	21	7	14	146
R Jill	J Slater	Touche	Sheepshead Bay	2	16	17	9	16	145
A Grovenor	R McGlohm	Flo	U S Naval Academy	5	22	13	17	5	143
D Knowles	S Farrington	Shooting Star	Nassau	6	Wdr	5	5	13	135
D Coley	R Gordon	Dorris	C Long Island Sound	21	11	19	6	20	128
R Ferguson	R C Ferguson	Finesse	Gull Lake	15	19	8	19	17	127
D Metcalf	F Schenck	Scout VI	Newport Harbor	12	15	18	21	12	126
H Halsted	W Halsted	Chuckle	Moriches Bay	16	9	11	Wdr	6	122
L Pirie	S Pirie	Twin Star	*Wilmette Harbor	Dsq	2	2	Wdr	3	116
E Vynne, Jr	R Watt	Alcor	Puget Sound	14	27	14	14	26	110
H Stephenson	R Lorenz	Havoc	Milwaukee	20	28	30	8	16	104
T Clark	E Schelin	Lyny	S Long Island Sound	38	5	16	13	34	99
J Price	E Navarro	Typhoon	Biscayne Bay	23	13	20	Wdr	18	90
R Blizzard	F Wolfe	Snowflake	Chesapeake Bay	28	1	26	Wdr	21	88
A Allardyce	A Robertson	Thistle II	Detroit River	27	32	23	31	7	85
J Forrington	E McCord	Picket	Great South Bay	31	26	22	18	27	81
C deCardenas	J deCardenas	Kurush III	Habana	32	17	37	12	28	79
C Ulmer	W Flynn	Scylla	East River	18	20	24	Dsa	24	78
J Capucho	A Heredia	Capucho IV	Cascais	19	Dsq	12	24	32	77
J Killeen, Jr	M Wynn	Urchin	New Orleans	17	23	34	25	31	75
E Fraker	H Durkee	Fracas	Raritan Bay	24	21	29	Dsa	19	69
P Woodbury	J Smollett	Flamingo III	Cape Ann	22	24	25	Dsa	25	68
F Macks	R Full	Laminar	Southern Lake Erie	25	30	32	27	29	62
R Bueno	J Bittencourt	Xodo III	Rio de Janeiro	35	33	31	23	23	60
D Birks	H Lankton	Desira	Illinois River	30	29	27	20	Wdr	58
C Ruble	R Williams	Barbaree	Lower Lake Huron	29	Dsq	28	22	30	55
G Dewar	H Riddle	Pasha	Oakmont-Allegheny	34	25	36	30	39	41
R Taylor	W Weatherly	Nike	Mississippi Sound	33	31	39	26	37	39
W Smith, Jr	R Armitage	Leatherstocking	Otsego Lake	24	Dsa	38	29	35	38
R Reithmiller	F Runnells	Para I	Belle Isle	37	35	33	28	38	34
C Korb	S Potter	Lady Veeco	Lake Arrowhead	39	18	40	Wdr	33	34
W Spencer	T McEnvoy	Ripple	L Ontario, Canadian	36	34	35	Wdr	36	23

Winning yacht No 2829 B—Old Greenwich Boat Works, 1949 Ch Meeting—H Halsted Ch
I R C --L R Bowden

1950—AT CHICAGO

Skipper	Crew	Yacht	Fleet	Daily Finish					Pts
R Lippincott	R Levin	Sea Robin	West Jersey	1	9	2	2	7	189
L Pirie	C Tuttle	Twin Star	Wilmette Harbor	6	2	5	5	8	184
E Etchells	M Etchells	Shillalah	C Long Island Sound	14	5	3	1	6	181
T Nordio	L deManincor	Luisa III	Trieste	5	12	10	6	1	176
A Straulino	N Rode	Merope	Se Ve Taranto	2	3	1	29	2	173
H Smart	P Smart	Hilarius	Milwaukee	3	4	11	9	10	173
R Miller	G Voss	Scout II	Central Lake Erie	12	6	8	12	3	169
J Tito	M Bramao	Golfinho	Cascais	8	8	14	14	4	162
C deCardenas	N Gelats	St Cristina	Habana	11	13	6	10	15	155
S Ogilvy	J Stephens	Flame	W Long Island Sound	4	7	4	Dsa	9	144
D Knowles	B Kelly	Gem II	Nassau	Dsa	1	7	8	11	141
W Nagle	A Nagle, Jr	Finagle	Moriches Bay	13	16	13	18	13	137
H Williams	D Sherwood	Kathleen	*S Lake Michigan	17	10	Dsa	7	5	129
L North	B Hanzal	North Star	San Diego Bay	9	Dsa	12	3	17	127
J Price	J Reid	Comanche	Biscayne Bay	18	Dsa	9	4	12	125
F Black	N Kershaw	Jet	Michigan City	10	11	20	13	33	123
H Havemeyer	J Hermus	Gull	Great South Bay	20	15	22	11	21	121
G Dewar	J Forrington	Stampede	Oakmont-Allegheny	19	14	18	16	24	119
S Lippincott	A Seither	Shooting Star	Barnegat Bay	29	19	15	21	14	112

(CONTINUED)

(1950 WORLD'S CHAMPIONSHIP CONTINUED)

Skipper	Crew	Yacht	Fleet	Daily Finish	Pts
E Fraker	L Smithline	Fracas	Raritan Bay	28 17 26 15 19	105
A Stoeffler	R Stoeffler	Hell's Angels	East River	21 22 23 17 22	105
T dePaula	O Dias	Bu II	Rio de Janeiro	23 21 28 19 34	85
W Ficker	B Hess	Chaser II	Newport Harbor	Dsq 23 16 26 20	83
J Cram	W Cram	Oregon Star	Puget Sound	31 29 30 20 18	82
J Killeen, Jr	H Killeen	Urchin	New Orleans G	25 25 27 23 31	79
G Parsons	G Forbes	Spitfire	English Bay	37 18 24 25 29	77
J Hansen	L Sobsted	Tulla	Sheepshead Bay	34 20 17 24 Dsq	73
D Burks	H Lankton	Desira	Illinois River	35 24 31 22 28	70
D Dunigan, Jr	R Jones	Lodestar	Chesapeake Bay	15 Dsa 19 Wdr 23	69
R Ferguson	W Bennett	Finesse	Gull Lake	16 Dsa 21 Dsa 25	64
A Fairhead	D Higgins	Ariel	L Ontario, Canadian	26 DNS Dsq 28 26	46
P Bishop	T Murray	Duchess	Boston Harbor	32 28 32 27 Wdr	43
M Amo	R Sutton	Mohawk	Detroit River	27 Dsa Wdr DNS 16	41
H Day II	T Nowlen	Seagull II	St Joseph-PawPaw Lake	38 Dsa 29 31 30	40
S Potter	W Kelly	Ecstasy	Los Angeles Harbor	33 Dsa 33 32 32	38
W Leirheimer	A Leirheimer	Idol	S Long Island Sound	22 Dsq 25 Dsa DNS	36
R Richmiller	F Runnells	Para I	Belle Isle	Dsq 26 DNS 30 35	35
W Myers	P Cox	White Shadow	Eastern Shore	7 Dsa Wdr DNS DNS	35
A Cosentino	C Rolandi	Fiamette	Naples	24 Dsa Wdr Dsa 27	33
W Stout	Pennewitt	Starduster	Lake Springfield	36 27 Wdr Dsa DNS	21
R Schluederberg	T Bundy	Flame	Southern Lake Erie	30 Dsa DNS DNS DNS	12

Winning yacht No 3002 B—Lippincott Boat Works, 1950 Ch Meeting—C de Cardenas Ch
I R C —G W Elder

1951—OFF GIBSON ISLAND

Skipper	Crew	Yacht	Fleet	Daily Finish	Pts
E Etchells	M Etchells	Shannon	C Long Island Sound	1 5 5 2 6	227
D Stearns	R Rodgers	Magic	Wilmette Harbor	1 2 15 4 2	226
S Ogilvy	W Stueck	Flame	W Long Island Sound	2 3 22 5 9	209
H Smart	P Smart	Hilarius	Milwaukee	12 17 2 10 8	201
J Price	J Reid	Comanche	Biscayne Bay	8 31 12 8 3	188
A Straulino	N Rodi	Merope	Se Ve Taranto	6 1 26 35 1	181
R Lippincott	R Lippincott	Sea Robin	*West Jersey	4 18 40 1 11	176
A Stoeffler	R Stoeffler	Hell's Angel	East River	13 15 17 13 16	176
D Bello	F Bello	Jade	Cascais	10 8 11 16 30	175
H Nye	S Fahlstrom	Gale	S Lake Michigan	14 19 24 6 12	175
D Knowles	D Pritchard	Gem III	Nassau	7 13 3 Dsq 4	173
W Myers	P Cox	White Shadow	Eastern Shore	9 11 1 Dsa 19	160
T Clark	J Bell	Mate	S Long Island Sound	19 7 18 23 17	156
D Bever	R Miller	Luscious Too	Central Lake Erie	Dsq 9 7 9 20	155
P Chancerel	J Lebrun	Gam	Seine	11 12 38 14 24	151
H Moore	E Prime	Wench II	Huntington Bay	35 25 4 25 10	151
H Halsted	E Pfrunder	Chuckle	Moriches Bay	15 27 9 15 35	149
D Jones	M Wynn	Pagan	New Orleans	27 20 28 12 18	145
C Dominy	J Dominy	Cygnet	Great South Bay	DNS 6 34 11 7	142
L North	B Hanzal	North Star II	San Diego Bay	Dsq 4 Wdr 3 5	138
F Zemina	C Storms	Pirene	E Long Island Sound	18 24 43 17 15	133
W Taylor	R Christensen	Dariabar	Puget Sound	21 34 8 33 22	132
J Todd	W Norris, Jr	Boomerang	Cambridge	20 22 20 19 38	131
H Witte	W Lawhorn	Not Given	Newport Harbor	25 14 21 22 39	129
G Dewar	W Flynn	Stampede	Oakmont-Allegheny	26 38 13 20 23	128
C deCardenas	deCardenas, Jr	Kurush	Habana	3 26 37 7 Wdr	127
A Karlson	J Karlson	Zippity	Old Orchard	31 23 19 32 21	124
C Stein III	J Nelson III	Snallygaster	Chesapeake Bay	22 37 14 18 37	122
W Hanson	R Whyte	Twinkle	Narragansett Bay	16 35 35 27 26	111
P Woodbury	E Hay	Dody	Cape Ann	40 30 6 36 34	104
R Kirkland	T Tranfaglia	Delight	Boston Harbor	28 32 23 Dsq 14	103
R Cameron	J Sennott	Lochinvar	St Joseph-PawPaw Lake	17 39 45 26 29	94
B Waddell	J Huntley	Trigger	Sarnia Bay	42 41 32 30 13	92
F Tobin	J Frey	Nibot III	L Ontario, American	37 28 30 34 31	90
W Hodges	F Gordon	Sampson	Lake Sunapee	32 29 47 28 27	87
C Sansoldo	E Simoes	Gem II	Rio de Janeiro	23 Wdr 10 40 40	87
S Lippincott	J Knight	Shooting Star	Barnegat Bay	19 16 33 Dsa DNS	82
R Craton	W Ester	Renaissance	Penn-Erie	34 33 36 38 28	78
P Hunt	S Biays	Draco II	Western Maryland	Wdr Wdr 27 21 23	79
P Barsolas	V Grant	Where Is It	Raritan Bay	33 21 29 41 Wdr	76

(CONTINUED)

Skipper	Crew	Yacht	Fleet						Pts
R Miller	R Villiers	Kahuna	Waikiki	36	40	42	24	33	75
J Hansen	J Smyth	Tulla	Sheepshead Bay	41	Wdr	25	31	32	71
D Spangler	C Bettcher	Naiad	Mid Connecticut	39	10	44	Wdr	42	65
R Riethmiller	G Sales	Para I	Belle Isle	45	44	16	42	Wdr	53
E Towl	D Schultheis	Miboubay	Peconic-Gardiners	43	42	31	Wdr	36	48
D Hubers	R McVey	The Chain	North Chesapeake Bay	24	Dsa	Dsq	29	DNS	47
A Allardyce	A Robertson	Thistle	Detroit River	30	36	39	Wdr	DNS	45
G Criminale	F Harrison	Aquila	Mobile Bay	38	Wdr	46	37	41	38
C Stewart, Jr	H Mahaffy	Fawn	Elk River	44	43	41	39	Wdr	33

Winning yacht No 3125 B—Old Greenwich Boat Works, 1951 Ch Meeting—H C Halsted Ch I R C—D J Dunigan, Jr
Note—It being impossible to establish a standard course at West Jersey, the Series was sailed at Gibson Island, Maryland

1952—AT CASCAIS

Skipper	Crew	Yacht	Fleet	Daily Finish					Pts
A Straulino	N Rode	Merope	Taranto	1	1	1	2	3	142
R Lippincott	D Hubers	Flower	West Jersey	6	6	3	11	7	117
D Bello	F Bello	Faneca	Cascais	7	15	6	1	8	113
J Fiuza	F deAndrade	Espadarte II	Lisboa	10	10	17	3	2	108
T Nordio	L Sangulin	Elletra	Trieste	8	5	2	Dsq	1	104
C Ulmer	S Farrington	Scylla	East River	9	11	5	19	9	97
J Schoonmaker	D Knowles	Dingo	Nassau	3	21	10	6	13	97
J Tito	A Graca	Ma Lindo	Porto	18	3	15	14	5	95
C deCardenas	deCardenas, Jr	Kurush IV	Habana	5	12	20	15	4	94
T Razelos	A Ziraud	Mari-Tim	Salamis	15	4	16	4	19	92
M Rivelli	G Schettino	Faneca	Formia	16	17	8	7	14	88
O Dias	T dePaula	Bu III	Rio de Janeiro	21	7	4	17	18	83
P Fischer	C Wunderlich	Paka V	Hamburger	11	18	18	18	6	79
J Price	P Smart	Comanche	Biscayne Bay	2	22	14	5	Wdr	77
P Chancerel	J Marzut	Gam	La Seine	12	9	19	23	10	77
E Mendonca	A Silva	Pedrito IV	Vila Franca	14	19	23	8	12	74
Y Lorion	J Lorion	Aloba V	d Alger	19	16	12	10	20	73
H Looser	J Both	Perfidia III	Rapperswil	22	23	11	13	11	70
H Bryner	K Bryner	Ali Baba IV	Zurichsee	17	2	21	Wdr	17	63
D Salata	A Pelloti	Fradolin	del Lario	Dsq	13	7	12	Wdr	58
F Mercier	J Rousse	Vega	Villefranche	13	20	13	Wdr	21	53
E Perrissol	A Moses	Ayoco	Cannes	24	14	22	9	Wdr	51
J Herbulot	A Debarge	Tramontanell I	Paris	Wdr	8	27	20	16	49
E Etchells	J Reynes	Shannon	C Long Island Sound	4	Wdr	9	DNS	DNS	47
C Blankenburg	O Schlenzka	Pandar III	Kieler	23	24	26	21	15	41
J Mitchell	Mrs Mitchell	Willy Nilly	Solent	20	Wdr	25	16	24	35
S Tay	F Thieck	Saucy Sue	Casablanca	26	26	24	24	23	27
P deMontaut	J deMontaut	Fada III	Seine et Oise	25	27	28	25	22	23
C Metral	J Coursol	Itrane	Rabat	27	25	Dsq	22	Wdr	16

Winning yacht No 2958 B—Old Greenwich Boat Works, 1949 Ch I R C—Beppe Croce Ch Meeting—Carlos deCardenas

1953—AT NAPOLI

Skipper	Crew	Yacht	Fleet	Daily Places					Pts
A Straulino	N Rode	Merope II	*Se-Ve-Taranto	1	1	11	1	3	188
D Bello	J Tito	Faneca	Cascais	2	3	10	5	1	184
T Nordio	L Sangulin	Asterope	Trieste	9	7	3	12	9	165
P Chancerel	C Gueullette	Myra	Seine	10	13	6	6	7	163
M Quina	E Cruz	Ma Lindo	Porto	11	5	19	3	11	156
A Cosentino	N Stella	Merope	Ischia	6	11	14	13	6	155
D Knowles	S Farrington	Gem III	Nassau	15	4	5	25	2	154
C deCardenas	deCardenas, Jr	Kurush IV	Habana	8	14	21	4	5	153
J Fiuza	M Ricciardi	Espadarte II	Lisboa	13	6	7	26	4	149
R Ciappa	C Rolandi	Caprica	Capri	16	8	16	2	18	145
C Lyons, Jr	Mrs Nina Lyon	Vega IV	Barnegat Bay	20	15	2	15	8	145
M Rivelli	G Schettino	Faneca	Formia	14	9	8	8	27	139
W Shehan	D Hubers	Vim	Eastern Shore	4	17	15	16	16	137
P Smart	J deCardenas	Melody	C Long Island Sound	5	21	25	9	12	133
F Mercier	G Pissani	Vega	Villefranche	21	12	23	11	10	128

(CONTINUED)

(1953 WORLD'S CHAMPIONSHIP CONTINUED)

Skipper	Crew	Yacht	Fleet	Daily Places	Pts
C Boselli	R Manara	Anna I	Alto Lario	7 Dsq 1 24 13	119
A Debarge	N Calonne	Candide	Paris	3 10 27 7 Dsq	117
C Ulmer	A deCardenas	Scylla	East River	25 16 20 14 14	116
U Fondi	G deLuca	Gloriana III	Sorrentina	12 2 22 18 Wdr	110
B Splieth	N vonStempel	Bellatrix II	Kiel	23 22 9 22 22	107
P Fischer	H J Renken	Paka VI	Hamburg	18 24 13 17 28	105
H Looser	H Rusterholz	Perfidia III	Rapperswil	22 18 18 23 20	104
R Bueno	A Torres	Xodo IV	Rio de Janeiro	27 28 4 19 31	96
E deMendonca	F Amorim	Pedrito IV	Vila Franca	29 25 17 31 15	88
A Moscovite	O Danelon	Elletra	Lignano	30 19 Dsq 10 24	81
D Salata	O Magnaghi	Fiadolin II	Lario	17 34 12 20 Wdr	81
H Bryner	U Bucher	Ali Baba IV	Lugano	19 31 26 29 21	79
T Rozelos	A Ziraud	Mari-Tim	Salamis	26 27 28 28 25	71
S diMaio	G Sangiovanni	Eolo	Leuca	33 23 24 30 30	65
J Both	C Joos	Blue Lei	Zuerich	24 20 Dsq 38 19	63
Y Lorion	J Carabia	Aloha V	Algers	28 29 34 21 32	61
J Pankofer	M Huber	Mechtild	Starnberg	36 33 29 35 17	55
O Lagos	A Vallebona	Susan	Olivos	34 30 31 36 26	48
H Day II	M Gray	Whirlpool	Paw Paw Lake	31 32 30 37 34	41
C Auteried	H J Wurmbock	Evita	Attersee	35 38 37 27 29	39
D Milella	G Modugno	Bufera	Bari	37 26 33 34 36	39
P Migliaccio	G Sartorio	Fiammetta	Napoli	39 35 32 39 23	37
P Bela	L Jolif	Fiadolin I	Cannes	32 37 35 32 33	36
M Taylor	M Taylor	Bimba	Lake Maracaibo	38 36 36 33 35	27
C Henrion	F Thieck	Old Nut II	Fedala	DNS DNS 38 40 37	8

Winning yacht No 3316 B—Lippincott Boat Works, 1953 Ch Meeting—Paul Smart Ch I R C —Beppe Croce Fourteen nations represented

1954—AT CASCAIS

Skipper	Crew	Yacht	Fleet	Daily Places	Pts
C deCardenas	deCardenas, Jr	Kurush V	Havana	1 1 1 2 1	169
D Knowles	S Farrington	Gem II	Nassau	6 5 2 3 4	155
A Straulino	N Rode	Merope II	*Se-Ve-Taranto	2 4 4 10 5	150
C Lyon, Jr	O P Merrill	Vega IV	Barnegat Bay	8 2 6 4 7	148
A deCardenas	J deCardenas	Kurush IV	Marianao	5 3 11 5 3	148
D Bello	J Tito	Faneca	Cascais	3 16 3 1 12	140
W Parks	R Ha'perin	Citation	S Lake Michigan	15 9 5 8 2	136
T Nordio	L Sangulin	Asterope	Trieste	9 6 7 14 11	128
J Fiuza	J Gorinho	Espadarte II	Lisbon	7 8 8 11 16	126
P Fischer	Baron v Stempel	Paka VI	Hamburg	16 10 13 9 10	117
P Chancerel	M Parent	Gais II	Seine	4 Wdr 9 7 6	116
D Salata	G Barnao	Nuvola Rossa	Lario	19 19 12 13 8	104
M Rivelli	R Camardella	Faneca	Formia	12 11 21 12 17	102
J Pontual	A Torres	Xodo IV	Guanabara	Dsq 22 16 6 9	87
F Mercier	G Pisani	Vega VII	Villefranche	23 23 14 24 13	78
M J Gautier	J L Domerc	Katia II	Safi	17 26 20 15 19	78
J Peytel	G deMontebello	Myra II	Paris	20 20 19 17 23	76
S Carlsson	O Carlsson	Mari	Rasta	28 Dsq 15 16 14	67
Y Lorion	J Hanin	Aloha VI	Algiers	13 12 17 — —	63
C Ulmer	C R Ulmer	Scylla	East River	14 21 27 Wdr 15	63
L Roboredo	D Roboredo	Luti	Porto	18 25 24 21 25	62
A Cosentino	N Stella	Merope	Ischia	11 7 26 Dsq Wdr	61
C Boselli	D Massa	Anna I	Alto Lario	21 28 29 18 18	61
P Hansohm	D Dotzer	Petrea II	Kiel	22 15 10 Wdr DNS	58
P H Smart	P G Smart	Melody	C Long Is'and Sound	29 13 Wdr 20 22	56
E Mendonca	E Cruz	Candide	Vila Franca	10 17 22 Wdr —	56
S H N Tay	Y Aillou	Gamm	Casablanca	25 18 Wdr 22 21	54
J Mitchell	Mrs Mitchell	Rig II	Solent	24 27 30 19 24	51
M Neiva	V Demaison	Rio II	Rio de Janeiro	26 24 23 Dsq 20	47
Lotar deDruet	A Ravazano	Pilantra	D Federal	30 14 18 Wdr Wdr	43
Roux-Delimal	A deBokay	Damoiselle II	Arcachon	27 29 28 23 27	41
Prince Bira	G Dagonnot	Tichiboo	Cannes	33 Wdr 25 Wdr 26	21
C Metral	Mme F Thieck	Itrane	Rabat	31 Wdr Wdr 25 —	14
R Taylor	O Ricupero	Frisette	S Olivos	32 Wdr — — —	3

Winning yacht No 3376 B—Old Greenwich Boat Works, 1953 Ch Meeting—Paul Smart Ch I R C —Beppe Croce

Continental Championships
(Winners Only)
EUROPEAN

Year	Skipper	Yacht	Fleet
1932	Aizpurua	*Izarra*	San Sebastian
1933	Peytel	*Moira*	Paris
1934	Giannini	*Orsa*	Napoli
1935	Postiglione	*Sirab*	Napoli
1936	von Hutschler	*Pimm*	Hamburg
1937	Bischoff	*Wannsee*	Berlin
1938	Straulino	*Polluce*	Sezione Velicia Taranto
1947	Nordio	*Titepi II*	Trieste
1948	Cosentino	*Hydra*	Napoli
1949	Straulino	*Poluuce*	Sezione Velicia Taranto
1950 to 1953	Straulino	*Merope*	Sezione Velicia Taranto

NORTH AFRICAN

1934	Grima	*Moira*	Philippeville (*Defunct*)
1934 to 1939	Lorion	*Aloha*	Alger
1942	Lorion	*Aloha II*	Alger
1946 and 1947	Lorion	*Aloha*	Alger

SPRING
Note — Mostly North American, but open to fleets on all continents

1934 and 1935	Iselin	*Ace*	Western Long Island Sound
1936	White	*Shucks*	Western Long Island Sound
1937	Smith	*Pioneer*	Otsego Lake
1938	Nye	*Gale*	Southern Lake Michigan
1939	Jahncke	*Scout*	New Orleans Gulf
1940	White	*Shucks*	Western Long Island Sound
1941	Nye	*Gale*	Southern Lake Michigan
1947	Ogilvy	*Whip*	Western Long Island Sound
1948	Knowles	*Cagin*	Nassau
1949	O'Gorman	*Wahini*	Western Long Island Sound
1950	Stearns	*Glider*	Wilmette Harbor
1951	Lippincott	*Sea Robin*	West Jersey
1952	Williams	*Kathleen*	Southern Lake Michigan
1953	Knowles	*Gem III*	Nassau
1954	Lyons, Jr	*Vega IV*	Barnegat Bay

NORTH AMERICAN
Note—Only held when World's Championship is elsewhere

1939	Sumner	*Whitecap II*	San Diego Bay
1948	Ross	*Cene*	Puget Sound
1952	Ogilvy	*Flame*	Western Long Island Sound
1953	Lippincott	*Flower*	West Jersey

SOUTH AMERICAN

1951	Samoldo	(*Skipper Series*)	Rio de Janeiro
1952	Bueno	*Xodo III*	Rio de Janeiro

AUSTRALIAN

1952	Whalley	(*Skipper Series*)	Pittwater

PICTORIAL INDEX

★

❂

I. S. C. Y. R. A.

TOP OFFICIALS

AND

PAST GREATS

There is insufficient space to include photographs of the many who have done most commendable work during their comparatively brief terms of office.

Commodore George W. Elder (the author) in his prime. President for twenty-five years prior to 1949, he is responsible for the Star's system of organization and many of its rules. Unopposed, he has been elected as a major class official forty-one consecutive times.

CONILL

ISELIN

CORRY

Commodore Enrique J. Conill (1947 and 1948) was vice-president for over a decade. He concentrated entirely on Star development in Europe. His insistance on the tall Marconi was justified.

Commodore Adrian Iselin II (1946 and 1945) was also vice-president for several years. Twice a Gold Star winner, he has raced every rig, starting in 1914. He has the best all-time record

Commodore George A. Corry, the dean of them all, held that office for twenty years. His lovable personality and infectious enthusiasm accounts largely for the Star's popularity. Pop, father of the Star, has become the legendary hero of the class.

International President Dr. Carlos de Cardenas and family. Also standing at his right is Alvaro. Seated left to right: Carlos, Jr., Maria-Luisa, Alberto on arm of chair, Jorge and Luisa, their mother. Charlie has the unapproached record of competing in forty-one major international events: sixteen world's championships, two olympics and twenty-three mid-winters. He and Luisa are popular in Star circles the world over. Each of their sons is a good skipper and the daughter a replica of her lovely mother.   —Photo by Varreno

Executive President
Paul H. Smart,
now at the helm
of the
I.S.C.Y.R.A.
Besides being
international
secretary, Paul was
legal advisor to
the governing
committee for many
years. In
addition to being
an olympic gold
medal crew, he has
represented his
fleet as skipper in
numerous major
championships.
—Photo by
Barcino, Havana

HALSTED

PEYTEL

LEE

Harold C. Halsted, president from 1949 to 1952. Previously vice-president and treasurer, he is still an active skipper, a two Silver Star winner. —Photo by Hansslar

European vice-president, J e a n Peytel. A Star skipper for over a quarter of a century, is the main-stay of the association in Europe

North American vice-president Cebern Lee, was Twelfth District secretary for many years and al-ternate on 1948 U.S. Olympic yachting team. He is famous for sailing Stars over bars—mahog-any ones. Seriously, he has given his best to the class at all times.

—Photo by Blair Studio

LOPES

HARVEY

South American vice-president Anchyses Lopes, the leading spirit on that continent. He has developed many new fleets and its Silver Star annual championship.

Austro - Malayan vice - president Bart Harvey. Responsible for the increase in Australian fleets and representative of that country in the Olympics. The able successor of Spackman and Jongelie (both lost in World War II) is gradually reorganizing the far flung islands

African vice-president Yves Lorion, represented Algiers for last world's title and France in the 1948 Olympics. Except for the Mediterranean coast, his is a large wild continent to develop.

LORION

W. T. Sampson Smith, international secretary during the years of plenty. Sam, unsung benefactor of the I.S.C.Y.R.A., provided its first central office and in many other ways is largely responsible for its enviable financial status today. A Silver Star winner, he has the best international record of any small lake skip-

Executive vice-president in 1954, C. Stanley Ogilvy is also editor of Log and Starlights and has been since World War II. His improvement of the Log and outstanding performance as a racing skipper is too well known to be reviewed.

—Photo by Parkville Studio

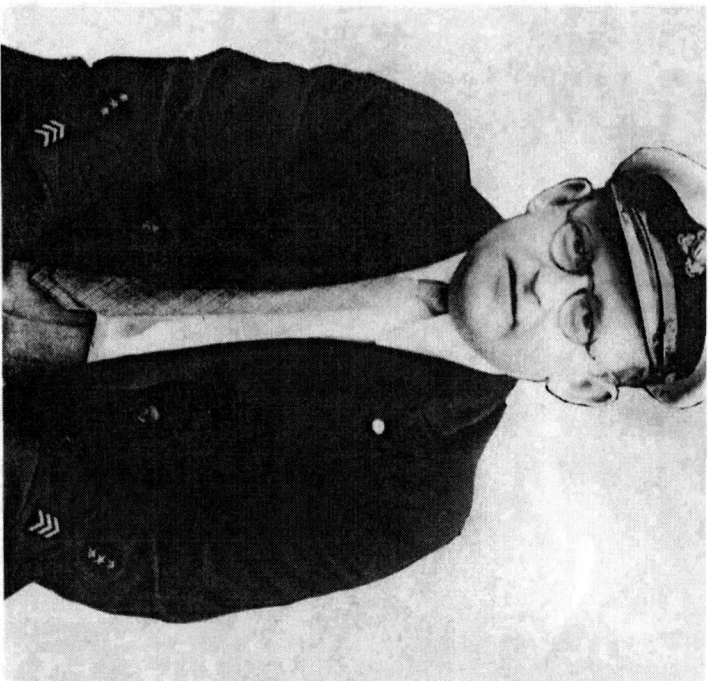

Timothy D. Parkman, international secretary and treasurer for fifteen years. Tim bore the burden of the detailed executive work through what might be called the middle phase of Star development. Youngest man to ever hold the office, he was at first forced to find time for his duties while working his way through law school, showing what can be done by one who has the interest of the Star at heart. Tim definitely ranks as one of the Star greats.
—Photo by Paul W. Davis

Corresponding secretary Edith U. Glass, for twelve years has handled the routine work of the central office. An efficient manager, she knows more about eligibility rules and the status of every fleet, skipper or crew than any other member, including the major officials themselves. She might rightfully be called "Miss Star Class."
—Photo by Vic Otis

DAVIS

GIDLEY

The late Arthur W. Davis, first official Star editor. Jeff was a most likable old fellow. A journalist, his original style and dry humor was enjoyed by many.

Bill Gidley, most famous of all Treasurers. He was more than a treasurer. Bill's sound, level-headed advice was most helpful in the early years of the I.S.C.Y.R.A.
—Oil painting by
Wilbur Fisk Noyes

Charles E. Lucke, former editor for two decades. Being in service during the last war, he did double duty, working at night so his Star publications could come out as per schedule. He also served on several I.R.C.'s.

LUCKE

EVOLUTION
OF THE
STAR RIG

For over forty years the basic hull design has not been changed. While by far the oldest, the Star remains the most popular, and in many respects, most modern one-design class in the world today.

The BUG, fifteen-foot prototype of Star, a 1907 Gardner creation. Picture shows Pop and Ma Corry in ''Big Bug.'' Note her yachting attire of that time—Tres chic, n'es pas?   —Photo by Francis Sweisguth

William Gardner, designer of the Star and other chine yachts, was convinced that this type of hull would make a popular and fast racing craft.
—Photo by Morris Rosenfeld

Francis Sweisguth, who put the Star on paper in 1910. Then a naval architect in Gardner's office, he was assigned to enlarging the lines of the Bug and making a few minor changes. Thus he produced the only successful exponent of Bill's pet theory.

GAFF RIGS, some of the first Stars built, racing on the Sound. No. 17 (leading) was Pop
Corry's original "Little Dipper."
—Photo by Morris Rosenfeld

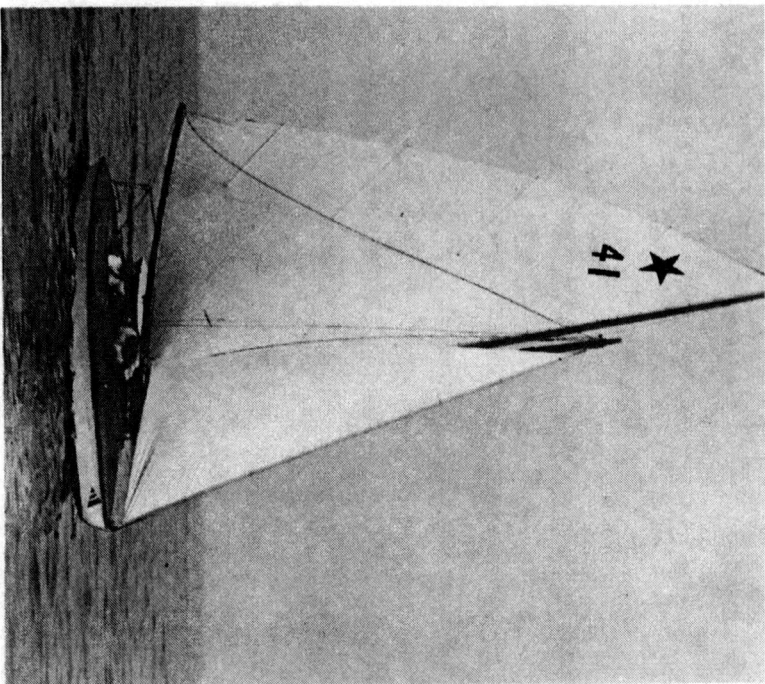

As owners became more tune conscious, the rig improved in the late teens. Keels were shifted about three inches aft and gaffs peaked up almost parallel to most, the first step toward the Marconi. Gordon Curry's "Aquilla" is a fair example. He won the first B title, forerunner to the Green Star Novice championship of today.

SHORT MARCONIES, off the Malecon, racing for the Bacardi Cup. The Star's second rig was adopted in 1921. The most being the same height as the old one plus its gaff, new sails were not absolutely necessary, hence conversion was inexpensive and rapid. Some had a single pair of wide wooden spreaders, others upper and lowers (mostly of metal tubing) and the author used none the first season.

"Rhode" started the gadget craze. First user of
"Rhody Runners" (backstay tracks) it was weighted
down with heavy hardware (mostly by Jock Wood)
that made almost everything adjustable. Many of
these fittings have been refined since for use on
modern Stars.

"Irex" with Ernest Ratsey at helm and his father
George as crew, was a very consistent winner in
the short rig decade. Ernest was allowed to test roller
reefing gear on "Irex" for a year before its use
was legalized.
—Photo by Morris Rosenfeld

TALL MARCONIES racing for the Chesapeake Lipton trophy. This, the third rig change, became optional in 1930. Masts were higher, booms shorter, but the sail area remained the same. Short and tall rigs raced together for a season, then the latter was made mandatory. Masts were raked, but kept straight. Any bend in a spar was thought harmful. Note how booms trimmed to the stern travellers.

"Merope" with which Straulino and Rode won their second World's title, is generally accepted as the last word in tune, condition and spar efficiency. In less experienced hands however, it would be JUST another also-ran.

"Iscyra IV" was among the early users of flex spars in America. Curves, often exaggerated ones, were at first obtained by force. It took a little time before skippers learned to stay masts, so they would flex automatically.

"Pimm", on which von Hutschler officially introduced SPAR FLEXING in 1937. It was an operation, not a rig change. Spar diameters, staying and trim had always been optional to promote improvement. Spar flexing could not be challenged, as it did not even violate the intent of the specifications. This policy of encouraging experiments, without affecting the design, has kept the Star modern.

—Photo by Ferd Urbahns

WORLD'S
CHAMPIONS
OF THE
STAR CLASS

Given in chronological order. The photograph of the crew, in every case, was not obtainable. Also the Olympic winners.

1923
Bill Inslee, Western L. I. Sound, crew Robert Nelson. Bill also won the 1922 National title, before the Star became international, with crew Harry Reeve.

1924
Jack Robinson, Western L.I. Sound, crew Arthur Knapp, see 1930.

1925 & 1936
Adrian Iselin II, left, and crew Ed Willis, Western L.I. Sound. Adrian's crew in 1936, Garret Horder.

1926
Ben Comstock, Narragansett Bay, crew Bill Gidley, see past greats. First to take title from the "Cradle of the Star Class."
—Photo by Oki Seizo

1927
Walton Hubbard, Newport Harbor, crew Dick Edwards, won after a three-cornered sail-off, taking event to California.

1928
Prentice Edrington, New Orleans Gulf, crew G i l b e r t Gray, see 1932 Olympics. Vice president five years.

1929
Graham Johnson, left, and his brother Lowdens, crew, Chesapeake Bay.

1930
Arthur Knapp, Western L.I.
Sound, crew Newell Weed,
won in a tall Marconi, only
series in which both tall and
short rigs participated. He
later wrote "Race Your Boat
Right" —Photo by Rosenfeld

1932
Eddie Fink, Long B e a c h ,
crew Edwin Thorne.—Photo
by W. Clifford Smith, Jr.

1931
Bill McHugh, left, and crew Fred Bedford, Central L.I. Sound.
—Photo by Jose Luis Lopez Gomez

Glen Waterhouse, left, and crew Woodie Metcalf, San Francisco Bay.

1934 & 1935

Hook Beardslee, right, and crew Barney Lehman, Newport Harbor, consecutive winners.

1937

Milton Wegeforth, San Diego Bay, crew E. Phillips, won, although von Hutschler took four straight races demonstrating flex spars to America.

1938 & 1939
Walter von Hutschler, Hamburg, crew Hans Weise, see 1936 Olympics, 1934 crew E. Beyn. First to take the event to Europe.

1940
Jim Cowie, left, Los Angeles Harbor, crew his brother Gordon. They tried the famous tent roach, before new rule barred its use.

1941 & 1946
George Fleitz, right, and crew Bill Severance, Los Angeles Harbor. Crew in 1946 W. Krug.

1942 & 1949
Harry Nye, right, and crew S t a n Fahlstrom, Southern Lake Michigan. The same combination won again in 1949.

1943
Art Deacon, Western L. I.
Sound and crew P. Roehm.
Art is now Executive Secretary.

1944
Gerald Driscoll, San Diego
Bay and crew Malin Burnham, see 1945.

1945
Malin Burnham, right, and
crew Lowell North, San
Diego Bay.

1947
Durward Knowles, right, and
crew Sloane Farrington, Nossau. The event, however,
had to leave North America
and went to Portugal.

1948
Woodie Pirie, left, Wilmette Harbor and crew Harry Rugeroni.

1950
Bob Lippincott, skipper, right, and Bob Levin, crew, West Jersey. 1950 Gold Star winner at Chicago.——Levin photo by Maura, Lippincott by Cuevas.

1951
Skip Etchells, right, and crew his wife Mary, Central L.I. Sound. Mary is the only girl to have won the World's title. Event had to leave North America. —Photo by Barcino, Havana

1952 & 1953
Agostino Straulino, left, and crew Nicolo Rode, Se Ve Taranto. Same combination of Italian Navy commanders won both years.

1954
Carlo de Cardenas, right, and Carlo, Jr., crew, Habana. Charlie came
within one point of a perfect score, establishing an all time record.

OLYMPIC
STAR
WINNERS

1932
Gilbert Gray, right, and crew Andrew Libano, Jr., U.S.A.

1936
Dr. Bischoff, left, and crew Hans Weise, Germany.

1948
Hilary Smart, right and his father Paul, crew, U.S.A., receiving their
Gold Olympic medals.

1952
Agostino Straulino and crew Nicolo Rode, Italy, receiving their gold
medals. Runners-up Price and Reid, U.S.A., left. Third, Fiuza and
Andrade, Portugal.

MISCELLANEOUS

Photographs of important person-ages, boats and events of the Star Class.

Nordico, Trieste, crossing Lippincott at Chicago in 1950.
—Photo by Fran Byrne

Stan Ogilvy, winner of many Star events, bringing "Flame" across line in near gale at Portugal.

Stars racing on Lake Lugano, Switzerland.
————Photo by Paolo Costa

Vesuvius in background, thirty-nine Stars before the gun, 1953 series
at Napoli, Italy.   ————Photo by Ugo Sarto

Spring Championship at Nassau, 1953, won by Gem III, Durward
Knowles. He also won the World's Title in 1947. Gem III is the darn
hull far to leeward, sixth from left.

North American Championship, '53, windward mark.
—Photo by Phil Nickerson

Harry Nye almost lost his mast.
—Photo by Barcino, Havana

"Wench II" with which Fleitz won 1946 World's title at Havana.

The late Charlie Pajeau, who for many years guided Star activities at Chicago.

Beppe Croce, second vice-president of Europe and chairman of the 1953 I.R.C.

Herb Dowsett, organizer and promoter of Star Class in Hawaii. A prominent figure in early Star days, he has been I.R.C. chairman, a Rear Commodore, District Secretary and established the Star's first foothold in bridging the Pacific.

Al Wakefield, veteran lake Star skipper since 1918. 1944 Great Lakes champion. He has been rear commodore, third vice president, international vice-president, chairman of the I.R.C. and G.C. member for many years.

J. Rulon Miller, who started Star racing on the Chesapeake, an important link in the development of the Class.

Bill Picken (South Bay) will long be remembered in many localities for an attribute that far transcended his outstanding racing record. Big jovial Bill was indisputably the most likable fellow that ever belonged to the Star Class.

Frank Robinson, Peconic Bay, winning Cup of Cuba in '28, after a sail-off with Tim Parkman.
—Photo by Kiko & Funcasta

Sig. Adler at helm of Canis Minor. Sig. is a contemporary of Iselin and the author. This trio have been Star members since 1914.

Sam Smith, most consistent winner in his beloved 12th, Small Lake, District.

Executive Vice President Reeve Bowden (forward) '51 to '53. Executive President Harold Halsted (aft) '49 to '52.
—Photo by Kiko & Funcasta

Rey Schauer and Ben Weston, crew and skipper of California's first international entry. Ben was also vice-president of the I.S.C.Y.R.A. at the time.

Charlie Davis, one of the best Star skippers in the teens.

The Havemeyers, three generations of Star skippers. (Standing left to right) Horace Jr. and his wife Rossie (nee Everdale), a Star skipper in her own right; Horace Sr. and his younger son Harry. Horace has owned thirteen Stars. (Seated are Horace's grandchildren) Dicky and Tommy Perkins, Danny and Briaan Cattin.

Alberto de Cardenas, Charlie's youngest, being presented with a trophy by Vice Commodore Rafael Posso. Alberto is the youngest skipper to have ever won a bona fide Star race.   —Photo by Barcino, Havana

After deck of the Columbia Y.C., headquarters of the 1942 title series. It is a converted lake steamer, with all the conveniences of a modern yacht club below deck, and is kept tied to one of the municipal wharfs. It was Pop's last big series. He can be seen in center talking to Ted Everitt.

Spring Championship of North America winners at Gulfport, La., Dick Stearns, Chicago skipper, runner-up. Farrington, Nassau, holding large tray. Commodore Cassibry G.Y.C. Morris Newman. Edward Jahncke, placed 3rd, his young son and crew in front. Elizabeth (Miller) Robin, famous secretary of the third district. Dave Wuescher (in white) veteran skipper of the New Orleans fleet. Durward Knowles, Nassau's winning skipper and Bob Rogers, Chicago, crew.

——Photo by Gulfport Photo Service

Contestants and band at flag raising ceremony opening the Silver Star Spring Championships. ——Photo by Gulfport Photo Service

H.R.M. King Paul of Greece, with hands clasped in center. King Paul was Vice-Commodore of the I.S.C.Y.R.A. for many years. Both he and his Queen sail their own Stars and are most enthusiastic skippers and loyal supporters of the Star Class, furthermore they do their own work on their Stars, are regular fellows and greatly admired by the entire membership.

1927 executives of the I.S.C.Y.R.A., left to right, Treasurer Bill Gidley, President George Elder, Commodore Pop Corry, Vice-President Prentice Edrington and Secretary Tim Parkman.

Left to right, the late John Pirie, Pop, Vice Commodore Rafael Posso and Woodie Pirie, winner, Midwinters.　　—Photo by Kiko & Funcasta

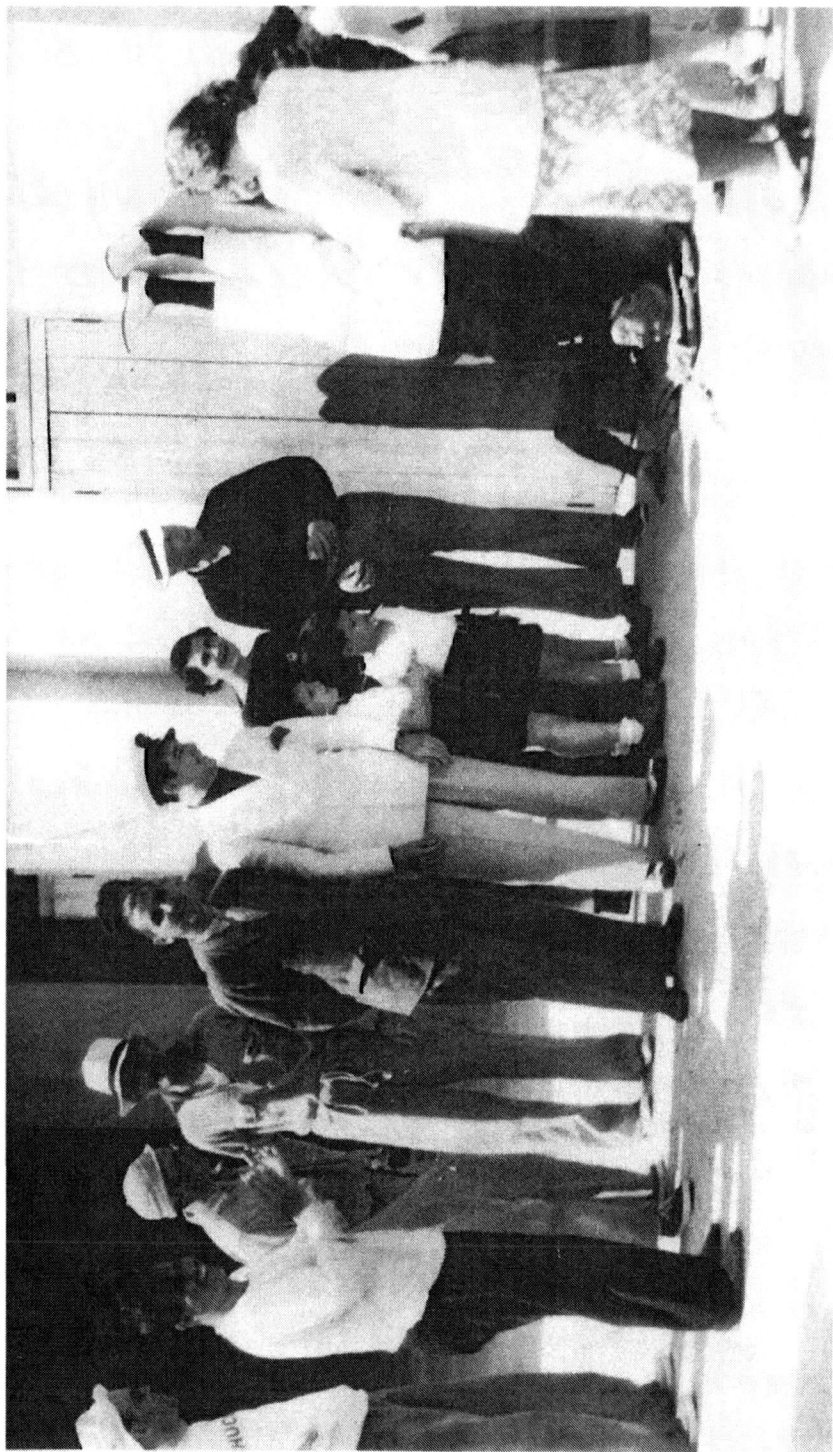

Pop Corry taking his usual reverse circulation exercise at the boat house, on the Almendares. Note two of the young de Cardenas boys with their mother Luisa, both are now winning races with their own Stars.

Clockwise: ● Skip and Mary Etchells racing Shannon at Nassau, 1953.
● A close finish at Puget Sound, Barbara Nettleton center. Photo by
Tom Lankford. ● Herb Dowsett towing home after an elimination race
of the Hawaiian Islands Fleet, Diamond Head in the background. ●
Barbara Lucke racing the Eel on Barnegat Bay. Photo by Edwin Levick.
● Stars racing in North Africa, Flotte d'Angiers.

Comet, first of the sixteen Stars owned by the author.

Ara, Jack Wood. Inventor of Rhody Runner and many other of the early adjustable Star fittings.
—Photo by Morris Rosenfeld

Mee Sing, first Star in Asia. Built by Baily 1923 and raced by Fred Tracy at Hong Kong during the early 20's.

351

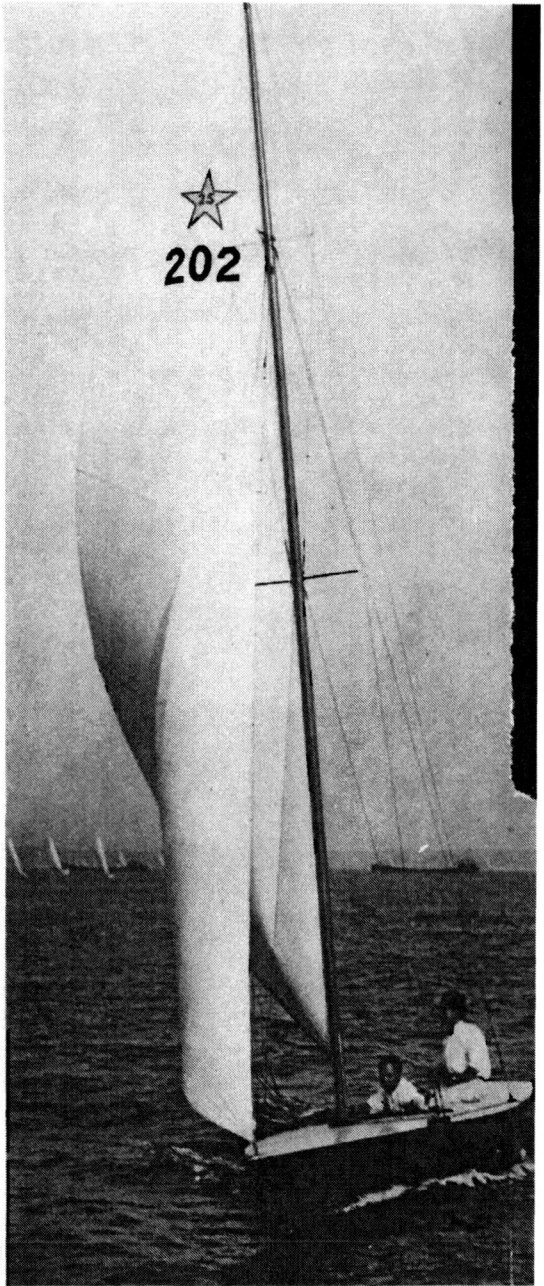

"Ace" won first Atlantic Coast Championship in 1925 and Adrian Iselin, with same boat, again won that title twenty years later.
—Photo by Ernest Tanare

Commodore Corry's second Star, also called Little Dipper. He acquired it from Bill Inslee, after the latter won the first World's Championship in 1923, because Pop felt he should be the perpetual owner of the first Star built.
—Photo by Edwin Levick

Juanita Elder, Commodore's wife, crew on Iscyra VI at Marblehead Week 1941, was also his crew in World's Championships of 1942.

CPSIA information can be obtained at www.ICGtesting.com
Printed in the USA
BVOW05s0046270315

393590BV00013B/89/P

9 781258 168018